*MY EARLY TRAVELS
AND ADVENTURES IN AMERICA*

Henry M. Stanley

December 1869.

My Early Travels
and
Adventures
in America

by
HENRY M. STANLEY

FOREWORD BY DEE BROWN

UNIVERSITY OF NEBRASKA PRESS
LINCOLN AND LONDON

Foreword copyright © 1982
by the University of Nebraska Press
Manufactured in the United States of America

First Bison Book printing: 1982
Most recent printing indicated by first digit below:
1   2   3   4   5   6   7   8   9   10

Library of Congress Cataloging in Publication Data
Stanley, Henry M. (Henry Morton), 1841–1904.
  My early travels and adventures in America.

  Reprint. Originally published: My early travels and adventures in
America and Asia. Volume 1. London : S. Low, Marston, 1895.

  1. West (U.S.)—Description and travel—1860–1880. 2. Indians of
North America—West (U.S.)—Wars—1866–1895. 3. Stanley, Henry
M. (Henry Morton), 1841–1904. I. Title.
F594.S79 1982   917.8'042   81–15941
ISBN 0–8032–4132–1   AACR2
ISBN 0–8032–9127–2 (pbk.)

Originally published in 1895 as Volume I
of *My Early Travels and Adventures in America and Asia*

FOREWORD

by Dee Brown

FOR most Americans the name Henry Morton Stanley summons up a vision of a sturdy explorer in a pith helmet cutting his way through the jungles of Africa to discover a long lost missionary. "Dr. Livingstone, I presume," are the words we remember him by. We should better remember him for his vivid record of experiences in western America that he preserved in a collection of dispatches published in book form almost a century ago and that has been virtually unobtainable for a generation.

Stanley's keen eye and his skill with the English language left a record that provides us with rare vignettes of that unique interval in the westward movement immediately following the Civil War. In contrast to the prewar period of the gold rushes and the era following completion of the first transcontinental railroad—both of which are abundantly documented—there is a sparsity of first-rate eye-witness accounts of the frontier during the turbulent months that followed the close of the war. Perhaps the better observers and writers—except for Stanley—were too busy elsewhere.

Certainly no one equaled Stanley in his reportage of

that exciting time when rails were first being laid across
the Great Plains, the stage was being set for the Indian
wars in the West, and the first trail-driving cowboys were
herding longhorns north from Texas. Without Stanley's
descriptions of these events, we would lack some of the
most spirited images of that colorful episode in our history.

Stanley's life in itself could provide the complete plot
for a mammoth picaresque novel. Born illegitimately in
Wales on January 28, 1841, as John Rowlands, he lived a
precarious existence until the age of fifteen, when he sailed
from Liverpool to New Orleans as a cabin boy. Rebelling
against his mistreatment at sea, he jumped ship and set off
down Tchoupitoulas Street in search of employment in
New Orleans. "I saw a gentleman of middle age seated in
front of No. 3 store, reading a morning newspaper," he
recalled in his autobiography. "From his sober dark alpaca
suit and tall hat, I took him to be the proprietor of the
building." In his English accent, young John Rowlands
asked for work.

After lengthy questioning, the Louisianian in the dark
alpaca suit took the runaway John Rowlands to a restaurant, saw that he obtained a haircut and a bath, and then
found a job for him with a wholesale trading firm. The
man's name was Henry Morton Stanley; he was a wealthy
merchant of New Orleans. Some months later that child-
less gentleman offered to adopt John Rowlands as his own
son and train him for a mercantile career, provided the boy
agreed to bear his name.

Thus did John Rowlands become Henry Morton Stanley. When he was nineteen, his foster father decided to
send him to an Arkansas River plantation to learn its
management from an associate. The younger Stanley

cared little for plantation life and thoroughly disliked the owner's treatment of slaves. He soon took a job as clerk in a store at Cypress Bend.

A few months later the Civil War began. Stanley was then twenty years old and small for his age—he stood only five feet, five inches—and was shy and lonely. He considered himself an outsider, an Englishman; the war was an American affair and of no interest to him. He was much more concerned with the whereabouts of his foster father than about the war. The elder Stanley had journeyed to Cuba, from where he had written his adopted son three letters, then for month after month absolute silence followed.

When enlistments started for the Confederate Army, Stanley made no move to join his young acquaintances in going off to war. But one day he received a parcel containing feminine underclothing—a symbolic presentation that he recognized as equivalent to an Englishman's white feather, a charge of cowardice. He joined the Dixie Grays the next day and in November 1861 found himself fighting under General Leonidas Polk against General U.S. Grant at Belmont, Missouri. Surviving the engagement, and the bad food and epidemics of the following winter, Stanley with his regiment arrived at Shiloh on April 6, 1862, to take part in one of the bloodiest battles fought in the West. His brief narrative of his part in the fighting, told in his autobiography, is as graphic an eye-witness account as one is likely to find in the literature of military combat.

During a hasty advance on the second day of battle, Stanley was cut off from his company by a surging line of Union soldiers. "Two men sprang at my collar, and marched me, unresisting, into the ranks of the terrible

Yankees. *I was a prisoner!*" Confined at Camp Douglas in Chicago, Stanley endured the misery of prison life, sleeping on flat boards and watching his comrades who died from disease being hauled away daily in wagons.

And then, unexpectedly, he was offered a way out. The prison commandant secured temporary permission from Washington to recruit foreign-born prisoners into a Union regiment. At first Stanley refused to consider the opportunity for freedom. "Every American friend of mine was a Southerner," he wrote, "my adopted father was a Southerner." But six more weeks of prison horrors, the useless flight of time, the fear of being incarcerated for years, all led him to change his mind. On June 4 he became a "galvanized Yankee." Out of fear that he might be returned to prison, he concealed from his superiors a severe attack of dysentery. Not long after reaching Harpers Ferry, however, he collapsed and was taken to a hospital, where eventually he was mustered out of service.

Adrift in Maryland, Stanley found work with a friendly farmer near Hagerstown, helped with the harvests, and then went on to Baltimore, where he obtained a berth on a sea-going ship. He was determined to make his way to Havana in hopes of finding some trace of his foster father, but when he reached Cuba he learned that the elder Henry M. Stanley was dead.

Completely alone in the world now, he returned to New York and enlisted in the U.S. Navy. He thus probably became the only man ever to serve in the Confederate Army, the Union Army, and the Union Navy. By now a fair sailor, he soon earned a rating on the *Minnesota* as ship's writer, his duties being to transcribe the log and other ship records. While the *Minnesota* was off Fort Fisher, North Carolina, Stanley witnessed at close hand

several sea and land battles. While recording these for the
ship's records, an idea came to him to compose some
narratives of the exciting events and send them to newspapers. Here began Stanley's career as a journalist. He
became so interested in writing for the press that he
wanted to do nothing else.

After a series of travels and adventures that would be
considered improbable had they involved anyone other
than the audacious Stanley, the *St. Louis Missouri-Democrat*
employed him in 1867 "to 'write-up' North-western
Missouri, and Kansas and Nebraska." The incidents and
scenes he depicted so fluently during that assignment
make up the contents of this book.

One of the remarkable elements of his talent was the
ease with which he acquired the style and flavor of American frontier humor. An example is his report of the birth
of the railhead town of Ellsworth, Kansas: "The population of the town of Ellsworth is estimated at forty men,
four women, eight boys and seven girls. There are also
fourteen horses, and about twenty-nine and one-half
dogs. . . . As Ellsworth is part and parcel of this great and
prosperous country, it is also progressive—for no sooner
has the fifth house begun to erect its stately front above the
green earth, than the population is gathered in the three
saloons to gravely discuss the propriety of making the new
town a city, and of electing a mayor." Mark Twain at
twenty-six could not have done it better, but unfortu-
nately Stanley lost that magic touch after he transferred
his reportage from the American West to darkest Africa;
he was later considered a humorless writer.

Stanley always seemed to know how to make the most
of a good story. When he was in Omaha he heard of how
the Cheyennes had wrecked a train near Plum Creek. The

wreck in itself was very newsworthy, but as usual Stanley capped it by tracking down one of the survivors, a fellow Briton named William Thompson. Thompson had been scalped and left for dead, and when he regained consciousness he retrieved his scalp and brought it to Omaha, carrying it in a pail of water so that it would not dry out, hoping to find a physician who could reset it to his head. "The scalp," reported the observant Stanley, "was about nine inches in length and four in width, somewhat resembling a drowned rat as it floated, curled up, on the water."

In later years, after achieving fame for stories of his African adventures, he credited his ability to deal successfully with the primitive tribes of Africa to his early experiences with American Indians when he accompanied General Winfield Scott Hancock on a 450-mile march through the country of the Southern Plains Indians, and to his observations of the Sherman peace commissioners with the Northern Plains Indians. Almost unconsciously, he said, he acquired lessons in dealing with primitive peoples.

Stanley's news letters for the *Missouri-Democrat* were so lively and well written that other newspapers were soon asking for similar pieces. James Gordon Bennett of the *New York Herald* was sufficiently impressed with the young journalist's verve and enterprise that he backed him on his first journey into Africa and in 1869 commissioned him to find Dr. David Livingstone.

In 1895, after he became world-famous, Stanley assembled some of the best of his newspaper dispatches into a two-volume work, *My Early Travels and Adventures*. Volume one is the American story, a brilliant series of first-hand accounts of our past told with gusto by a sharp-eyed observer endowed with a remarkable gift for the English language.

INTRODUCTION.

THE letters from the Indian country which are contained in the first volume were not written with a view to permanent publication, but for the exacting and imperious necessities of American newspapers, principally for the *Missouri Democrat* of St. Louis, and a New York paper. Previous to the period at which they begin, I had been only an Occasional Descriptist of battle scenes and important public events ; but in my twenty-fifth year I was promoted to the proud position of a Special Correspondent, with the very large commission to inform the public regarding all matters of general interest affecting the Indians and the great Western plains.

The incidents to which the letters relate occurred in 1867, during two Indian Campaigns. When General Hancock's Expedition first set out from the Missouri River, it was generally expected that there would be a good deal of fighting ; but the General's disposition, and management of the Indian chiefs, were such that he had only to conduct a series of tactical marches through the red men's domains. Later, General

Sherman took charge of the operations. He was accompanied by several of the most renowned American Generals, such as old General Harney, Generals Augur, Terry, Sanborn and Hardie, who with a couple of Chief Indian Commissioners, and Senator Henderson, constituted a Peace Commission. On discovering that there was not much need of his military services, Sherman soon retired, and left the Indian affairs in the hands of the Peace Commissioners. To hold the councils with the principal Indian tribes, the Peace Commission made prolonged excursions through a wide tract of the plains, altogether travelling about 2000 miles. The incidents on these journeys afforded abundance of interesting matter to the press of the period, and were not without benefit to me in after years.

Scarcely twenty-eight years have elapsed since these letters were hastily written amid the bustle of military life, and yet what a change has come over the face of the land! I find that many of the predictions then ventured upon have been more than realised. Kansas, which contained in 1867 only 350,000 inhabitants, now possesses a population of one and a half millions. The several isolated forts at which we halted have become thriving towns and cities, connected by railways. Dodge City, near old Fort Dodge, has 2000 people. Cheyenne City—then only a tented camp—numbers 12,000 inhabitants. Junction City and Abilene, its neighbour, have over 6000. Laramie City in 1890 contained 6400 inhabitants. The territory of Colorado, which in 1867 had only 35,000, is now a State with over half a million of people, while the population of Nebraska has increased from 122,000 to 1,100,000. In their respective capitals, Denver and Omaha, will be found the greatest marvels of growth and prosperity; for Denver has increased from 3500 to 106,000 people, while Omaha, from 11,000, has risen to 145,000. We may well look back " bewildered, and wondering how it is " that such prodigious and extraordinary results have taken place.

From the letters in the first volume it may be gathered what this portion of the United States— Nebraska, Eastern Colorado and Western Kansas— was like in 1867. It was chiefly an ocean of prairie untenanted by the white man, except at the Forts. It was one vast pasture plain, trodden by buffalo, and ranged over by thousands of audaciously hostile Indians. It is now intersected by railways—as many as nine lines cross Kansas—the buffalo have been exterminated, the Indians are rare visitants, and may be said to have disappeared ; and over their hunting-grounds, about which they were so anxious and appealed so passionately, there are scattered 750,000 orderly and law-abiding white citizens.

Few can read the speeches of the Indian chiefs without feeling deep sympathy for them. They move us by their pathos and mournful dignity, for it must be admitted, now that we know what has happened, that the speech of Black Foot, for instance, is solemn and depressing reading. What has taken place was inevitable. It is useless to blame the white race for moving across the continent in a constantly increasing tide. If we proceed in that manner, we shall presently find ourselves blaming Columbus for discovering America, and the Pilgrim Fathers for landing on Plymouth Rock. The whites have done no more than follow the law of their nature and being. Moreover, they had as much right to the plains as the Indians, and it would not be a difficult task to prove that they had a better right.

The mounds in the Mississippi Valley, the temple ruins of Central America, and the silent cities in Arizona prove that there once existed in America semi-civilised millions. But the Pilgrim Fathers found no such people when they landed in America in 1620, they found only war-bred savages, who were devoted to internecine strife, descendants, probably, of those nomads who had dispossessed the true aborigines. When the white race appeared, it was the turn of the haughty savages to be dispossessed, and driven back to the West, where, in 1867, we find them cooped up between the Missouri River and the Rocky Mountains. The whites were, however, kinder to them than their fathers had been to the industrious mound-builders. For two hundred and fifty years the whites persisted in offering terms of peace, but during all that time the slightest cause had been seized by the Indians for renewing the strife. Had not the American Government restrained them from their inter-tribal wars, protected them from un-scrupulous traders, and from the just revenge of settlers, the tribes treated of in these letters had long ago been exterminated. Savage and implacable humanity of the Indian type need expect no other fate than that of extinction.

In commenting upon the causes of the red men's disappearance, writers have been in the habit of imputing the blame to the white colonists. From the pulpit and the press, as well as on the floors of the congressional halls, the diatribes have issued in eloquent streams. There is no doubt that the rifles and "firewater" of the colonists have slain a great many, but the principal causes of their disappearance have sprung from their own innate savagery. It was in their nature to destroy their own families, tribes, and each other. The "firewater" of the whites undermined the constitutions of a comparative few, but with the firearms, of which they obtained pos-session by trade and war, and as peace offerings, the incorrigible Indian spirit of revenge led them, upon the most trivial affront, to remorseless slaughter of each other. It would be no exaggeration to state that twenty times more Indians fell by the hands of rifle-armed Indians than by the arms of the whites.

Added to the fatal habit of Indians to resent their petty spites with midnight massacre of entire families, communities—aye, even of tribes—were the thousand and one accidents of savage life, the ravages of infectious diseases, the cruel indifference to childhood and infirm age, the neglect of the sick, the lack of means and knowledge to arrest illness, their ignorance of medicine, and profound faith in the incantations of their "medicine-men," the insanitary condition of their camps, their coarse and precarious manner of existence, their sudden exposure to wintry blasts after being overheated in their wigwams, the brutal treatment and heavy labour to which they subjected their females, old and young, and the natural sterility of their women consequent upon privation and inter-marriage between relations, or "breeding in." These, and hundreds of kindred causes, prove that the nature of Indian life and temper killed thousands where the whites killed scores.

When the hot-headed and fiery braves, whose chief glory lay in the number of scalps taken, exchanged their primitive weapons for the musket, their power of inflicting loss upon their race increased tenfold, but when they exchanged the flintlock or single-shot rifle for the fifteen-shot Winchester, any one who reasoned might perceive that their annihilation was not far off.

The lessons derived from the near extinction of the Indian are very applicable to Africa, and it was my principal reason for advocating the prohibition of trade in breech-loading rifles with Africans. To produce the same effects on the African aborigines as have resulted in the almost total destruction of the North Americans, all we need do is to freely permit the carriage of modern rifles and their ammunition into Africa, and in a few years we shall find the same rapid process of depopulation going on there. Savages have the minds of children and the passions of brutes, and to place breech-loaders in their hands is as cruel an act as to put razors in the hands of infants.

These letters describe two great efforts made by the United States Government to save the unfortunate Indians from the consequences of their own rash and heedless acts. The speeches of Generals Hancock and Sherman and the Peace Commissioners faithfully reflect the sentiments of the most cultivated Americans towards them, and are genuine exhortations to the Indians to stand aside from the overwhelming wave of white humanity which is resistlessly rolling towards the Pacific, and to take refuge on the reservations, where they will be fed, clothed, protected, and educated in the arts of industry and Christian and civilised principles. The replies of the Indian chiefs no less faithfully reflect their savage, indomitable spirit, their proud contempt of danger, and betray in many instances a consciousness of the sad destiny awaiting them.

The second volume begins in 1869 and treats of widely different topics. The success of my Indian letters induced Mr. Gordon Bennett of the *New York Herald* to appoint me his special correspondent on the Abyssinian Expedition in 1868. Having by good fortune succeeded in sending news of the fall of Magdala many days in advance of the Government and English correspondents, I was sent on a roving mission to Egypt, Crete, and the Levant, and finally to Spain—whence in October, 1869, I was summoned to Paris to receive a commission for the finding of Livingstone in Central Africa. But previous to embarking on the last enterprise, which was great for a young journalist, I was instructed to report on the inauguration of the Suez Canal, to write a kind of guide to the Nile, to visit Captain (now Sir Charles) Warren, and give an account of his explorations underneath Jerusalem, and finally I was to proceed through Persia to India, viâ the Caucasus, and send a series of letters upon all subjects that I might find worth describing on the way.

These letters are the result of that long journey which was a kind of apprenticeship to the longer and more difficult one I was to continue into Unknown Africa. Most of them have been shorn of their original redundancy, because of the exigencies of space. Many of them were never published, because, as I presume, some were lost on the way, and others were left out through pressure of matter more immediately affecting Americans. Fortunately for the purposes of this book, I had preserved copies of them ; and as they contain many facts of lasting interest concerning Eastern lands, both publishers and author have deemed them worthy of reproduction in book form.

HENRY M. STANLEY.

RICHMOND TERRACE, WHITEHALL.

CONTENTS.

———•◦•———

I.

c

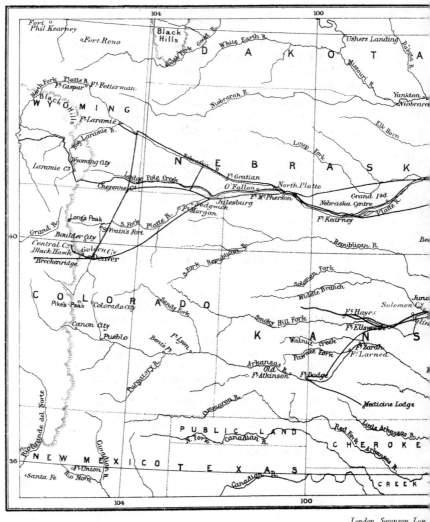

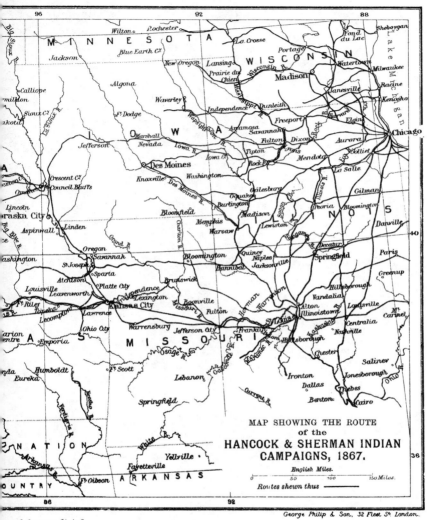

MAP SHOWING THE ROUTE
of the
**HANCOCK & SHERMAN INDIAN
CAMPAIGNS, 1867.**

English Miles.

Routes shewn thus ————

George Philip & Son, 32 Fleet St. London.

ston & Company, Limited.

EXPERIENCES

TWO INDIAN CAMPAIGNS.

———◦———

Office of the *Missouri Democrat*, St. Louis,
March 1867.

Our special correspondent, whom we lately sent to
accompany General Hancock's expedition, overtook
the command on the banks of the Saline, and in a
letter which has been delayed writes thus :—

"A ride of forty-seven miles (from Solomon City)
brought us within view of General Hancock's expedition, encamped on the banks of the Saline River,
a small, muddy, but swift stream, which empties
itself into the Smoky Hill River five miles below
the town of Salina.. The white square tents and
the blue uniforms of the soldiers were well-remem-
bered scenes, and recalled vividly to our mind the
late civil war.

"Alighting from the coach, we made our way, valise
in hand, toward the General's quarters. The General
was asleep, and we preferred to wait his pleasure
before making our presence known. In the mean-

I.

B

while we took a quiet stroll through the camp. Groups of soldiers were discussing gravely the probability of a fight with the Indians, some were busy preparing for supper, cleaning their horses, their arms and accoutrements, others were arranging their beds, or playing chess, cards, dominoes. After a while the drum and fife announced 'Retreat.' Every soldier dropped his work, took his place in line, and answered to his name. Mysterious evolutions followed, after which came the order, 'Break ranks—march!'

" Fresh sentinels are stationed, and darkness rapidly approaches. Eight o'clock comes, and 'Tattoo' is beaten. The soldiers form line once more, the rolls are called, and they are dismissed for the night. Nine o'clock, and two taps on the drum order ' Lights out.' One by one lights are extinguished, and darkness and quietness reign throughout the camp. While we were jotting these notes down an orderly approaching, said, 'The General wishes to see you, sir.' On entering the tent, we saw standing before us Major-General Winfield Scott Hancock, the leader of the expedition, who is a hale, hearty, and tall gentleman, in the prime of life. On reading our credentials, he said, 'You are welcome, sir'; and after a few unimportant discussions we bade him good-night, and proceeded to our assigned quarters to indite you this first letter.

" The troops will proceed to a point where Hancock has arranged a meeting with the chiefs of the different hostile Indian tribes. If they evince a disposition to be submissive and peaceable they will be allowed to depart in peace. If they are fractious, and prefer war, General Hancock will at once commence hostilities.

"Accompanying the expedition, under the special charge of the commanding General, is a little Indian boy, about five years old, the son of a chief who fell at the Sand Creek massacre. He is a boy of extraordinary intelligence, and shows the true spirit of the savage by drawing his jack-knife on any one who attempts to correct him. He is called Wilson Graham, and was for a time with Wilson and Graham's circus, where he was exhibited as a curiosity. The Indians, before assenting to a meeting, expressly stipulated that this boy should be delivered up to them."

Fort Harker : its Associations and its Celebrities—Express Riders of General Hancock—"Wild Bill," Jack Harvey, and Tom Atkins—The General Order of the Expedition.

FORT HARKER, *April 4th*, 1867.

TOURISTS through Kansas would call this place dull enough, but then so much of the interest of a place depends upon its traditions. For a passing traveller, in search of pleasure, it certainly possesses few attractions. But a "special," in the pursuit of useful knowledge for the reading public, observes things differ-

ently.   When I mention a fort, you need not imagine
one of those formidable affairs as built in ancient
times, with moat and drawbridge, towers and battle-
ments, but a simple square, surrounded by some
wooden shanties, situated on a gentle eminence,
whence there is a commanding view of the great
naked prairie.   There are neither flowers, shrubs,
nor trees planted in its vicinity, and the only signs
of vegetation around are the various kinds of grasses,
" buffalo," " swamp," and " herd."   Where the buffalo
and swamp grass throve the whole scene appeared like
a vast brown sea.   Perhaps the neighbourhood of
Fort Harker, in summer, when blossoming with
flowers, may appear more interesting, but the fort
in its present naked state appears like a great wart
on the surface of the plain.

The fort is situated about eighty miles due west
of Junction City, on the open prairie, and close by
the Santa Fé road.   It was formerly known by the
name of Ellsworth, after an officer of that name.
The officer having lost his commission, the fort lost
its name, and received the more reputable one of
Harker.   General Harker was a distinguished officer
of the Union army, who fell gallantly at the head
of his troops at the battle of the Kenesaw Mountains.
Two companies of cavalry and two of infantry are
stationed here under the command of Major Gibbs,
who was once called Major-General Gibbs of the
volunteers.

All sorts of men can be found here.   Living so far

on the frontier, and thrown so much together, they are thoroughly known to each other by their vices and virtues. It is a miniature world, a faithful duplicate of the big world we live in.

Among the celebrities of the fort is the sutler, Snyder, who is well read, and a man of the world, and "Big Goat," a negroid Indian woman. She has travelled over the United States, following the pursuits of a man, dressed in a man's clothes, and has, altogether, seen a good deal of rough life. As she advances to middle age she commences to make provision for old age, and, it is said, has already a snug sum laid by.

Looking from the fort towards the north-east, the eye lights upon Fremont's Rock which rises abruptly from the level prairie to the height of about twenty feet. From the top of that elevated platform General Fremont made a speech some years ago to a large assemblage of Kaw Indians. He impressed on them the necessity of keeping at peace with the whites, who would otherwise come with their "big thunder" and destroy them. Since that time the rock has retained the name of "Fremont's Rock."

General Hancock has three famous express riders— "Wild Bill," Jack Harvey, and Tom Atkins, who are widely known for courage, endurance, and faithfulness. A slight sketch of each of them may not be amiss, as they may be destined to take an important part in this expedition.

James Butler Hickok, commonly called "Wild

Bill," is one of the finest examples of that peculiar class known as frontiersman, ranger, hunter, and Indian scout. He is now thirty-eight years old, and since he was thirteen the prairie has been his home. He stands six feet one inch in his moccasins, and is as handsome a specimen of a man as could be found. We were prepared, on hearing of "Wild Bill's" presence in the camp, to see a person who might prove to be a coarse and illiterate bully. We were agreeably disappointed however. He was dressed in fancy shirt and leathern leggings. He held himself straight, and had broad, compact shoulders, was large chested, with small waist, and well-formed muscular limbs. A fine, handsome face, free from blemish, a light moustache, a thin pointed nose, bluish-grey eyes, with a calm look, a magnificent forehead, hair parted from the centre of the forehead, and hanging down behind the ears in wavy, silken curls, made up the most picturesque figure. He is more inclined to be sociable than otherwise ; is enthusiastic in his love for his country and Illinois, his native State ; and is endowed with extraordinary power and agility, whose match in these respects it would be difficult to find. Having left his home and native State when young, he is a thorough child of the prairie, and inured to fatigue. He has none of the swaggering gait, or the barbaric jargon ascribed to the pioneer by the *Beadle* penny-liners. On the contrary, his language is as good as many a one that boasts "college larning."

He seems naturally fitted to perform daring actions. He regards with the greatest contempt a man that could stoop low enough to perform " a mean action." He is generous, even to extravagance. He formerly belonged to the 8th Missouri Cavalry.

The following dialogue took place between us : " I say, Mr. Hickok, how many white men have you killed to your certain knowledge ? " After a little deliberation, he replied, " I suppose I have killed considerably over a hundred." What made you kill all those men ? Did you kill them without cause or provocation ? " " No, by heaven ! I never killed one man without good cause." " How old were you when you killed the first white man, and for what cause ? " " I was twenty-eight years old when I killed the first white man, and if ever a man deserved killing he did. He was a gambler and counterfeiter, and I was then in an hotel in Leavenworth City, and seeing some loose characters around, I ordered a room, and as I had some money about me, I thought I would retire to it. I had lain some thirty minutes on the bed when I heard men at my door. I pulled out my revolver and bowie knife, and held them ready, but half concealed, and pretended to be asleep. The door was opened, and five men entered the room. They whispered together, and one said, ' Let us kill the son of a —— ; I'll bet he has got money.' Gentlemen," said he, " that was a time—an awful time. I kept perfectly still until just as the knife touched my breast ; I sprung aside and buried mine in his heart, and then used my revolver on the others right and left. One was killed, and another was wounded ; and then, gentlemen, I dashed through the room and rushed to the fort, where I procured a lot of soldiers, and returning to the hotel, captured the whole gang of them, fifteen in all. We searched the cellar, and found eleven bodies buried in it—the remains of those who had been murdered by those villains." Turning to us, he asked : " Would you not have done the same ? That was the first man I killed, and I never was sorry for that yet."

Jack Harvey is a specimen of the same kind, but rather more reckless than Hickok, and has won, for his wild and daring deeds, a name second only to that of "Wild Bill."

Tom Atkins has also been proved in many a skirmish with the rebels and Indians. In 1861 he took command of a train for Santa Fé. He had twentynine men with him. When about half-way his train was attacked by a mounted band of seven hundred Indians, mostly Comanches and Apaches. After a fight of four hours, during which many an Indian bit the dust, the Indians retreated, leaving Atkins' little band masters of the situation.

The train consisted of twenty-seven waggons, which were filled with costly merchandise. Three days after the fight the teamsters went in a body to Captain Atkins, and informed him that they had determined to drive the train to Texas. "Well, boys," said

he, "that was just the thing I was thinking of, so
you will have to take me along ; but I want to make
a speech to you first, and tell you of a plan better
than that." His men gathered about, and were
impatient to hear his plan. " Sit down, boys, and let
us discuss things sociably." They all ranged themselves before him on the grass. When all were
seated he drew his revolvers, and presenting them
at the trembling party, informed them that he
would most certainly blow out the brains of the first
man who should attempt to rise. Not one dared to
move. Then calling his assistant waggon-master, he
sent him off with a despatch to Fort Garland
for a squad of soldiers to arrest his men, who had
mutinied. His waggon-master saddled the best
horse in the train, and galloped full speed to the fort,
and returned with a strong detachment which took
the whole party prisoners. During the time that
intervened between the departure of his waggon-
master and the arrival of the soldiery, which was
fully four hours, Tom Atkins kept guard over twenty-
eight men, until they were marched off to Fort
Garland. Atkins was then obliged to employ
Mexicans, and in due time delivered his freight
safely at Santa Fé.

Such are the three men whom General Hancock
has engaged for his express riders and scouts through
the Indian country.

The following is an abridged copy of the general
order by which this expedition is governed :—

HEADQUARTERS, DEPARTMENT OF THE MISSOURI,
IN THE FIELD.

[General Field Orders, No. 1.]

1. While on the march, and in camp, the troops composing the present expedition will receive orders from Major-General Smith, commander of the district of Upper Arkansas, in whose territory we are about to move. When instructions may be necessary, General Smith will receive them from the Major-General commanding.

2. It is uncertain whether war will be the result of the expedition or not ; it will depend upon the temper and behaviour of the Indians with whom we may come in contact. We go prepared for war, and will make it if a proper occasion presents. We shall have war if the Indians are not well disposed towards us. If. they are for peace, and no sufficient ground is presented for chastisement, we are restricted from punishing them for past grievances which are recorded against them ; these matters have been left to the Indian Department for adjustment. No insolence will be tolerated from any bands of Indians whom we may encounter. We wish to show them that the Government is ready and able to punish them if they are hostile, although it may not be disposed to invite war. In order that we may act with unity and in harmony with these views, no one but the commander present, on detachment or otherwise, will have interviews with the Indians. Such interviews as may be necessary

with them will be reserved, and corresponding reserve will be required from those under his command. No Indians will be allowed in camp, and no "talks" will be had with them, except for the purpose of explaining to them the facts herein stated. The chiefs of any bands of Indians, who may wish any information, will be referred to the Major-General commanding, who will see them at his headquarters.

3. Straggling is dangerous in an Indian country, and will not be tolerated.

4. Firing of guns or pistols will not be permitted without authority. For hunting, details may be made, but permission for such purpose will be required from these headquarters, which will be granted, as a rule, only when necessary to procure meat.

5. Guard will be kept up as in a state of hostility.

By command of Major-General Hancock.

W. G. MITCHELL, Capt. and A. A. General.

We move to Fort Zarah to-morrow.

From Fort Harker to Fort Zarah—Description of Fort Zarah— The Oft-Mooted Indian Question—The Agent Leavenworth —The Military and the Agents—Backsliding and Double Dealing.

FORT ZARAH, *April 6th,* 1867.

IT was a clear, bright, and frosty morning when, after a two days' rest, the drums of the 27th Infantry announced "Réveille."

"Oh, the drum, the drum, it rattles so loud,
  There is no such stirring sound
  Is heard the wide world round
  As the drum."

The sound woke us all from our dreams. Another day's fatigue and weary riding lay before us, and as we threw off the warm blankets, the keen, cold air rushing in from under our tent made us sigh for the comfortable quarters of some hotel, rather than be exposed to the cutting morning blast that sweeps over these plains on a raw March morning.

The journey from Fort Harker to this place occupied two days. It is about one hundred and fifteen miles west of Junction City. Two houses, placed about three hundred yards from each other, are by a stretch of courtesy called the fort. These houses are built of adobe and brown stone, roughly hewn. Their low, flat roofs are covered with earth, like the houses of Syria and Palestine. Fort Zarah is named after a son of General Curtis, Zarah M. Curtis, who was killed by a guerilla party at Buckster's Spring, near Fort Scott, at the affair generally known as Blunt's Massacre. At this post are placed fifteen men under a lieutenant, to guard the Santa Fé route; hence, probably, the name of *fort*. One house is occupied by a fellow called Charley Rath, a notorious desperado, who has contributed not a little to the Indian disturbances which have occasionally broken out in this vicinity. He has sold revolvers, knives, and powder to the

Kiowas. He has been warned by the Indians not to approach their villages, and yesterday he was warned off the Indian Reserve by Inspector-General Davidson for selling whisky to soldiers and Indians. There are five graves not a hundred yards from the fort, where the victims of Indians lie buried.

The Indian—the poor red man—has been used and abused by the military and civil authorities. Special legislating has been done for him time out of mind, and still he is "the poor Indian." Treaties have been made repeatedly with him, and then some unaccountable cause occurs, and the treaties are broken. Lately the War Department and the Indian Department have been exercised over the same question. The result is that all control over the Indians has been handed over by Congress to the Indian Department. We do not imagine it will mend matters in the least, but, on the contrary, will only increase the hostility and impudence of the Indian. If the War Department took charge of the entire thing we might hope, if reliable and energetic commanders were placed at the head of a sufficient number of troops, of hearing less of the hellish outrages lately committed. Of late years we have had many treaties with the Indians, but they have been as often disregarded. The butchering, murdering, and torturing of the frontier settlers have been continued in a manner that only savages could conceive. The late massacre of Phil Kearney is an instance of the horrible way in

which Indians avenge their grievances. The Indians
seem to be regarded as special *protégés* by the
Department which presides over them ; and their
unparalleled barbarities appear to be winked at.
This causes them to unduly exult, and many of them
believe that they will again be in undisputed possession of the vast territory over which they ruled
before the whites appeared in their country. To
make a war of extermination would involve vast
expense ; besides, it is not enterprise becoming a
great nation. Everything points to the coming destruction of the aboriginals of North America, but
we should not hasten their doom, if it be possible
to avoid it. There ought to be a large tract of land
given them, where they may hunt the buffalo, the
antelope, and other game, as of old. We should
keep them there ; and when any of the inhumani-
ties with which they are charged are again committed, let them be punished, man for man, blood
for blood, injury for injury, and by so doing we may
avert their speedy destruction, and avoid the terrible
murders and massacres which every now and then
visit these western military posts and frontier settlements, and the heart-rending lamentations, the

> " Widows, maidens, mothers, children,
>   Shrieking, sobbing in despair,"

will be heard no more.

Colonel J. H. Leavenworth, the Indian agent for
the Kiowas and Comanches, has arrived at Fort Zarah,

the headquarters of that agency. He has been the object of a good deal of censure from all parties, both civil and military. The military imagine he has infringed on their rights and privileges, and the civilians find fault with him because they think he cheats the Indians. As the post at Fort Dodge is in proximity to Fort Zarah, its commander, Major Douglass, and the agent, Leavenworth, are reported to be constantly at "loggerheads," and to indulge in mutual recriminations and insinuations. The gallant Major bases his charges against him on the following letter received by him from a deputation of Indians :—

"*Commanding Officer at Fort Dodge—*

"The Kioways want to know why Leavenworth does not have the goods intended for them carried to them. They say they want them. They cannot go after them ; it is too cold. Horses is poor. They have a long ways to go after buffalo. Squaws making robes. Four days to buffalo. Grass covered with snow. For them to go after the goods it would kill more horses than the goods is worth. Leavenworth has corn to feed his mules. They will not die. They want you to rite to Leavenworth and send him this also. If Leavenworth lisens to this and holds the goods, it is all right ; if not, Kioways get mad. They will not go after them. It is cut off. The dore is shut ; but they will not fight. Leavenworth can keep them. The Kioways want me to be sure and rite this, as they tell me those men were present when I rote this.

"(Signed) JOHN DODGE.

"On behalf of the following chiefs : Satanta, Poor Bear, and others."

This John Dodge, the writer of the above letter, is a half-caste trader in the Indian camp. The Major encloses it with one from himself to Colonel Leavenworth, which runs thus :—

"This letter, with bitter complaints on the part of the principal men of the Kiowa tribe, leads me to believe that there may be some possible grounds of complaint of which you may be ignorant; and I am confident that when such are brought to your knowledge you will use every means in your power to secure these Indians their just rights."

The Indians who affixed their marks to their names on the precious document above alluded to were the leaders of the bands that raided into Texas last September, where they massacred unoffending whites, and took white women prisoners. At the approach of winter the women were brought to Fort Dodge, where they were ransomed for $2,800 by the Quartermaster. They were the daughters of Mr. Box, a farmer, who was killed during the Indian raid in Texas. The guilty Indians are even now hanging around in the vicinity of the fort, endeavouring to sell the mules, horses and other stolen property. The Indian Department, on receipt of the intelligence of the raid, sent positive orders to Colonel Leavenworth not to distribute the annuities until the Indians delivered up the captive females and stolen property, and gave assurances not to repeat their raid. In compliance with those instructions the agent deemed it his duty to withhold the goods intended for distribution. Those who were penitent received their portion, but those who "rode the high horse," and failed to make restitution, are still encamped at Fort Dodge, swearing dire vengeance on the white man when the young grass of spring appears.

I am told that there are about five hundred lodges of Sioux, Arapahoes, and several bands of Kiowas, gathered together for hostile purposes.

In the last treaty, made May 20th, 1866, between General Sanborn, Kit Carson, Colonel Leavenworth, and others on the part of the United States, of the first part, and Ton-a-en-ko, Satanta, Satank, Boyah-wah-to-yeh-be, Quel-park, Pecha-naw-quoip, Esh-e-tave-pa-rah, Oh-to-ah-ne-so-to-wheo, Ah-cra-kah-tan-nah, or Parry-wah-say-mer, and several other Indians with equally unpronounceable names, chiefs of the Comanches and Kiowas, of the second part, it was expressly agreed that perpetual peace should be maintained between the people and government of the United States and the Comanche and Kiowa tribes of Indians, and that those tribes would abstain from all depredations and raids against the whites. Yet, no later than September last, these tribes went to Texas and committed most diabolical atrocities,

I. C

and then, at the approach of winter, appeared at Fort Dodge to claim their annuities.

The eldest Miss Box, in presence of Major Douglass and his subalterns, pointing to Ton-a-en-ko, said, with horror written in every lineament of her countenance: " There stands the man who slew my father. I saw him stab him in the breast, his knife reeking with his blood when he pulled it out ; and he has my father's clothes on, even now, and oh, my God ! you are giving him flour, sugar, and silver medals. Shame upon you, sir ! Why don't you arrest him ? "

Ah ! that is the question. Why not ? Instead of harbouring the red fiends within the walls and enclosures of his fort, the Major ought to have sent them out bag and baggage to take care of themselves. Details that would shock even the most callous are daily poured into our ear of the scenes which have been enacted at Fort Dodge. But we shall see for ourselves, whether it is possible these things which I have heard from Colonel Leavenworth and his friends can be true.

From Fort Zarah to Fort Larned—Scenes on the Route--
   Buffalo, Antelope, Wolves, *Mephitis Americana*, and Prairie
   Dogs—Pen Sketches of Hancock, Smith, and Davidson.

FORT LARNED, KANSAS, *April 10th*, 1867.

EACH State in the great confederation has its peculiarities and wonders. California boasts her

monster trees and her precious metals ; Kentucky her
"Mammoth Cave"; Missouri her iron mountain;
New York, the Croton aqueduct and its metropolitan
city and harbour ; Pennsylvania her vast petroleum
fields and her inexhaustible mines of anthracite coal,
etc., etc. ; but Kansas boasts, and that justly, of her
boundless grassy prairies.

Many readers may not be aware that Fort Larned
is in Kansas. Fort Larned is 275 miles west of
the Missouri River, and Kansas extends almost
100 miles further west; from which we gather that
Kansas is a large State, and her prairies of great
magnitude. She has also many fine rivers. The
Arkansas, Kansas, and Republican may be mentioned as noble specimens, while she has scores of
streams, abounding with various kinds of fish.

Throughout the many hundred miles which it
traverses from its sources to its confluence with the
Mississippi, the Arkansas River flows through no
district so wild, so primitive, or so untrodden by
civilisation, as that part of Kansas which is watered
by it, and which opened to our view as we journeyed
from Zarah to Larned. For centuries the painted
Indian has lorded over it, and careered over the
pathless plains after the American bison in the wild
exuberance of freedom. Celebrated chiefs renowned
for valour, after their own fashion, have departed one
after another to the "happy hunting grounds."
Generations after generations have been swept away,
mingling their dust with the common mother, and

leaving to their successors their ancient traditions and usages, as well as their darkness and barbarism. The Indians of the present day hunt the buffalo and the antelope over this lone and level land as freely as their ancestors, except where the white man has erected a fort.

The country through which we are travelling grows wilder in its aspect, and the plains more immense as civilised Kansas recedes from touch with us. The whole of the journey from Zarah to Larned was crossed with more circumspection and discretion than distinguished any of our previous marches. The long commissary, quartermasters' and baggage trains were kept closely together by detachments of cavalry. The infantry marched in close, compact columns, and the veteran commanding officer was often seen casting glances of pride at the fine body of men under his command. The 7th Cavalry presented a good appearance, and their Colonel, General Smith, took every occasion to drill them in cavalry tactics. When not practising, they marched in solid squadrons, the sight of which must have struck with terror any observing bands of Indians. Old hunters shook their heads ominously when they heard the hoarse *ca-au* of the crows and the howl of the *cuyote*, and they asserted most emphatically that Indians were not far off the line of march. But there was nothing to apprehend so long as we had five experienced Generals with us. The march after a while became rather monotonous, and no amount of jests and songs, and a variety of sights and scenes incidental to a march could enliven it. The same perpetual prairie could be seen stretching away as far as the eye could see, till sky and land seemed merged together.

While scanning the horizon, hoping that some object would heave in sight to relieve the dreadful sameness, we were greatly gratified to hear some officer on our left exclaiming, " What huge moving objects are those ? " indicating with his finger the objects he referred to, which were shadowed out into grand proportions by the vapour rising out of the ground. One man hazarded the opinion that they were buffalo, which remark was met by a diminutive specimen of humanity, saying, " You git ; them 'ere are some stray mules." Some of the youngest of the party were for instantly galloping towards them for the purpose of satisfying any doubts there might be upon the subject, but they were checked from pursuing that course, because of the stringent and positive orders of Hancock. Constrained by curiosity, blind instinct, or some wayward impulse of their own, those uncouth objects advanced towards the column, and near enough to prove to us that they were *bonâ fide* buffalo. They stood still for a while, about a dozen in number, great, shaggy, powerful beasts, tempting-looking objects for an amateur sportsman. Evidently they did not relish our proximity, so they wheeled around, and, galloping away, were soon lost to view in the distance.

We now and then caught a glimpse of ante-

lope bounding and racing away at a remarkable pace.
We also saw the grey wolf as he prowled around in
the neighbourhood of the trains, ready to pounce
upon anything that promised to allay his hunger.
The grey wolf grows to the size of a big sheep-dog,
and has the appearance of a savage and dangerous
beast; but prairie travellers unite in saying that he is
a cowardly animal, and unless reinforced by great
numbers will not attack man. In this respect they
differ from Russian wolves. Another species of animal
was seen in great numbers, whose presence caused
us great annoyance—*i.e.* the *Mephitis Americana*,
yclept the pole-cat, which invariably at our approach
turned its dorsal extremities towards us, at which we
all evinced a tendency to keep aloof, as it was anything but pleasant to breathe the fetid odour.

Prairie dogs, also chirped away defiantly at us, and
causing one of our party to remark, "Just look at
the impudent little devils, will you?" The sight of
these little dogs caused an almost endless discussion
regarding the manner in which they live. These
animals are so called by hunters from a fancied
resemblance between their chirping cry and a dog's
bark. They live principally on grass, and burrow
far-reaching holes in the ground at the extremity
of which they build their nests of buffalo grass.

On the Denver route, about nine miles from Fort
Kearney, is a settlement which is called by the inhabitants "Dog-town," from an extensive village of prairie-
dogs in its immediate vicinity. It is said to be about

seven miles long, and the burrows are found at nearly regular intervals, from twenty to thirty feet apart. As a stranger approaches, they chirp, and jerk their tails, hopping about as if undecided how to act. If they see the stranger advancing rather too near they immediately descend to their holes, where they are secure from intrusion. The animal is a little larger than the common squirrel. It is a matter of great difficulty to secure one, as at the least approach of a stranger it descends with remarkable rapidity, and if shot, it always contrives to drop "indoors," and disappear underground. An apparently ill-assorted neighbour is commonly found sharing the parts of the prairie occupied by the prairie-dogs—that is, the small owl (*Strix hypogæa*). It builds its nest in the deserted holes, and keeps "watch and ward" at the entrance, like its former occupant. When a strange object approaches their holes, these birds, which are seen standing on the little hillock of earth by the edge of the burrows, retire, leaving nothing but their heads above the ground. They then commence chattering and bowing, presenting quite a ludicrous appearance. On a nearer approach they either disappear into their burrows altogether, or skim over the plain, where they again commence their chattering and bowing.

On commencing this epistle we had not intended to write about animals, but we have been led on to it. We will now beg permission to refresh the public mind concerning the principal officers of this expedition.

Major-General Winfield Scott Hancock was born in Montgomery county, Pennsylvania, February 24th, 1824. He graduated in 1844 at West Point Military Academy, after which he was sent to the Indian Territory, where he remained until the breaking out of the Mexican war. For brilliant services at Cherubusco he was brevetted first lieutenant. When the rebellion broke out Hancock was stationed at Los Angeles, Lower California. He was then appointed Brigadier-General of volunteers in the army of the Potomac. His heroic conduct is too well known to be described here. The crowning proof of his military abilities, and his valour, came off at Gettysburg. Unawed by the furious storm of shot and shell, belched from one hundred and twenty guns, directed under the personal supervision of the most eminent Southern General, he stood at his post, freely exposing his own life, and exciting his troops by his presence and example, until victory was announced for the Union armies. He was seriously wounded in that battle, and still suffers occasionally from the wound, although to all appearances he is as active as ever. He is of a tall stately figure, in the prime of life, with a commanding appearance, and excites admiration and respect wherever he goes.

Brevet Major-General Andrew Jackson Smith, Colonel of the 7th United States Cavalry, is also a Pennsylvanian by birth. He is now about forty-seven years old. He distinguished himself at the battle of Pleasant Hill, and in the disastrous campaign of General Banks, while Generals Emory and Franklin were retreating, he continued fighting, and stubbornly contested the ground inch by inch with the enemy. When he fully realised the defeat of Banks it is said that he " sat down and wept." He has a grey head, but is as active as any young blood in the command. He is a tough old soldier ; laughs at the " dandified young bucks " who wear shoulder straps and are afraid of a little snow. During the wildest snowstorm that has visited this part for many a year, and which we experienced yesterday, the General was out on foot, tramping through the snow, performing duties with as much celerity as the youngest subaltern. Being of a kind and genial disposition, he has many friends and admirers. He commands the department of the Arkansas.

Inspector-General J. W. Davidson is a Virginian by birth. He graduated at West Point when twenty-one years of age. He served under General A. J. Smith in California for four years. During the war he commanded the troops in south-east Missouri, and the people of St. Louis will bear witness how well he performed the onerous task imposed on him in a country infested by the guerillas. He is very temperate in his habits, and never smokes, satisfied with holding an unlit cigar between his lips all day. He is attentive to duty, and somewhat of a disciplinarian. He is considered to be one of the most efficient officers on Hancock's staff. He has hosts of friends and admirers ; and no wonder, for he has " a taking way " with him.

But my letter has spun its length.

Appearance of Fort Larned—Sketch of an Officer's Life on the Frontier—Serious Accident—Learned Disquisition on the Indian—Pow-wow with the Chiefs of the Cheyennes—Speech of General Hancock—Reply of " Tall Bull "—Grand Stampede of Indians—Horrible Outrage on a White Captive—General Custer in Pursuit—Post Scriptum —Suspicious Conduct and apparent Hostility of the Indians —They decline a satisfactory Conference—Decisive Steps by General Hancock.

FORT LARNED, KANSAS, *April 13th*, 1867.

WERE you to catch a glimpse of our present forlorn condition, you would pity us, compelled as we are to transmit to you as early as possible all the news that we can glean.   This letter, like all my previous ones, is written amid the confusion which prevails in a soldier's camp—·the lively conversation of the officers pouring in at one ear, and at the other the continuous palaver of the " coloured folks " as they are preparing some officer's meal.   Our manuscript is tacked to a thin board, which forms a partition between the two halves of our valise, to escape the fate which befel the sibylline leaves of old.   A small " monsoon " is blowing, which makes our tent to reel like a drunken man, and to keep a terrible racket with its flaps.   It has started to rain ; there are holes in the tent ; drops of rain fall through on the letter like great welling tears. . . . Yet notwithstanding the unfavourable circumstances under which we daily labour, we feel in duty bound to do the best we can.

Standing on the summit of the hill that overlooks the plain of Larned as we approach it from the eastward, our eyes were gladdened by the sight of the fort, and close to it could be traced the tortuous course of the Pawnee Fork. As we advanced nearer to the fort, we obtained a better view of its surroundings. The banks of the Pawnee, whose waters flow from the slopes of the Rocky Mountains, are adorned with plants, umbrageous shrubbery, and patriarchal trees, whose freshness pleasingly contrasts with the naked tops of the hills in the distance. The spot on which the fort is situated is a green oasis in the Sahara of bleached grass. Beautiful as the plain is at present, it was lovelier by far before the volunteer soldiers came and destroyed more than two-thirds of the trees that lined the Pawnee's banks. From the top of one of the barracks can be seen a wide area, stretching away in all directions, the hills swelling into every variety of form, until the indistinct outline of their summits blends with the sky where it touches the horizon. The course of the Pawnee may be traced by the trees, whose dark foliage indicate the windings of the stream. The whole, to be appreciated, must be seen as we saw it just then, in the approaching twilight, through a bright, clear atmosphere, and amidst the opening foliage and bursting blossoms of early spring.

Fort Larned is commanded by Major Henry Asbury, a gentleman who served with some distinction in the late war. It is a model of neatness. Everything is carried on according to the strict letter of the military code. Guard mounting, inspection, and dress parade are announced by the familiar sounds of the fife and drum, accompanied by all the pomp and circumstance of military form. The officers are affable with their equals, and gracious towards their subordinates. The quartermaster is a linguist, and takes to all sorts of trades kindly ; acts as commissary, superintendent of Government works, and a general referee on all subjects.

This fort also boasts of its characters. One of them is an old soldier seventy-two years old, who has served forty-three years in the United States army and is still straight as an arrow, and of undiminished vigour. The post surgeon gives him great praise as a nurse, and from what we saw of the tender manner in which he handled the sick, we think he is certainly efficient. Another is a soldier named Klein, who has served sixteen years, and is now within ninety-three days of the end of his last enlistment. As each day passes, he rubs the mark of it off a board which he has hanging in his room, and in this way reminds himself of the time he has yet to serve.

Dave Butterfield, of Butterfield's express notoriety, has a trading camp near this post. He has obtained about three thousand fine buffalo robes.   In his camp we met Mr. Charles Tracy, a gentleman of St. Louis, who looks hale and hearty, and evidently enjoys himself in the wilderness.

According to invitation from General Hancock, fifteen chiefs of the Cheyennes, or " Dog soldiers," came to camp last night, that the General might impress on their minds the necessity of keeping to the strict letter of their treaties.   The Council which followed their arrival presented a most curious yet somewhat imposing sight by the light of the fires. The military officers were dressed in full uniform— gold epaulettes, tall hats glittering with gold.   The artillery especially made a fine show, with their red horse tails.

On one side of the great camp fire sat Generals Hancock, Smith, Custer, Davidson, and Gibbs, and a score of other officers ; while on the other sat the Indian chiefs with Major Edward Wynkoop, their agent and interpreter.   The Indians were dressed in various styles, many of them with the orthodox army overcoat, some with gorgeous red blankets, while their faces were painted and their bodies bedizened in all the glory of the Indian toilette.   To the hideous slits in their ears were hanging large rings of brass ; they wore armlets of silver, wrist-rings of copper, necklaces of beads of variegated colours, breast ornaments of silver shields, and Johnson silver medals, and their scalplocks were adorned with a long string of thin silver discs.

Generals Hancock and Smith were introduced to "Tall Bull" and "White Horse," the two principal chiefs, after which Hancock, taking off his overcoat, and standing in all the bravery of a Major-General's uniform, spoke as follows :—

"I told your agents some time ago that I was coming here to see you, and if any of you wanted to speak to me they could do so. I don't find many chiefs here. What is the reason? I have a great deal to say to the Indians, but I want to talk with them all together. To-morrow I am going to their camp. I have an Indian boy with me, whom the Cheyennes claim. We had made a promise to find this boy, and a girl, who were somewhere in the United States. We have found the boy—and here he is, ready to be delivered to his nearest relative. I will leave him at Fort Larned with the commander. He will deliver him up to them. The girl is near Denver. We have written for her, and she will be sent here, either to your agent or to the commander at Fort Larned, for delivery to her relatives. You see the boy has not been injured ; the girl will be delivered by us also uninjured. Look out that any captives in your hands be restored to us equally unharmed. Now I have a great many soldiers— more than all the tribes put together. The Great Father has heard that some Indians have taken white men and women captives. He has heard, also, that a great many Indians are trying to get up war. That is the reason that I came down here. I intend not

only to visit you here, but my troops will remain
among you, to see that the peace of the plains is preserved.   I am going also to visit you in your camps.
The innocent, and those who are truly our friends, we
shall treat as brothers.   If we find hereafter that any
of you have lied to us, we will strike you.   In case of
war, we shall punish whoever befriends our enemies.
If there are any tribes among you who have captives,
white or black, you must give them up, safe and
unharmed.   I have collected all the evidence of all
outrages committed by you, so that your agents
may examine into the matter and tell me who are
guilty, and who are innocent.   When your agent
informs me who the guilty are I will punish them ;
when just demands are made I will enforce them,
if they be not attended to.   I have heard that a
great many Indians want to fight ; very well, we
are here, and are come prepared for war.   If you are
for peace, you know the conditions ; if you are for
war, look out for its consequences.   Your agent is
your friend, but he knows his friendship will not save
you from the anger of your Great Father if we go to
war.   If we find any good Indians, and they come to
us with clean hands, we will treat them as brothers,
and we will separate them from the malcontents, and
provide for them, if necessary.   This we will do that
the innocent may escape the war which will be waged
against the guilty.   The soldiers are going to stay in
the country, and they will see that the white man
keeps his treaty as well as the red man.   We are

building railroads and military roads through the country ; you must not let your young men stop them, and you must keep your men off the road. These roads will benefit the Indians as well as the white man in bringing their goods to them cheaply and promptly. The steam-car and waggon-train must run, and it is of importance to the whites and Indians that the mails, goods and passengers carried on them shall be safe. You know very well if you go to war with the white man you would lose. The Great Father has many more warriors. It is true you might kill some soldiers and surprise some small detachments, but you would lose men, and you know that you have not a great many to lose. You cannot replace warriors lost ; we can. It is to your interest to have peace with the white man. Every tribe ought to have a great chief, one that will command them. For any depredations committed by any one of his tribe I shall hold the chief and his tribe responsible. Some Indians go down to Texas and kill women and children. I shall strike the tribes that they belong to. If there are any good Indians who don't want to go to war, I shall help them and protect them. If there are any bad chiefs, I will help the good chiefs to put their heels on them. I have a great many chiefs with me that have commanded more men than ever you saw, and they have fought more great battles than you have fought fights. A great many Indians think they are better armed than they were formerly, but they must recollect that we are also. My chiefs cannot derive any distinction from fighting with your small numbers. They are not anxious for wars against Indians, but are ready for a just war, and know how to fight, and lead their men. Let the guilty then beware. I say this to you to show you the importance of keeping treaties made with us, and of letting the white man travel unmolested. Your Great Father is your friend, as well as the friend of the white man. If a white man behaves badly, or does a wrong to you, he shall be punished, if the evidence ascertained at the trial proves him guilty. [Great sensation among the Indians.] We can redress your wrongs better than you can. [Groans of "Waugh, waugh."] I have no more to say. I will await the end of this council, to see whether you want war or peace. I will put what I say in black and white, and send it to each post commander in the country I command. You can have it read to you when you please, and you can come back after a while and read it, and you will know whether we have lied to you or not."

General Hancock sat down, and deep silence prevailed in the council. The grave, taciturn countenances of the red warriors indicated deep consideration of the words they had heard. The officers, on their part, were also silent. Then a chief lit the calumet of peace, inhaled two or three whiffs, and handed it around to his compeers. When that important ceremony was over, the chief, with much dignity in his bearing, sprang to his feet, and folding his red and black robe around him, so that he could have the

I.   D

free use of his right arm, extended his hand towards General Hancock, and uttered the word " How ! " at the same time.   To each of Hancock's soldier chiefs he spoke the same word, and gravely shook hands with them.   Then moving to the centre of the council, " Tall Bull," a chief of the Cheyennes, addressed it in the following words :—

" You sent for us ; we came here.   We have made a treaty with our agent, Colonel Wynkoop.   We never did the white man any harm ; we don't intend to.   Our agent told us to meet you here.   Whenever you want to go on the Smoky Hill you can go.   You can go on any road.   When we come on the road your young men must not shoot us.   We are willing to be friends with the white man.   [A pause.]

" This boy you have here, we have seen him ; we don't recognise him ; he must belong to some tribe south of the Arkansas.   The buffalo are diminishing fast.   The antelope that were plenty a few years ago are now few.   When they will all die away we shall be hungry.   We shall want something to eat, and we shall be compelled to come into the fort.   Your young men must not fire on us.   Whenever they see us they fire, and we fire on them.   [A pause.]   The Kiowas, Comanches, Apaches, and Arapahoes, you should send and get them here, and talk with them.   [A pause.] You say you are going to our village to-morrow. If you go, I shall have no more to say to you there than here.   I have said all I want to say here. [Interrupted by the General—" I am going, however, to your camp to-morrow."]   I don't know whether the Sioux are coming here or not.   They did not tell me they were coming.   I have spoken."

We saw a great many noble faces among the Indians around the council fire.   One of them somewhat resembled President Jackson, according to the average picture of him.   We were formerly under the impression that there were no noble-looking Indians, save in the fervid fancies of a Fenimore Cooper, but we must confess that they do exist, even at the present day, and that we have seen them.

The Indians lately have horrified the people of the United States by diabolical and cruel massacres. These called for instant retaliation and severe punishment.   Detachments from this expedition have been already sent to punish them.   Though the Indians south of the Platte were entirely innocent of any participation in the atrocities, it was rumoured that, elated at the success of the tribes in the north, they likewise intended to try the same game in the south. In that case, the southern Indians, upon seeing the extensive preparations the President has made to meet them, will be awed into quietness, and will be rather inclined to keep to the strict letter of their treaties, and on terms with the whites.   Any confederations they may have formed will be crushed and annihilated, and for that reason alone the present expedition will have produced beneficial results.

The Indians, in times bygone, kindled their watchfires on the Atlantic coast, to the infinite terror of the Pilgrim Fathers, and on the slopes of the Alleghanies, to the dismay and discontent of the Quakers.   Their descendants kindle their signal-fires on the slopes and on the snow-clad peaks of the Rocky Mountains, on the Pacific coast, and in the prairie. The same system of violence that the Indians of yore pursued is followed at the present day by their descendants, to the detriment of agricultural enterprise, and the development of the country.   The pertinacity with which they resist the advance of the whites, the hatred with which they bear the yoke of civilisation, their unshrinking hardihood, and their contempt of death, will, for years to come, employ the sober pen of the historian.   The expectations of the Indian, cherished now and then as some mad dream flits across his poor brain, concerning the repossession of the entire lands of his fathers, turn out repeatedly ephemeral and illusory.   As the buffalo and antelope vanish, so will they, and that before many years have elapsed.   Annihilation of the many and absorption of the remainder is clearly their doom.   But extermination, which is often urged by vindictive Western men, is alike impolitic as it is barbarous.   Let us hope, however, that the awful and heartrending scene of homesteads turned into pyramids of flame, making the dark night lurid with destroying fire, and the morning sun dawning on smouldering masses of embers, bones, and blood, will no more electrify the nation with the horrible details.   " Taps." The lights must be out.

CHEYENNE CAMP, FIFTY MILES FROM FORT LARNED,

April 14th, 1867.

P.S.—We have a chance to send you a hasty account of what happened yesterday. General Hancock, perceiving that the principal chief of the Cheyennes did not intend to present himself, determined, as he informed the chiefs at the pow-wow, to move to the Cheyenne camp. When half-way to it he was met by three hundred and twenty-nine chiefs and braves of the Cheyenne and Sioux nations. The troops advanced and formed line quietly, and halted within one hundred and fifty yards of the Indians. The Indians also stopped to await Major Wynkoop, their agent, who was coming towards them. Each chief and brave had his arrows in his hand, and his bow drawn. "Roman Nose," the chief of a band of Cheyennes, bore a white flag, but, although there were no signs of hostility on our part, when they saw the formidable appearance of our troops, they became immediately disturbed, and many of them were seen to edge gradually off, and presently to set off for their camp at a run. "Roman Nose" himself drew up near the General's staff with a small company of chiefs and warriors. He had a fine pair of gold epaulettes, and was otherwise dressed magnificently. General Hancock sharply demanded of him whether the Indians wanted peace or war, to which "Roman Nose" replied, "We don't want war; if we did, we would not come so close to your big guns."

General Hancock introduced General Smith as his big chief, who would remain with his troops in the country, and he wished him respected as such when he returned home.   Hancock then asked "Roman Nose" why he did not visit him at the fort as requested; to which he replied : "My horses are poor, and every man that comes to me tells me a different tale about your intentions."

The General told him then that he was going to visit their camp, and as he had a great deal to say to their chiefs, he wished them all to come and see him at his tent when in camp.   The troops then moved on, and arrived near the Indian village about two o'clock P.M.   We afterwards camped near it.   A few Indians stood outside the village, evidently observing our motions.

Towards night, three or four chiefs came to the General's quarters, and informed him that all the women and children had left, and had scattered over the prairie, because they were afraid of the troops. About eight o'clock that evening it was ascertained that mostly all the Indians had left with every article of value they could lay their hands on, leaving their hide wigwams standing.   The troops were immediately mustered, and General Custer, with the 7th Cavalry, was sent to scout the neighbourhood.   The battery was also planted, so as to command each side of the camp. The soldiers remained under arms during the whole night. General Custer has not yet returned from the pursuit.

There seems to be a confederation between the Cheyennes and Sioux for evil purposes. The Indian village consists of about three hundred hide lodges. They show unmistakable traces of the haste of their owners to get away,—dogs half eaten up, untanned buffalo robes, axes, pots, kettles, and pans, beads and gaudy finery, lately killed buffalo, stews already cooked in the kettles, are scattered about promiscuously, strewing the ground. Detachments of infantry guard the camps to prevent spoliation by the troops. But in spite of the strict guard kept, the "boys in blue" are continually carrying away mementoes of their bloodless victory, such as stiff buffalo robes, dog skins, calumets, tomahawks, war clubs, beadwork, moccasins, and we saw one officer of the artillery carrying off a picininny Indian pup which looked very forlorn. Arrows and knives are picked up by the dozen, and also little dolls, which had been the gratification of the papooses. The soldiers rummage and pick up things in the most senseless manner, and after carrying them a few yards throw them away, when they are soon picked up by somebody else, and thrown away again. We saw plenty of dog hash and dog heads cooked. The chiefs' wigwams were painted in a gaudy manner. A young white girl has been found who, according to the surgeon, has been outraged by no less than six

Indians. She is now in our camp, and is a most pitiable object to look at.

General Hancock is so angry that he intends to burn the camp to-day.   But the mail is closing, and I must close.

Indian Incendiarism and Murder—Scalping and Burning—
General Custer's Command divided and pursuing.

DESERTED CHEYENNE VILLAGE, THIRTY MILES FROM
FORT LARNED,

April 18*th,* 1867.

DISPATCHES received last night at headquarters from General Custer announce that the fugitive Indians had burned three stations on the Smoky Hill route, and killed three white men, and scalped and burnt them.   Orders have been sent to each post, both on the Santa Fé and Smoky Hill routes, warning all posts to be on the alert, as the Indians had broken out at last, and intended to be true to the threats they uttered during the winter.   This outbreak is attributed to the Sioux, who encamped with the Cheyennes in this village.   General Custer has divided his command, taking five companies of cavalry himself to pursue the main body of Cheyennes and Sioux, while three companies of cavalry have been sent after that particular band which committed the raid, and is supposed to belong to those Sioux who were in the massacre lately at Phil Kearney.   We strike out for Fort Dodge to-morrow,

A Paradise of Nature—The Cheyenne Eden-Beauty and Squalor—Indian Courtship and Marriage—A Wigwam—The deserted Camp—An Ancient Couple—An Outraged Captive—Burning of Cheyenne and Sioux Lodges by Hancock—$100,000 Worth destroyed—The Conflagration a Necessity—Hancock and the Indian Department.

CAMP NEAR CHEYENNE VILLAGE, THIRTY MILES FROM FORT LARNED, KANSAS,

April 20th, 1867.

THE Cheyenne village is located in the centre of a grove of noble elms, which covers a square area of three hundred paces along the banks of the Pawnee River. From our tent door the white tops of the Indian wigwams may be seen, gleaming through the trees. The aborigines undoubtedly display great taste in the selection of their camping grounds. Water and wood are indispensable necessities to the Indian, as well as to the white settler. But the savages, roaming at large over the whole country, can select, of all the thousand and one lovely spots which Nature has so bountifully provided, the loveliest of all. And it is without exaggeration we style the spot on which the Indians pitched their village as scenically pretty. But within, the village is foul, so foul, indeed, as to defy description.

We may shock the sensibilities of romance-loving boys and girls by relating the manner in which the dark-eyed aboriginal damsel is espoused. There have

been poems sung on the beauties of Pocahontas and
Hiawatha, but we have not seen an Indian girl yet
that we could compose an ode upon.   The voluptuous
form, olive features, ripe, red lips, delicate feet, well-
formed ankles, humid eyes, wavy masses of raven hair,
a queenly head and a swan-like neck, as described
by the Cooper and Murray type of romancers, we
have not seen.   But we have seen matter-of-fact,
and most unromantic Indian girls handling dextrously
the axe, cutting wood for their liege lord's supper,
who were remarkable for coarse black hair, low fore-
heads, blazing coal-black eyes, faces of a dirty, greasy
colour, who were not over modestly dressed, and who
sometimes carried staring, round-eyed, and grinning
papooses, on whom they seemed to scorn to bestow
the maternal endearments so natural to a mother's
heart.

When an Indian wishes a squaw to attend his
lodge, cook his meals, and wait upon him, he does
not launch into lyrical enthusiasm ; nor does he think
in his wooing mood of the existence of a sky or the
green woods about him, but simply asks the prosaic
question, "How much is she worth ?"   The amount
being ascertained, and if he has the means, he lays
it at the feet of her father, and takes her to his lodge.
From that time she is his own.   Probably the manner
in which he has been raised accounts for his matter
of fact manner of treating the *fair* sex.   When an
infant, he was looked upon as an encumbrance, by
his inexpressive mother.   This treatment probably

called forth that Spartan stoicism and hardihood
for which the North American savage is celebrated.

The style and architecture of a "wigwam" is
almost invariably the same, its size varying from
fifty to seventy-five feet in circumference at the base,
and in height from the base to the apex of the tent
about twelve feet. Twenty poles planted around and
meeting at the top, where they are tied firmly with a
covering of tanned buffalo robes, form the wigwam.
The top is left open to represent a window, and a flap
in the side represents a door, by which the Indian
enters *on all fours.* In this unpartitioned lodge sleep
the Indian, his wife (or wives), and children, and
frequently his children's husbands and their wives.

The furniture is quite in keeping with the "house."
Name the saucepan, camp-kettle, three or four horn
spoons, of home manufacture, two or three wooden
dishes, likewise of home manufacture, and you have
as thorough an inventory as any auctioneer could
make. It is not by inadvertence that the coffee-
roasting, grinding, and boiling apparatus are absent
from the list, for the luxury of a cup of coffee is not
amongst the home comforts of the Indian, unless he
has lately visited a Government fort. Half-a-dozen
buffalo robes are the only articles approaching bed
furniture which he possesses, all of which contain an
accumulation of filth and vermin. Towels and soap
are of course unknown luxuries, and his personal
costume entirely accords with his other domestic
equipments, his scanty and only covering being a

" breech-clout," generally ragged, and never washed. Of course in winter the Indian covers his nakedness with a red blanket, or a buffalo robe, or an army overcoat.

Morality is hardly known amongst the Indians ; but it frequently happens that when a squaw is unfaithful to her spouse *her nose is cut off* (!), which, surely, does not add to the beauty of her countenance. As a mother, the squaw ranks but little above the lower animals, she makes no preparation for child-birth, and possessing, apparently, no instinctive fore-thought, she as frequently introduces her young into the world on the open prairie as under the friendly shelter of the wigwam. The papoose is swaddled in any chance rag that offers, and the mother resumes her work or journey as if nothing had happened.

Among the only living beings found in the deserted village were one old warrior and his squaw, one little captive girl, two grown dogs, one young Indian "purp," and five or six miserable Indian ponies. The old Indian warrior had seen, as he himself expressed it, "eighty summers," and with his squaw was found in the most sorry plight, and when brought into our camp to be fed, expressed a wish to be taken into his own lodge to be left there to die in peace. He had been left, according to the tradi-tional custom of the Indians, to die. Being old, decrepit, and useless, and of no earthly use to his tribe, he had been left there to starve with his squaw. The squaw was found busily preparing a dog for supper. They were provided with five days' rations, which would prove sufficient, while we stayed to watch proceedings in the neighbourhood of the Cheyenne camp. The outraged girl seems to be eight years old, and is undoubtedly white. She was taken care of by our surgeon, Dr. Breuer, and is at present doing as well as could be expected.

This morning General Hancock ordered the Indian lodges to be burnt. He was compelled to adopt this course, because, after the delivery of his speech to the fifteen chiefs, they went and burnt three stations on the Smoky Hill route, and scalped, disembowelled, and burnt three men employed at Fossil Creek station, ran off several mules and horses on that route, and gave a good scare generally to the traders. According to Custer's official report to General Hancock, the station hands are leaving for "America," east of the Missouri River, and the ranche men are barricading their ranches, and preparing for a desperate resistance.

At a council of war, it was deemed advisable to retaliate immediately by burning the Indian village.

The following is a true list of the miscellanea which were consigned to the flames this morning : 251 lodges, 942 buffalo robes, 436 horn saddles, 435 travesties, 287 bead mats, 191 axes, 190 kettles, 77 frying-pans, 350 tin cups, 30 whetstones, 212 sacks of paint, 98 water kegs, 7 ovens, 41 grubbing horns, 28 coffee mills, 144 lariat ropes, 129 chairs, 303 parflecks,

15 curry combs, 67 coffee pots, 46 hoes, 81 flicking irons, 149 horn spoons, 27 crowbars, 73 brass kettles, 17 hammers, 8 stewpans, 15 drawing knives, 25 spades, 4 scythes, 8 files, 19 bridles, 8 pitchforks, 15 teakettles, 90 spoons, 15 knives, 10 pickaxes, 1 sword, 1 bayonet, 1 U.S. mail bag, 74 stone mallets, 1 lance, 33 wooden spoons, 251 doormats, 48 raw hide ropes, and 22 meat stones.

The loss of these articles will be severely felt by the Indian tribes—Cheyennes and Sioux. It will require 3,000 buffaloes to be killed to procure enough hides to make their " wigwams." The whole outfit of an entire wigwam costs, on an average, one hundred dollars. Six different stacks were made of the effects taken from the village ; everything was promiscuously thrown in, and fire set to them all at the same moment. The dry poles of the wigwams caught fire like tinder, and so many burning hides made the sky black with smoke. Flakes of fire were borne on the breeze to different parts of the prairie, setting the prairie grass on fire. With lightning speed the fire rolled on, and consumed an immense area of grass, while the black smoke slowly sailed skyward. Every green thing, and every dead thing that reared its head above the earth, was consumed, while the buffalo, the antelope, and the wolf fled in dismay from the destructive agent.

At this retaliation the Indian agents cry with hands aloft, " Oh, Lord, what will become of Hancock ? " The General commanding has been very kind and courteous to the agents, but everything that he has done, so far, has been met by them with acrimonious censure. Considering the explicit nature of his instructions from the War Department, there is no necessity for the deference which he pays them, but he has wished to show them and the country at large that if they have more experience in Indian affairs than himself, he is quite willing to profit by their advice. But the Indians deceived him and commenced hostilities, and he was compelled to burn their villages. He had waited patiently at Larned for the chiefs to come to the council, but they only came in groups of twos and threes five days after the day appointed for it, which involved him in endless embarrassment.

Custer has gone northward in hot pursuit on the trails of the Indians, and will probably not halt until he reaches their encampment on Beaver Creek.

Hancock's reception at Fort Dodge—The awakening of the Government — Satanta's discretion — A spirited fight — Another pow-wow.

FORT DODGE, KANSAS, *April 25th.*

AFTER three days' march across the barren, bleak, and sandy hills, beyond Larned, we arrived at Fort Dodge.

As soon as we were seen descending the brow of the hill that shut off Fort Dodge from our view, the commanding-General was greeted by a salute of fifteen guns, and the garrison at the same time was turned out, and presented arms, under command of Major Douglass, its commander.   Hancock seemed pleased with the manner of his reception, and paid great attention to the soldierly appearance of the men.   The old fort in which the garrison resides is surrounded by embankments with sallyports, moat, and wooden drawbridges.   Some former commander evidently bestowed great care on it, and it has been planned with an amount of skill that was unexpected in the middle of the plains, and the fort is kept as neat as possible.   The approaches to it are commanded by a battery of four howitzers.

We discarded all proffers of hospitality with a remarkable degree of self-denial.   The hard-cracker, counterfeit coffee, hog meat, pork and beans, and the suavity of our Irish cook, with an overflowing plenty, sweetened and seasoned with hearty friendship, reconciled us to our lot.

The Government apparently is awakened to the following facts : First, that the Santa Fé route is important ; second, that soldiers are enlisted to do military duties—and not to be quarrymen, common labourers, and clodhoppers ; third, that the frontier should be protected ; and fourth, that Indians should be regarded otherwise than as special *protégés*, licensed to commit all sorts of depredations unpunished.   As proofs that the Government has awakened from its apathy, General Smith's brigade will remain to guard the Santa Fé route, and the 7th Cavalry will act as patrols in the country ; civilian-mechanics and labourers are to be set to work on Government fortifications, and instead of the miserable adobe hovels, termed stations, strong, substantial buildings, are to be erected at intervals along this road ; and Hancock was permitted to inform the Indian chiefs at Larned that they were to be punished " like the white man " if found guilty of committing any depredations. Escorts sufficient for the protection of the mail will be furnished at each station. It has frequently been the custom for overloaded stages to dump the mail into some of the creeks that run across the road. In Plum Creek, above Fort Larned, when the expedition passed over it, were found five bags of mail matter, and one sack of books, which consisted fortunately of only agricultural reports.

On hearing of the destruction of the Cheyenne village, Satanta and Satank, with their Kiowa bands, emigrated to distant parts on the Arkansas, doubtless believing that discretion is the better part of valour. " Little Raven's " band of Arapahoes also took flight with almost as much rapidity as the ominous bird from which the chief derives his name. With the exception of Ton-a-en-ko, or " Kicking Eagle's " band of Kiowas, who came to the fort to the pow-wow with the " big chief," there are no Indians at present in the immediate vicinity of the fort, and the disgraceful scenes we expected to see were not realised. All was order, neatness, and strict discipline.

I.   E

A spirited and exciting little affair occurred five miles above Cimmarron Springs, which is about thirty miles above this place. On learning that the Cheyennes and Sioux had decamped from the banks of the Pawnee, General Hancock immediately despatched his express riders to all the posts on the Arkansas River, warning the commanders of each post to be on the alert, as the Indians were on the war-path, and at the same time he ordered two companies of cavalry under Major Cooper to intercept the Indians should any undertake to cross the Arkansas at Cimmarron Springs, the nearest fording-place. On Friday last, while one of the cavalrymen was out grazing his horse, he was shot at by an Indian. Mounting his horse, he galloped to camp and gave the alarm. Major Cooper instantly sent with him a scouting party of fifteen men, who, on arriving at the place designated, could see no enemy at first, but were soon made aware of their presence by being fired upon from an island in the Arkansas. A few volleys from the scouts soon made the island untenable for the Indians, who beat a retreat across the Arkansas, throwing away their rifles into the river. The soldiers crossed after them and commenced an exciting chase of ten miles right into the heart of the Indian country, which seemed to be alive with the red men ; and not until six Indians had been killed did they cease the pursuit. On inspection of the bodies there was found in the girdle of one of them the scalp of a woman with long auburn hair attached to it, which so angered the soldiers that they refused to bury the dead. These Indians were probably *avant couriers* of the main body of the Cheyennes. They were painted for war, and stripped to the "buff." The main body, we presume on the non-arrival of their scouts, went higher up the river, but a party of them returned last night and robbed the Cimmarron mail station of eleven mules, the property of the mail company. A detachment of cavalry is hotly pursuing them and on their trail, and they will probably pay dearly for their temerity.

In accordance with the invitation of General Hancock, which was sent to the chiefs of the Kiowa tribe of Indians, Kicking Eagle, Stumbling Bear, and Atalie, brother of Ta-hawsen, late head chief of the Kiowas, with a few braves, came into the fort yesterday, and held a pow-wow with Hancock and General Smith who is in command of this department. As we have already copied his speech, we will only give a portion referring expressly to the Kiowas, as rendered officially. General Hancock, after the calumet of peace had as usual been passed around the circle, rose and said :—

"It will not be safe for any Indians to roam between the Arkansas and Platte Rivers, for our soldiers will not be able to distinguish friends from foes, or Kiowas from the Sioux and Cheyennes, unless those soldiers happen to have scouts who could give the requisite information. Our soldiers might fire on them, and by so doing might injure our friends. We

E 2

shall require all Indians who are friendly to stay south of the Arkansas, and then no mistakes will occur. If everything is quiet here, our soldiers will be stationed on the Smoky Hill and the Platte, but should they have occasion to come to the Arkansas, they may not be able to discern their friends from hostile Indians. Last year I had but a small force of troops, but now I command more soldiers than all your warriors together. My intentions were to have brought them down here, that you might see them, but as the Cheyennes and Sioux had dug the hatchet and behaved falsely, I was compelled to send them after those Indians. We wish to engage friendly Indians as scouts, either Kiowas, Comanches, or Arapahoes. We will not have others. They shall receive the same pay as our soldiers, besides horses, guns, blankets, etc. They will be commanded by white officers, who will inform them of their necessary duties. We shall require them to keep the Cheyennes and Sioux away from this route. Whenever they desire to quit our service they are at liberty to do so. In the meantime, while engaged in this capacity, their families will be provided for. They shall be dressed finely and in suitable clothes. They will be soldiers of the Great Father, sharing the same privileges as the white soldiers. Report to other chiefs what I have told you, for I wish to know if the terms are agreeable. We expected to see more of your chiefs in this council. We intend going south to see if we can meet other Kiowas and Comanches. Then we

intend going north of the Arkansas, on some of the
creeks, to look for Sioux and Cheyennes. We shall
not come back unless there arise some disturbances
which will compel us to return. That's all I intended
to say to you."

Atalie, "the man that moves"—half brother to
Ta-hawsen, late chief of the Comanches—rose, and
opening wide his arms, clasped General Hancock
to his heart convulsively, and said : "What the Big
Chief says I believe—so will all of the chiefs, every
word of it. I am an old man, brother to Ta-hawsen.
What this Big Chief says, listen to, you young men."
After a short silence Kicking Eagle stood up and
said : "I know you are a big chief. I heard some
time ago that you were coming, and am glad to see
you, and glad that you have taken us by the hand.
Our great chief, Ta-hawsen, is dead. He was a great
chief for the whites and Indians. Whatever Ta-
hawsen told them in council they remembered, and
they would go the road he told them ; and were
friendly to the whites. Ta-hawsen always advised
the nation to take the white man by the hand, and
clear above the elbow. I, Kicking Eagle, advise the
same. We lie south of the river. We all in our
hearts want peace with the whites. We have seen
you, and our hearts are glad. Our goods are coming
this spring. When they arrive, that will be the time
to pick out young men for guides and scouts. When
there is no war our squaws and papooses can sleep in
peace, without fear of being disturbed."

"My heart is big, and glad that you have told us that you will not make war upon Indians whose consciences are good. We are encamped close to the river, and you see that we act peaceably toward you. I have spoken."

Hancock then replied : "Your temper is good. Be assured that there will be no trouble with you. I command now all the country down to the Red River, north of the Platte and New Mexico. No one can harm you unless by orders through me. It is important, therefore, that you should make friends with the white men, so that they will protect and feed you if necessary. [Cries of "A-hou," "A-hou,"—"It is well."] The whites are getting very numerous, and they are coming West like the mighty wave of a sea. [Cries of "Se-ka," "Se-ka,"—"Wonderful."] You should settle in your own country, and begin to teach your children to raise corn and animals, as Indians further east are now doing."

General Hancock intends soon to cross the river to the Indian country.

General Topics—A Thunder Gust on the Plains—Beautiful Islands—Pow-wow with the Arapahoes—Satanta, Chief of the Kiowas—Departure for Fort Hayes.

FORT LARNED, KANSAS, *April 29th*, 1867.

AT these isolated camps on the plains soldiers are engaged in a variety of things between the rising of the sun and the going down thereof. The early morn is sounded in the sleeping camp by beat of drum and echoing bugle. The soldier wakes from his dreams to hear the many feathered songsters around, as they welcome the advent of day. After rising, he hastily performs his morning ablutions, and then prepares his breakfast. If he is an energetic man, and has a " live mess," the important ceremonies of preparing and eating breakfast will be despatched in half an hour, and then begins the task of wearing the day out. He will, doubtless, find many of his comrades disposed to ramble or for play. He is nothing loth to engage in wrestling, sparring, or leap-frog. Those who have been nominated for guard by the orderly sergeant, look with envy on their comrades' liberty. The new guard are bound to have all their arms clean and bright. They have been industriously at their operations since breakfast. They have rubbed their Spencer rifles scores of times, burnished their brass buckles till they shine, and brushed their clothes, already clean, repeatedly.

Nine o'clock has been announced by a premonitory tap of the drum, and as a warning note to the fifer and the new guard to stand by. Ten minutes elapse, and the sounds for which they were waiting are heard. Forthwith from each company a squad of men file off, under a corporal, towards the guard tent, where they are formed into line, and inspected. A portion of the new guard relieve the old guard, who have been wearily expecting the relief for the last hour, and wondering what caused the delay. The relieved guard are disbanded, and go to their quarters to sleep.

On looking into the tents we see one where there are five soldiers, and each of them is busy at something. One is ransacking a plethoric knapsack (he is evidently a German), hunting for fouled clothes to wash ; two are engaged in mending and patching their well-worn blue clothes, that have seen their best days months ago. One young lad is reading a Bible, and another is reading a yellow-covered novel, and, as we live! it is the life of that prince of highwaymen, " Dick Turpin."

In another tent was seen a soldier sitting *à la Turque*, with paper spread out on his knees, who was evidently trying to gather his senses so as to compose a proper letter such as would affect the heart of some young lady in his native village, or—who knows?—he may be writing a letter to his mother full of filial affection, or a letter to his brother, who was never a soldier, enlarging on the comparative enjoyments and luxuries of home and the camp. An old man was engaged inditing a letter to his child at home. In one tent soldiers seemed piled on the ground without regard to propinquities, indulging in the lazy gossip of the camp—and in a crowded wall tent there is banjo playing and fiddling, and among the listeners there is a jovial general-officer. One of the players breaks out into song. All enjoy it, from the Major-General to the infantry private, who is trying to catch a single note of the melody. The fiddler sings in a sentimental voice that beautiful song, " Father, dear father, come home with me now."

When the day is worn out down come the stars and stripes, the boys drop all work and play, and hasten to roll call, and " Retreat" is sounded. Eight o'clock comes, " Tattoo"; another roll call, and they are all dismissed for the night. Some retire to sleep, and some linger to exchange topics. Nine o'clock, and then "taps"; the lights are put jout, the soldiers have gone to rest. The deep silence of the night is broken only by the watchful sentinel, who paces his beat with the cry of "All's well," or by the yelping snarl of the hungry cuyote as he is disturbed in his feed upon some morsel of corruption.

On the first day's march from Fort Dodge to Larned, the black masses of cloud that began to ascend above the horizon in the morning were quickly followed by others of a still more portentous aspect. These soon invaded the whole heaven, and with gathered depths hung over us menacingly. The wind appeared obstructed in its passage. The very atmosphere seemed dead, and not a blade of the long prairie grass rustled; yet, a stranger to these phenomena would have anticipated only a shower of rain. Not so with the experienced and sunburnt scout, who was familiar with prairie life. In a short time the black brooding mass above was riven by lightning. The wind came, and moaned and sighed, until it increased to the force and power of a hurricane, bearing along in its wild and impetuous course

whirling clouds of dust. Nothing could be seen
twenty yards off. The straggling body of troops,
and the long zig-zag lines of trains groped their way
along, choked and buried out of view with dust.
The army was converted from Yankee soldiers to the
dingy colour of Confederate greys. Water was in
great demand, and the more provident of the soldiers
had cause to bless their forethought in filling their
canteens with the precious liquid, and providing
themselves against such contigencies. Equestrians
who had prided themselves upon their magnificent
appearance looked now woebegone and miserable.
Friends and acquaintances were unrecognisable.

During the whole march the gale lasted, rendering
travelling extremely uncomfortable. Neither was
there peace after we reached camp. The tents reeled
like surging waves. The dust came in powerful
currents from under the flaps. Visions of the Turkish
bath flitted across our minds, which rendered the
state of affairs worse ; and yet it seemed that without
some operation of the kind, we should never be able
to remove from our bodies the layers of dirt that
encrusted them, and bring us to a proper state of
mind. It started to rain at last, and large drops
pattered on the tent. Immediately our baggage was
in requisition, and from the shallow depths of our
valise, clean toggery was brought to light, and in a
very short period, after a thorough cleaning of the
outer man, we sallied out of our tents feeling as if we
had thrown away the incubus of years with the dust.

We were not alone in this happy state of mind. From every tent issued out gay, cavalierly-looking gentlemen, with shining epaulettes on their shoulders. Quiet rapture beamed from every feature, and the change which had come over their limbs and gait was like the resuscitation of the dying to the energies of a fresh life. Rain is a great blessing, after being half-smothered with fine prairie dust.

There are a great many islands in the Arkansas River, and they are extremely beautiful. They abound in green shrubbery. Some of them are of great size, but not the less charming. They are the green *oases*, on which the wearied eye loves to dwell ; and when compared with the naked and level land which extends in all directions, they loom up from the caressing bosom of the Arkansas with inviting aspect.

Here, at that still hour of evening, a happy pair might wander at will, without a fear (except of Indians) ; no jealous eye to circumscribe their steps, no censorious tongue to mar their peace, and no obtrusive curiosity to create distrust. But we advise no one to try a residence here until the country is settled. Then let them come to Kansas, which opens wide her arms for the indigent, and all other sorts ; let them pre-empt one of these islands ; and with this very sensible and practical advice we turn to our next theme.

When we were at Fort Dodge General Hancock intended to cross over to the Indian country, which lies south of the Arkansas, but, owing to the continued absence of his most effective arm, Custer's Cavalry, he thought it an imprudence. With "Kicking Eagle" he sent a scout and interpreter, named Apache Bill, after the Kiowas, to request all the chiefs to a conference with the "Big Chief." Apache Bill, who is a white man, returned with Yellow Wolf, brother-in-law of Little Raven, chief of the Arapahoes. He stated that he had been in great danger of losing his hair, but that Satank saved him by rousing him early in the morning, and sending him on his way to our camp. He also states that some of the chiefs told him that "If Hancock is a big chief, let him prove it by sending two waggonloads of ammunition and three waggonloads of provisions and clothes. Let him leave them south of the Arkansas, and we will then believe him to be a big chief." It must not be supposed that Hancock sent them the goods as proofs of his bigness. Nor did he attempt to follow them, as his inadequate force would not permit him to adopt such a course. Kicking Eagle remained behind, and acted honourably. It remains now for Hancock to bend his course for Fort Hayes, and then to Fort Harker, when the expedition will be virtually ended.

The forces that composed his expedition will be sent to their several destinations. Forts Lyon, Dodge, Larned, and Hayes will each receive two companies. A fort will be built at Monument Station, and some companies will be stationed there.

A council was held with the Arapahoe chiefs under Little Raven, Yellow Bear, Cut Nose, and Big Belly, at Fort Dodge, on the 28th instant. Hancock made a speech begging them to cultivate feelings of amity and friendship towards the whites. He also made a demand on them for the immediate restitution of twenty-five mules, which were taken by them from Put-in-encampment. This place is situated east of Port Lyon, on the Arkansas River. To this demand Little Raven replied, "We Arapahoes have always been the last to go to war with the white man, and the first to desire peace. We will return the mules to this fort" (Dodge) "as soon as we reach our village."

To-day we had the extreme pleasure of seeing the redoubtable chief, Satanta, who has made such a terrible name on this road. He came to this fort to have a "talk" with the big chief. He is dressed in a captain's regulation coat, with epaulettes to match, leggings ornamented and decorated in the most gaudy manner, with small brass bells attached. He seemed pleased when Dave Butterfield exhibited some comical pictures representing parlour scenes, but this pleasure was manifested in grimaces on a much painted and vermilionish face.

The Last Pow-Wow—The Irrepressible Satanta in Council—
His Speech—His Views of War and Peace—He accuses
the Indian Agent at Leavenworth—Hancock's last Speech—
Leavenworth's Reply to Satanta.

FORT HAYES, KANSAS, *May 3rd*, 1867.

THE last and most important "talk" with the Indian
chiefs took place at Larned on the 1st inst.   Satanta,
the chief of the Kiowas, appeared in person, accompanied by a small and select body of lesser chiefs.
Satanta has won a great name for daring and reckless-
ness from the Republican to the Rio Colorado.   His
name is on every lip, and his praises are sounded
by the young damsels of his tribe as the chief and
greatest warrior of the red men !   His figure is large,
and very muscular, showing great strength, and at the
council was adorned in a unique manner, the colour
of red predominating.   As he stood before the
glittering council, his sharp, brilliant eyes wandered
incessantly around the circle.   All the officers in the
command were assembled in the tent which had
been erected and set apart for the important occasion.   There were present, also, Colonels Edward
W. Wynkoop and Jesse H. Leavenworth, Indian
agents.   It will be remembered that the latter per-
sonage is agent for the tribe of which Satanta is
chief.   His father built the well known fort of that
name in the twenties.   Some time ago we stated that
the civilians and the military had censured Leaven-

worth. We have reason to believe that the censure was not undeserved, as may appear from a careful investigation of the evidence.

Colonel Leavenworth is now a cripple, and his beard is silvered by age. He has an astute look, and is devoted to red tapeism. His coat pockets are always full of official documents, and the ends of said papers can be seen sticking out an inch or so, and on each and all will be found legibly inscribed, "Leavenworth, Indian Agent."

Preceding the grave charges of Satanta, we had confessions from three men, Frederick Jones, John A. Atkin, and Kin-caid, who by profession are Indian interpreters. In their confessions they stated that for their services they had received as compensation Indian annuity goods ; that they had been engaged at various times in trading Indian annuity goods in Indian camps, for buffalo robes, furs, and lariats ; that Leavenworth conveyed the goods received in exchange to Leavenworth City, and there, to their certain knowledge, the said Leavenworth did receive for the goods several sums of money amounting to several thousands of dollars, from a merchant bearing the name of Durfy ; and that Leavenworth, to their certain knowledge, did bury in the earth, with intent to conceal, several bales of Indian goods.

Frederick Jones was employed as interpreter at this Council. Before proceeding with the regular business, he rose and said : " I have learned that Colonel Leavenworth has told Satanta not to talk much to-day, but to go down to Fort Zarah" (head-quarters of his agency) "to-morrow, and he would make it all right. He may not, therefore, talk as much as he would have done."

On hearing the above, General Hancock said : " Colonel Leavenworth is here, and can answer for himself."

Leavenworth : "All I have to say in regard to that is, that not a word of that kind has passed between us. I did not ask him to come to Zarah, nor tell him anything about talking."

Hancock : "Now, Mr. Jones, if Satanta wants to proceed, you can let him do so whenever he is ready."

Then Satanta very seriously rose and said :—

" I look upon you and General Smith as my fathers. I want friends, and I say by the sun and the earth I live on, I want to talk straight and to tell the truth. All the other tribes are my brothers, and I want friends, and am doing all I can for peace. If I die first, it is all right. All the Indians south of here are my friends. When I first started out as a warrior I was a boy ; now I am a man.

" I want the Great Father at Washington and all the soldiers and troops to go slowly. I don't want the prairies and country to be bloody, but just hold on for a while. I don't want war at all. I want peace. As for the Kiowas talking war, I don't know anything about it. Nor do I know anything about the Comanches, Cheyennes, and Sioux talking about war. The Cheyennes, Kiowas, and Comanches are poor. They are all of the same colour. They are all red men. This country here is old, and it all belongs to them. You are cutting off the timber, and now the country is of no account at all. I don't mean anything bad by what I say. I have nothing bad hidden in my breast at all; everything is all right. I had heard that there were many troops coming out to this country to whip the Cheyennes, and that is the reason we were afraid and went away. The Cheyennes, Arapahoes, and Kiowas heard that there were troops coming out to this country; so did also the Comanches and Apaches; but did not know whether the soldiers were coming for peace or for war. They were on the look-out and listening, and hearing from down out of the ground all the time. They were afraid to come in. I don't think the Cheyennes wanted to fight; but I understand that you burned their village. I don't think that is good at all. To you, General, and to all these officers sitting around here, I say that I know that whatever I tell you will be sent to Washington, and I don't want anything else but the truth told. Other chiefs of the Kiowas, who rank below me, have come in to look for rations and to look about, and their remarks are reported to Washington; but I don't think their hearts are good. [Interrupted by Colonel Leavenworth : " What he means by that is that other chiefs come in to make speeches for nothing else but to get something to eat."] Lone Wolf, Stumbling Bear, and Kicking Eagle, all come

I.   F

in with that object, and their speeches amount to
nothing. The Cheyennes, the Arapahoes, Comanches,
Kiowas, Apaches, and some Sioux, all sent to see me
—for they knew me to be the best man—and sent
information that they wanted peace, and nothing but
peace. They do not work underhanded at all, but
declare plainly that they want peace. I hope that
you two Generals, and all these officers around here,
will help me, and give me heart, and help the
Cheyennes, and not destroy them; but let them live.
All of the Indians south of this desire the same; and
when they talk that way to me I give them praise
for it. Whatever I hear in this council, and whatever
you tell me, I will repeat when I reach my villages;
and there are some Cheyennes over there whom I
will tell and induce to preserve peace. But if they
will not listen to me all my men and myself will have
nothing more to do with them. I want peace, and I
will try to make them keep peaceful. The Kiowa
braves have grown up from childhood obtaining their
medicine from the earth. Many have grown old, and
continue growing old, and die from time to time, but
there are some remaining yet. I do not want war at
all, but want to make friends, and am doing the best
I can for that purpose. There are four different
bands of Comanches, camped at different points
in the south along the streams, and there are five
different bands of Kiowas, 'Lone Wolf,' '—— Wolf,'
'Heap Bears,' 'Timber Mountain,' and 'Stumbling
Bear.' They profess to be chiefs, although they have

but two or three lodges each. They are waiting, however, to hear what they can learn before taking the *warpath.* The Kiowas do not say anything ; and whatever the white man says is all right. The Kiowas and the white men are in council to-day, but I hope no mistake will be made about what the Indians say, and that nothing will be added to it, because I know that everything is sent to Washington. [Interrupted by General Hancock : "There are two or three interpreters here to witness, and prevent mistakes in the translation, so that all will be properly written down."] About two o'clock to-day I want to start back to Fort Dodge, and I want you to give me a letter."

General Hancock : "As soon as I can copy it I will give you the written proceedings of this council, but cannot say that I can give it to you as soon as that."

Satanta : "I simply want a letter when I go into camp so that I can show it."

General Hancock : "I will give you a copy of the proceedings to take with you, so that you may show it to any man who may be able to read it to you."

Satanta then resumed his oration : "As for this Arkansas waggon road, I have no objection to it, but I don't want any railroad here ; but up on the Smoky Hill route a railroad can run up there, and it will be all right. On this Arkansas, and all these northern streams, there is no timber ; it has all been cut off ; but if anybody knows of anything bad being done I

do not like it. There are no longer any buffaloes
around here, nor anything we can kill to live on ; but
I am striving for peace now, and don't want anything
construed to be bad from what I say, because I am
simply speaking the plain truth. The Kiowas are
poor. Other tribes are very foolish. They make
war, and are unfortunate, and then call upon the
Kiowas to aid them, and I don't know what to think
about it. I want peace, and all these officers around
this country know it. I have talked with them until
I am tired. I came down here, and brought my
women with me ; but came for peace. If any white
men steal our stock I will report it openly. Now, I
am doing the best I can, and the white man is looking
for me. If there were no troops in this country, and
the citizens only lived around here, that would be
better. But there are so many troops coming in here
that I fear they will do something bad to me.

"When Satank shot the sentinel here at the post "
(Larned) "some two or more years ago, there was
then war, and that was bad. I came near losing my
life then. The Kiowas have now thrown him "
(Satank) "away. If the Indians up north wish to act
foolishly, that is none of my business, and is no reason
why we should do so down here. If the Indians
further south see the white man coming, they will not
come up on the warpath, nor fight. They will call a
council to come and talk, as they do here now.
To-day it is good, and to-night it is good, and when
the grass comes it will be good ; and this road, which

runs up to the west" (Santa Fé), " is good also. Everything is all right now.

"If you keep the horses herded around here close to the fort they will never be good. Let them run away off on the prairies ; there is no danger ; let them get grass, and they will get fat. But do not let the children and boys " (young soldiers) "run away off on the hills now. That is not good. I don't do it ; nor do the Cheyennes. I think that is a very good idea. You are a very big chief; but when I am away, over to the Kiowas, I am a big chief myself.

" Whenever a trader comes to my camp I treat him well, and do not do anything out of the way to him. All the traders are laughing and shaking hands with me. When the Indians get a little liquor they get drunk, and fight sometimes ; but when they get sober they are all right. All the white men around here can look at me, and hear what I say. I am doing all I can to keep my men down, and doing the best I can to have peace. Down at the mouth of the Little Arkansas, where a treaty of peace was made, Colonel Leavenworth was present, and I was the first man who came in there to make peace with Colonel Leavenworth ; and I did it by my word.

" Little Mountain, the chief of the tribe, is now dead. He did all he could to make peace, and kept talking, and talking, but the white man kept doing something bad to him, and he was in so much misery that he died. The white men and Indians kept fighting each other backward and forward, and then I came in and made peace myself. Little Mountain did not give me my commission; I won it myself. These three braves" (pointing to some Indians near him) "are chiefs also, and are not afraid of soldiers, and the sight of them does not frighten these chiefs at all. This prairie is large and good, and so are the heavens above, and I do not want it stained by the blood of war. I don't want you to trouble yourself about bringing out too many trains in this country. I don't want to see any waggons broken or destroyed by war.

"Now, I want to find out what is the reason that Colonel Leavenworth did not give me some annuity goods. I don't want to talk bad, but want to find out the reason why I did not get my annuity goods. There are Lone Bear, Heap of Bears, Stumbling Bear, and Little Heart, and others—six chiefs with very small bands, and they have all received their annuity goods, while those of my tribe are as plenty as the grass, and I came in for my goods and did not see them. You can look upon us all here present, and see if we have any of those goods. All that we have we have bought and paid for. We are all poor men, and I think others have got all the goods; but let them keep them. I want peace, and don't want to make war, on account of our goods. I expect to trade for what I get, and not get anything by making speeches. My heart is very strong. We can make robes and trade them. That is what we have to live upon. I have no mules, horses, nor robes to give Colonel Leavenworth for my goods. I am a poor

man, but I am not going to get angry and talk about
it. I simply want to tell this to these officers here
present. Such articles as the white man may throw
away we may pick up, and use, and make out the
best we can ; and if you throw away any provisions we
will use them also, and thus do the best we can. I
see a great many officers around here with fine
clothing, but I do not come to beg ; but I admire fine
clothes, although I never did beg, or anything of that
sort. I have no hat, and am going about without
one, the same as all other Kiowas. Colonel Bent,
of St. Louis (who was present, and was an interested
spectator), used to come over often to my tent, and the
Kiowas went there to him very often, and were glad,
and shook hands with him ; and Mr. Curtis went
there, and he was treated in the same way. All were
treated the same. But I am not poor enough to die
yet. I think my women can make enough to live off,
and can make something yet.

"When Colonel Bent was our agent, and brought
our goods out to us, he brought them out and kept
them in a train, and when we arrived he unloaded all
our goods to us, and that was the way to do it. But
now there is a different way of doing things. That
different way of doing things is, that the agent lives
away from the Indian tribes, about two hundred miles
apart from them, and he keeps their goods in his back-
room, and when the chiefs come for them he denies
that he has any. At my camp I waited and sent for
the agent, and did not see him ; but other chiefs

mounted their horses and went there, and claimed to be the principal men.

" I heard that this railroad was to come up through this country, and my men and other tribes objected to it. But I advised them to keep silent. I thought that by the railroad being built up through here, we would then get our goods sure, but they do not come. I would like to get some agent who is a good and responsible man, one who would give us all our annuities. I do not want an agent who will steal half our goods and hide them, but an agent who will give all my goods. I am not talking anything bad or angrily, but simply the truth. I don't think the great men at Washington know anything about this ; but I am now telling your officers to find it out.

" He gave goods to Stumbling Bear and Mah-way, two chiefs who were with me in Texas.

" Now, I am done, and whatever you " (General Hancock) " have to say to me I will listen to, and those who are with me will listen ; so that when we return to camp we can tell the others the same as you tell us."

Major-General Hancock said : " We have heard always that you are the great chief of the Kiowas, and that is the belief among the white people whom I have seen. I am very glad to see you here for that reason.

" The Great Father did not send me here to make treaties with you, but we came to see who are respecting the treaties which have already been made ; to find out those who are not respecting them ; and if there are any guilty, as their agent tells us, we are ready to punish them. We do not come down here to make war ; but with the hope of avoiding war. We came prepared for it, however, and if we found anybody here who wanted war, as we heard, we were ready to meet it. When I first came to Fort Larned I went up to Pawnee Fork ; I had more soldiers with me in my command than all your men together.

"Your Great Father has many more soldiers. You know this very well. If we lose soldiers we don't have to wait for them to grow up. Your Great Father will send us more—a great many more. You know very well that when you lose a man you cannot send another but you must wait until your young men grow up. It is for your interest, then, to have peace ; and the white men do not want war, and the Great Father is as much a friend to the Indian as to the white man. He learned that there were a great many murders and depredations committed upon the trains and travellers on the Smoky Hill, and sometimes on the Arkansas, and sometimes in Texas, and he became angry. I have been sent here to find out who those persons were that committed the depredations. Some time ago we were at war with Texas. They were a great people, but rebelled against their Great Father, but they have now been punished, and they are now his children, and you must not make war upon the people there. As I have told the other

Indians before, I command all of the country down
to the Red River and New Mexico, and up to the
Platte on the north, so that when any orders to fight
Indians are made by the Great Father the orders pass
through me.

"I like to see tribes, too, who have one chief, to
whom I can talk, and whom the young men will
obey, instead of two or three chiefs.

"The Great Father will not permit all these young
men to run around. And if there is no great chief,
who can prevent it? The Great Father must do it
with his soldiers. When I started out I intended to
go south of the Arkansas and see the Kiowas and
Comanches, as well as the Apaches and Arapahoes;
but I got into the war with the Cheyennes and Sioux,
and have sent all my cavalry after them. I don't
want to call them back here, because they have plenty
to do where they are. Nor do I want to go south of
the Arkansas, because they told me that the Indians
were afraid of the troops, and ran away. I don't want
to frighten the families of those who are at peace with
us. I will not go south of the Arkansas River, unless
I find that we have enemies there. The Cheyennes
and the Sioux at the north are fighting and behaving
very badly, and a great many troops are in pursuit of
them. A great many Sioux and Cheyennes came down
south here last winter. I learnt that they were coming down here to induce these Indians to join them.
Satanta told Major Douglass so, and others told him
so, and told Major Douglass that they must get off

from this road, and that they intended to make war here, and that is one of the things that brought me here. We know that the depredations that were committed last summer and winter, and recently, were by the Sioux and Cheyennes. We know this, and have satisfactory evidence of it. You say the Indians do not want to make war? Is not that war? What do you call war if that is not war? The other day I came here and sent for the chiefs of the Sioux and Cheyennes to come to my camp at Fort Larned. Only two chiefs came, although I waited here for several days, and although they were only thirty miles away from here.

"They told me the young men were out buffalo hunting, and that was the reason the young men could not come. But I know the reason. I soon found out that the young men were out on the Smoky Hill. Their agent was with me, and I took him along so as to convince them that I did not mean to harm them unjustly. I told them that whatever their agent told me they had been guilty of I would make a demand for if the agent considered it was clear; and I told them that we didn't go there to make war upon them. When I got up near their camp I met Pawnee Killer, who promised to come and see me the next morning at nine o'clock to have a talk. Pawnee Killer and some of the chiefs of the Cheyennes remained in camp all night. He sent a messenger to their camp. I was then ten miles from them, and told them that after our talk I would come

up and encamp near them on my road to the south.
They did not come out the next day at nine o'clock,
and then I ordered my camp to be struck, and some
time after that we received notice that they were coming, but it was so windy that we could not have a conference ; and we said that we would talk with them in
the evening. They spoke very well, and said that they
would be in camp in the evening, and have another
talk. And all this time they were telling me they
were going to talk with me, the Cheyennes and
Sioux, and all, excepting a few warriors, were running
away. When I reached their camp, and encamped
quietly by them, and sent their stray mules to them,
Bull Bear and Roman Nose came to me and told me
that the women and children were frightened and ran
away. They did not tell me though that the Sioux
and nearly all of the Cheyennes had run away, but
that if I would give them some horses they would
go and bring them back that night, and they promised
to keep their warriors in camp that night. I told
them very well. I put an interpreter there to see if
they remained in camp, and instructed him to come
and tell me if they remained in camp all night.

" He came and told me just after dark that they
were all running away ; and thus they lied to me. I
then concluded that it was a nest of conspirators,
and that they were there for mischief, as Satanta
had told me and all the others. I believe they ran
away because they were guilty, fearing that we would
punish them. I sent my horsemen after them, and I

waited there nearly a week to see whether they commenced war or not. I had made no war yet ; I placed a guard around their camp so as to allow nobody to touch it. I wanted to see if the Sioux and Cheyennes committed any murders, and I waited there for that purpose. They started so early that they arrived on the Smoky Hill a good while before the cavalry arrived, and they burned one station and tried to burn another, and burned three white men. That I consider war, and then I ordered their camp to be burned, and everything they had in it to be destroyed. They fired upon my expressmen.

"I wanted to ascertain whether the Cheyennes went north or south, and sent a few of the cavalry up to the Cimmarron crossing, with orders that if any Cheyennes came there to take them prisoners. There were some horses out herding and grazing, and six Cheyennes came along and tried to sneak up and shoot the herders. I don't think they saw the cavalry. The commander of the troops thinks that the Indians did not know that the cavalry were there, and twenty soldiers happened to come up just then and demanded that they should surrender, but they, in answer, fired upon the troops. The troops then killed them all. I then wrote to all of my commanders and to General Smith, who commands in this part of the country, that we were at war against the Cheyennes and Sioux. When the Great Father knows all that has taken place out here, he will see what has to be done with the Cheyennes and Sioux.

"It is very difficult for soldiers to tell one tribe from another, and therefore during the time this war is going on with the Cheyennes and Sioux, you had better remain south of the Arkansas, unless they go north from the south, or south from the north. But there must be peace south of the Arkansas; there must be no trouble, nor on this road. Otherwise I shall have to bring my troops here. If these Cheyennes cross the river, and we see their trails, we shall have to follow them. We shall soon know whether the Cheyennes mean war or not, and whether the Sioux do, and whether they both do, and whether any other Indians do, and we shall then know what to do ourselves. If we have war with the Sioux and Cheyennes, I will not make peace with them until the Great Father tells me to do so. They will have to show by their acts that they are honest, that they are not telling me lies. If the Kiowas, Arapahoes, Comanches, Apaches, or either of them keep this road clear, I will not have to send any soldiers down here, and then their families will not be frightened, and you will not have to go to war unless so disposed.

"If this war continues with the Cheyennes and Sioux, I would like to get two or three hundred of your tribe for scouts. I will clothe, feed, and dress them well, and arm them well and furnish them with horses and blankets. I want them to keep this road clear, and tell us who are the Cheyennes and the Sioux, and who are the other Indians, so that we may kill only the guilty. I prefer to have some Kiowas, some Arapahoes, and some Apaches, but if I can't get them from all the tribes I will take them from one tribe. I wish you would think over it, and let Major Douglass know at Fort Dodge what your conclusion is. I will put a white officer with them, so that our troops can know who they are, and will give them the lodges of the Sioux which we did not burn up to put them in if they are short of lodges. The most important thing I have to say to you now, is to keep this road upon the Arkansas River clear, and allow no depredations, and allow no horses nor mules to be stolen, so that I will not have to collect all this force out here and come down again to see who are committing these depredations.

"You see that you cannot travel in winter. We have forage and storehouses, and can move in winter when horses are fat. I may not come down south of the Arkansas this month, nor the next month, but whenever I find out anything is going wrong, I shall come, even though it should not be until next winter.

"You know very well that in a few more years the game will go away. What will you do then ? You will have to depend upon the white man to assist you, and depend upon the Great Father to feed you when hungry. Your children will have to depend upon raising corn and stock, as other Indians do. This generation may not have to do it, but the next generation will have to do it. Then you should cultivate the friendship of the white man now, in order that he may be your friend when this time

comes. The white men are coming out here so fast
that nothing can stop them—coming from the east
and coming from the west, like a prairie on fire in a
high wind. The reason of it is because the whites are
a great people, and they are spreading out and we
cannot help it. Those on one sea in the west want
to communicate with another sea in the east, and that
is the reason they are building these waggon roads,
and railroads and telegraphs. The Great Father had
a council with these tribes, and asked their permission
to run roads through here, and you and the others
gave your permission. That treaty was made at the
mouth of the Little Arkansas ; and last fall it was
signed again, and it is too late to reconsider it now.
I don't know where the railroad is going to run. It
may run on the Smoky Hill, and they may find a
better road on this line. At any rate, if the road
comes here I cannot help it, and you have already
given your assent to it.

"You say the wood is all going. So it is in the
east where the white man lives, and they will soon
use up the wood there, as soon as the Indians
are out of it here ; but we have found other things
that answer the purpose as well as wood ; and the
same will be found here when the white men have
explored here. They will find it somewhere in this
country. It has been found up on the Smoky Hill.
In the east, where the Great Father lives, they all
burn coal. You need have no fear on this point.

"We build these garrisons as places of rest for the

travellers and for soldiers in case the travellers are disturbed ; but they will disturb no Indians unless they have sufficient cause. We will also protect the Indian in his property, and if he loses property and the white man commits a depredation, you must not take it upon you to redress these wrongs, but come to us, for we can do it better. We will arrest the offender if there is any danger of his escaping, and if you should arrest offenders, you must bring them to us.

" I have listened to what you have said about your annuity goods ; I have nothing to do with that matter. What you have said here, however, and what I have said will go to Washington. I cannot tell you anything about your agent ; after I have finished, if he" (the agent) "desires to say anything, he can do so ; I have no control whatsoever over him. I have said everything now which I desire to say ; I do not expect to see you for some time again, unless we go south of the Arkansas River."

Colonel Leavenworth said :—

" These are the men who killed the Box family in Texas, and my instructions were not to give them any annuity until the conditions of my written in- structions were complied with. I accordingly file copies of these instructions for record in the pro- ceedings of this council, as an explanation why these Indians have not received their goods. These papers are from Washington. The Commissioner at Wash- ington told me in these papers that until all these captives were returned without ransom of which he "

I.   G

(Satanta) " knows, and we obtained sufficient assurances that no further depredation would be committed, no annuities should be given. But Satanta has never come and given any assurances in the matter."

Satanta said : " Stumbling Bear was in that raid, and why should he get so many goods ? "

Colonel Leavenworth : " Because he had come in and given the assurances that had been required of him."

Satanta : " Why was Mah-way given so many goods ? "

General Hancock said he did not wish to be questioned upon this matter.

" This council will now end unless Satanta has something more to say. This man is General Smith, an old soldier on the plains, and was here a great many years ago, and was here twenty years ago with General Harney. He commands in this country when I am not here."

General Hancock's speech is well worthy of study. To the reports of the three interpreters about a dozen names of the most respectable citizens on the route are attached, certifying that they are correct in every particular.

After the council was over Satanta was presented by General Hancock with a major-general's coat and yellow sash. He seemed fully aware of the high rank to which he had been elevated. Had General Hancock encouraged Satanta we have no doubt that he could have disclosed other dark deeds of Indian agents ; but, we presume, he did not feel himself licensed to play the inquisitor.

These speeches reveal many true facts about Indian matters. The speakers appear to be on their honour to tell the truth ; and between the Indian chief and the great General we get a good deal of it.

From Fort Larned to Fort Harker *viâ* Fort Hayes—Homeward Bound—The End of the Expedition—Its Mission—Its Results—Departure of Hancock for Leavenworth—Custer's Cavalry and its Conditions—Scurvy among the Troops— Ellsworth City—Intended Meeting with " Black Kettle "— " To the West."

FORT HAYES, KANSAS, *May 9th*, 1867.

AFTER the important council held at Larned with Satanta, we set our faces towards the north. Two days of rapid marching across country brought us to Fort Hayes.

Fort Hayes is built on a space of level ground completely surrounded by a deep ravine, at the bottom of which trickles during all seasons a stream of pure water. The men's quarters are built on the edge of the ravine, in the form of a square, and consist of small log shanties, with wide and capacious stone chimneys. Major Howe, the commander of the fort, has been at great pains to make it as thorough and complete a place of defence as the short space of four months would allow. The garrison consists of two companies of the 37th Infantry. The commanding

G 2

General is not well pleased with the site, and a special council has already determined upon a spot more eligible for a fort. This place received its name after Brigadier-General Alexander Hayes, who fell during the battle of the Wilderness. It is fifty-eight miles from Fort Harker, and two hundred and forty-five due west from the Missouri River.

We found General Custer with the 7th Cavalry at this post, waiting patiently for our arrival. His horses are in a very poor condition, from lack of forage. Before starting on this campaign, General Hancock had taken great precaution to have sufficient subsistence for both troops and horses, and had ordered it to be forwarded at once to different posts, to await our arrival, but owing to the dilatoriness of quartermasters the animals have suffered greatly. Neither hay, oats, nor corn could be found at the fort, which caused great inconvenience to Custer, who had been ordered to pursue the Indians to the death. It has also occasioned excessive disappointment to General Hancock, who had been expecting daily despatches from him, announcing a successful result. Horses have been daily dying at the camp, to the number of four and five ; and to add to the inconveniences of an early spring campaign, thirteen men have sickened of that terrible disease, the scurvy. There were also symptoms of that disease in the 37th Infantry. The surgeons are, however, sanguine of their entire recovery, and no case so far has proved fatal. On the whole, the troops have been remarkably healthy, taking into consideration the fatiguing marches the infantry were compelled to make.

Though our experience on the plains has only been limited, we think it a foolish policy to take foot soldiers on a campaign against mounted Indians. Even if infantry were only needed as escort for trains, still we are of the opinion that they would be productive of more harm than good. Four or five soldiers cannot ride on loaded waggons, and they must, therefore, necessarily walk. It is an old saying on the plains, and one which has been repeatedly proven to be true—viz., that "A man without a horse has no business on the prairie." When General Custer was ordered to pursue the Indians, he thought that travelling fifty miles a day would bring him up to them. But if he failed with fresh cavalry to overtake Indians, how is it possible for infantry loaded and encumbered with heavy knapsacks and muskets to do so? Fifteen miles a day on an average is the utmost a foot soldier can travel. The dullest mind will perceive the use-lessness of infantry travelling at that rate to over-take Indians who travel fifty or sixty miles a day. We only mention these facts because we were led to reflect on them at observing the weary foot soldiers struggling on with heavy clothes, accoutrements, and knapsacks, under a broiling hot sun, and the copious perspiration rolling down their sunburnt faces. Many of them were mere boys from fifteen to nine-teen, and others were aged men. It is said that the soldiers desert at the first opportunity offered. Can you wonder at it ?

The infantry have now been detailed to the different posts in Western Kansas. Forts Dodge, Larned, Hayes, and Lyon have each received an addition of two companies from the 37th Infantry, and one company has been stationed at Fossil Creek station, which has lately been made memorable by the brutal murder of three white men by the savages. The 7th Cavalry, under Custer, must remain in the neighbourhood of Fort Hayes until the grass appears, and the horses are in a better condition. He is then to commence active and offensive operations against the Sioux and Cheyenne tribes. Custer is precisely the gentleman for that job. A certain impetuosity and undoubted courage are his principal characteristics. From all we hear from persons qualified to judge, he must be a first-rate cavalry officer, and will no doubt perform any task allotted to him to the entire satisfaction of the western people. Let those who are in authority see that quartermasters supply him with all the forage and stores he needs, and some extra horses, and the people of the west will not, for a time at least, have cause to complain of the laggardness of the military, or of the danger of travelling to the Rocky Mountains. The battery has been ordered to Fort Riley this morning, and with it all the waggons in the command. The waggons are then to return from Riley immediately, for the transport of provisions to the several posts already mentioned.

When I commenced this rambling correspondence I was under the impression that General Hancock had undertaken his campaign on the plains for the sole purpose of punishing the Indians for the innumerable outrages which they were alleged to have committed Indeed, it was the common belief out west. But lately the commanding General very affably favoured me with his views—when I learned that his mission had been to feel the temper of the Indians—to see who were guilty and who were not—to convince himself and others whom it might concern, which tribe was for war, and which was for peace—to sign a treaty, if necessary, with any tribe or tribes peaceably inclined—to separate the peaceful tribes from those disposed for war—and lastly, to post more troops on the Smoky Hill and Santa Fé roads.

The progress and results of this expedition have been already given in detail, but with your permission I will take a summary view of the late operations.

Congress voted $150,000 to pay the expenses of this short campaign. The troops have marched over 450 miles. The guilty tribes—viz., the Sioux and Cheyennes—have been separated from their ancient allies, the Kiowas, Arapahoes, and Comanches. One hundred thousand dollars' worth of Indian property has been burnt, and the guilty tribes have been despoiled of everything save their horses, squaws, and papooses. The wigwam poles lately burned cannot be replaced without going to the mountains, which will involve them in war with their hated enemies, the Utes. The Santa Fé and Smoky Hill routes will in future be better guarded. Kansas is now free from all hostile Indians, and is open to the emigrant. Briefly, that is all that the expedition has accomplished. Of one thing we are certain, Major-General Hancock obeyed his orders to the very letter. While General Hancock is east, Brevet Major-General Andrew J. Smith remains in command of the department of the Upper Arkansas, and will make his headquarters, for the present, at Fort Harker, but his intention is to make his permanent headquarters at Pueblo, Colorado.

Major-General Hancock left for Leavenworth this morning, to receive his final instructions from the " great flanker," Sherman, before the latter starts on his excursion to the Holy Land.

As the " iron horse " advances towards the west, settlements spring up as if by magic along the intended route. The locomotive is the true harbinger of civilisation. About three miles from Fort Harker a speculative company has bought and apportioned some " bottom " land close to the Smoky Hill River into town lots. This same land about two years ago was entered under the Homestead Act, by one Charles Kingsbury. This person sold it to a company, who offer it now at $300 per town lot. At the time of my visit there were four houses already completed, and three of them were lager beer saloons, while one, a log shanty, bore the euphonious title of Kingsbury Hotel. The locomotive will pass through

the town in less than eight weeks from the date of
this letter. When that important event occurs all
intending settlers in this infant town should provide
themselves with the necessary articles for table use.
They should also be supplied with some warm
blankets or rugs. In the matter of provisions they
need have no fears, as these are abundant everywhere.
We took a glance at the list of good things prepared
for guests at the hotel, of which the following is a true
transcription to wit; that is to say: "Breakfast—real
and fresh buffalo broiled, bread and canned peaches.
Dinner—canned peaches, bread, and fresh roast
buffalo hump. Supper—bread, canned peaches, and
fresh buffalo steak." You will observe, by glancing
at the above, that the articles set forth promise a
healthy diet, which the hotel proprietor out of infinite
love prescribes for his boarders. There are thirteen
buildings in course of erection at the present moment.

The population of the town of Ellsworth is estimated, according to the latest census, at forty men,
four women, eight boys, and seven girls. There are
also fourteen horses, and about twenty-nine and one-
half dogs. There is neither a cow, hog, cat, nor
chicken around, but there are plenty of rattlesnakes,
copperheads, gophers, owls, mice, and prairie dogs
within the limits of the town. As Ellsworth is part
and parcel of this great and progressive country, it is
also progressive—for no sooner has the fifth house
begun to erect its stately front above the green earth,
than the population is gathered in the three saloons

above-mentioned, to gravely discuss the propriety of making the new town a city, and of electing a mayor. An enterprising citizen of Leavenworth has announced his determination of setting up a printing establishment, and of issuing a daily paper, which is to be a model of enterprise and intelligence. As houses are only built of rough boards, the new town has quite a rough appearance. The men are rough, the women and children are also rough, and they have a certain rough hospitality, geniality, and kindness, which is beyond criticism.

The inhabitants of Ellsworth are fair types of the western people. They are rough diamonds. The stranger is not turned from the door—the hungry traveller is not compelled to beg—the thirsty obtains the wherewithal to appease his thirst, diluted with something strong if necessary ; for the tired and wearied body, a corner, with a buffalo robe, is always reserved, and if the stranger can play a fiddle, the best in the house is at his command.

Wonderful, indeed, is the rapidity with which the rolling hills are cleft, roads graded, ties laid down, and the rails secured in their places by the railroad-makers. The regularity and order of the operations are as perfect as could be devised. Within the short space of five weeks a most surprising change has happened. From Harker to Junction City the bottom lands are studded with ranches lately built, and the voice of the ploughman is heard where but two short months ago the war whoop of the savage Indian

echoed in the green woods of the Smoky. Pedestrians bound for the west line the road. Pilgrims
with their little all, their wives, children, and earthly
substance, flock in numbers, and answer your queries
as to whither bound, with " To the west." The
energy of the tracklayers seems to be infectious ;
everybody seems imbued with railroad haste and
vigour. The city of Salina commences to raise her
head. A magnificent depôt is to be built to meet the
demand for storage addressed to this live city. The
cars run here regularly, passengers alight and inquire
anxiously, "How is biz ?" and go away again,
delighted to hear that "biz is tip-top." Passengers
can procure tickets for Salina, and four weeks hence
will be able to get them for Fort Harker. Squads of
Irishmen, under energetic taskmasters, are scattered
all along working with might and main, as if they
had an interest in the road apart from their daily
bread or monthly wages. "Excelsior" is the motto
all round, and westward do empire and civilisation
wend their way.

General Subjects continued—Junct:on City—Arrival of Citizens
    of St. Louis—The Future of Junction City—Government
    Mules—Hancock's Express Riders chased by Indians—
    Wild Bill kills Indians, etc.

JUNCTION CITY, KANSAS, *May 11th,* 1867.

As this city is destined, in my opinion, to become an
important one, I feel in duty bound to describe it,

so that, should it attract the attention of the public in the future, some slight idea of what Junction City really was at this date may be formed.

Its location is admirable and picturesque. It is situated in a valley surrounded entirely by commanding elevations, and its position is well chosen, not only for protection against the chilly winds of the plains, but also for its future commercial interests. The Union Pacific railroad runs through the city, which was, until a few days ago, the terminus. The southern branch of the railroad will intersect at this point with the eastern division. Extensive quarries of beautiful and durable stone are found about one mile from the city limits, which will undoubtedly prove, when fully developed, to be of great importance in forwarding the rapid growth of the young city. It is a kind of light freestone, so soft, when freshly quarried, as scarcely to impede the carpenter's plane, and yet it has been proved to be most durable. The romantic shores of the Smoky—the river that moves with a silvery voice, and which runs through the green valley of Junction—afford pleasant sites for private residences. The country immediately contiguous is noted in the geography of Kansas for its fertility, and approaches in appearance to the wooded parks and verdant glades of France. With all these attractions, we may rest assured that this city is destined to considerable expansion. The population at present, is estimated at 1500 souls.

Lieutenant-General W. T. Sherman is expected

here to-night, and rooms at the Hale House have been engaged for himself and lady. He is *en route* to Fort Harker on a short tour of inspection, preparatory to giving final instructions to General Hancock.

The Methodists, Baptists, and Episcopalians have each a church, well attended by respectable and orderly congregations. There are also three hotels.

The streets of Junction, or "Junk town," as the plainsmen love to call it, present to the casual observer the most striking contrasts. Perhaps the solemn and the ludicrous were never found in closer connection than they are in this truly western-featured city. The swarthy Mexican, and the scowling major-domo with their wide sombreros and the graceful serapes of variegated hues—the keen, blue-eyed and benevolent-looking Yankee—the patient phlegmatic Dutchman, the restless and refractory Irishman—the eagle-eyed Israelite—the overbearing southerner, and the independent frontiersman, can be met here. Parading the streets at all hours may be seen generals, colonels, captains, judges, and professors. In our perambulations through the streets we heard almost every other pedestrian addressed by some magnificent title, which was, to say the least, startling when we looked at the man and his garb.

During my experience with the military trains on the prairie I have noticed that there are four distinct classes of mules—viz., the sleepy, the cunning, the dainty or Government mule, and the hard-working, ever-willing species. Each has its peculiar traits.

The sleepy and sluggish mule is a ridiculous-looking animal, with a somnolent look, requiring the frequent application of the "black snake." When punishment is thus administered, it seems roused to momentary activity, but soon relapses into the same melancholy, apathetic walk, with head and ears drooping heavily downward. The cunning mule seemingly works hard, and a stranger to its habits and mode of work would be deceived; but the experienced express driver knows its tricks. On the march this species generally contrives to keep its traces taut, and I have seen it often unmercifully belaboured by the driver, when, to all appearance, it worked hard enough; but as an apology for the severe treatment the driver would say, "You see, sir, he is playing possum, but he can't fool me nohow; he is the cunningest, darndest mule (Go-'lang; go-'lang there, you, Jake!) that I ever saw." The dainty or Government mule prides itself greatly on its appearance. Possessed of a style entirely and peculiarly its own, somewhat similar to the superb prancing of a stallion of noble pedigree, it is always chosen for that quality by superintendents of transportation and waggon bosses as their pets. Hence the rough frontiersmans' pertinent epithet, "As proud as a Government mule," bestowed on any young man of presumptuous manners fresh from big cities. The hard-working, willing, and perseveringly industrious mule is a valuable acquisition to a teamster. Unflagging in its efforts, always on the pull, and steadily putting its whole strength forward, these qualifications make it eagerly sought after. When the train is halted he rests with its whole weight thrown forward, in order to be ready at the first word to move on.

When the mules in the van reach camp they are sure to set up a bray. That one braying note is distinct and peculiar, and clearly understood by all the rest of the braying animals. One team after another catches the cry, and such a chorus of dying, distressing, lugubrious cadences, the natural result of that one signal note, the great prairie never heard before. Some cry in tones almost human, a few like mules, but the majority of them like donkeys. These last begin at the very top of their whistle, and then, as if overstraining in an effort to heighten the pitch, break down through an ag-on-yet-ical succession of abortive and horrible efforts, till they finally drop their ears as if ashamed of their utter failure, and were indescribably confused thereby. An animal of this kind is just such an one as a young man should ride home after having confidently addressed a young lady and received her absolute refusal. He must undoubtedly have been intended for the use of those who were thus taken all aback in their matrimonial enterprises. We should not close this essay on " Government mules " without adding something in their praise. They carry their burdens, and haul precious freights with a slow but sure progress from the Missouri River over the interminable plains, through winding gulches, and cañons, and over broad streams, to the golden shores of

California, and with a fidelity and certainty not to be realised amid the fickleness of winds and waves, by the sailing packets.

What we are about to relate concerns the *Democrat* and its readers a great deal more than they would imagine on glancing at the heading. You should know that the daring express rider, who faithfully conveys in his saddle bags the plethoric and important official document, bears also the letter from the newspaper correspondent across the burning plains, and desert wastes, alone, dashing through black night and the chilling storm of sleet and rain, with such an enduring spirit, that the very tempest itself might pause and admire. While performing this errand two days ago the scout Atkins was chased by Indians for about five or six miles. One bold savage overtook Atkins, and raising a sabre, manifested an intention to cut short his career by decapitation, but, taught by long experience to be wary, Atkins presented a long dragoon revolver so suddenly before the Indian's triumphant face, as to cause in him an immediate revulsion from hatred to amity.

The Indian informed Atkins, in "pigeon English," that he had no cause of quarrel with him, but that on the prairies every one was bound to be on his guard. Atkins, as a matter of course, laughed at him, and strange to say, forgave him. Touched by " the magnanimity of his white foe," the Indian warned off his comrades. Atkins continued his gallop, and thus our letter from Fort Hayes reached you.

" Wild Bill," who is an inveterate hater of the Indians, was also chased by six Indians lately, and had quite a little adventure with them. It is his custom to be always armed with a brace of ivory-handled revolvers, with which weapons he is remarkably dexterous ; but when bound on a long and lonely ride across the plains, he goes armed to the teeth. He was on one of these lonely missions, due to his profession as scout, when he was seen by a group of the red men, who immediately gave chase. They soon discovered that they were pursuing one of the most famous men of the prairie, and commenced to retrace their steps, but two of them were shot, after which Wild Bill was left to ride on his way. The little adventure is verified by a scout named Kincaid, who, while bearing despatches for General Custer, was also obliged to use his weapons freely. The lives of these Indian scouts are made up of these little experiences.

A Trip up the Missouri—The Cities on its Banks—St. Joseph and its Circus—A Waif—The Steamer, the Captain, the Clerk, the Pilot, the Passengers—Arrival at Omaha— General Augur—His Intended Expedition—War with the Indians.

OMAHA, *May 20th,* 1867.

THE vast body of water that rushes everlastingly from the most northern part of this continent to the Gulf of Mexico, and divides it into almost equal halves

I.   II

has been aptly termed by the native red man Min-ne-ook-ta, or Much Water, which is a true description of the Missouri River. On gazing up the dark, muddy river, the same outlines of the land, the same eternal objects present themselves to the view above, as we observed below. Now and then square specks of white can be seen afar off, sometimes on one bank and sometimes on the other. These turn out on a nearer approach to be embryo "cities." Many of them are comparatively old, and present quite a finished appearance. There is none of that American energy which is visible in the lower portion of the river, in the neighbourhood of St. Louis. There is no apparent advancement, and but little desire for progress manifested by the citizens. In these cities each resident's peculiarities and eccentricities are well-known to his neighbour. Each maiden's "points" have been noted down long ago by her swain, even to the number of teeth in her little coquettish head. A new-comer is regarded as an unwelcome visitor and a curiosity ; at least, it must be presumed so, judging from the manner in which the northern Missourians stand and regard *us* passengers. The girls appear pretty, virtuous, and happy. Contentment beams from the countenances of the men ; and cleanliness, thrifty, economical, industrious, housewifery, early rising, vigorous health, and virtue, sit enthroned on the features of the dames. A boyish bashfulness pervades the overgrown youths, who, if not blessed with much worldly conceit and knowledge, are evidently endowed with an abundance of bone, sinew, and muscle that is really delightful. You catch a glimpse now and then of a rude log hut almost buried out of view by the dense forest around it. In that hut reside some coloured man's family, revelling in its newly acquired independence and liberty. The wood-piles which are arranged in three long rows along the margin of the river, in close proximity to the huts, exhibit the freedmen's occupation and industry and their whole worldly wealth. Much toil and fatigue have the late contrabands experienced before the tall, upright cotton wood was cut and split into firewood. Their dark-skinned children now play under the greenwood trees free!

While stopping at St. Joseph, previous to taking the steamer, we visited the great attraction of the season in that Christian city—viz., the circus, which has had such an unprecedented attendance each night since its arrival. On the night of our visit there were about 1000 persons present.

Wandering around the extensive circle was a golden-haired little boy of scarcely four summers, who had been attracted by the lively music, as played by seven female musicians, or fascinated by the gaudy attire of the gymnasts. He had strayed away from home unknown to his fond parents, and now gazed on the extraordinary scene with unspeakable wonder. He now and then gave vent to his childish glee in ringing peals of laughter, which caused the respectable citizens of St. Joseph to smile tenderly on the innocent.

Moved by sympathy for a mother's anxiety, some good-hearted citizens took charge of him, and carried him from the circus to gladden some distracted mother with the sight of her "sugar-plum."

We took steamer from St. Joseph to Omaha, to join General Augur on his intended northern expedition. It has been generally conceded that travelling on a steamboat is far superior as regards personal comfort to any other mode of travelling. The western river steamers are famous for their luxurious fare, and consequently, in this region, are more patronised than any other means of transit from one city to another; though, to the disgrace of the builders and owners of these boats, be it said, they have thus far been rather careless of the personal safety of the passengers. The countless shoddy steamers which have been blown up and sunk in the capacious bosom of the Father of Waters, have contributed in a great measure to retard travelling in this manner. Delicate ladies and nervous gentlemen withhold their patronage, and shrink from entrusting themselves on board, preferring to undertake the fatigue of railroad travelling. Still, on the late occasion, we found the steamer excellent, "barring" a little rudeness on the part of independent waiters, and a little grumpiness on the part of the upper officials towards the passengers.

The steamer groaned and gasped, and moaned and sighed continually. The cabin floor rose visibly at each pulsation of the engines as they drove the frail vessel. On account of the curious impulse of the captain to "pile on," I fear there will be a "fine bust-up" some of these days.

At the head of the long table at meal time sat the middle-aged, florid-faced captain. His office appeared to be to escort the old ladies to the table, and to smile condescendingly on the young misses. In our ignorance we committed an unpardonable breach of western etiquette by sitting down simultaneously with the captain. The waiters were excessively indignant, and looked horrified, and in more ways than one showed that their tender "feelin's" had been outraged. After the captain and ladies had sat down, the autocratic steward rang a second bell, and with a majestic wave of the hand, and a calm, benignant smile, signified his pleasure that we should sit down.

The clerk of the steamer, or purser, is the man of business, and the prime minister of the gay vessel. In his limited den forward, he is assailed by steward, waiters, cook, deck boys, cook's boy, captain, pilots, engineers, and passengers, who are continually asking questions. As he is responsible for the good name of the boat, he is expected to be invariably gracious and polite.

The pilot is aloft at the wheel, and oblivious to everything save his duty. With what skill he manages the craft! How gracefully he steers her through, and between the myriad snags—any of which might rip her keel open—around the tortuous banks, and up again straight on her course! With what care he approaches the treacherous shoal and sandbar! At one stroke of the bell the boat relaxes her speed ; another stroke warns the leadsman of his duty, who instantly sings out, in a chanting voice "By the mark twain," "Quarter less three," "Nine and a half," "Se-ven feet," the boat proceeding still slower till the cry is heard, "No-o-o-o bottom," at which the vessel plunges on her course again as if released of an incubus, to plough the reddish water till it rages around her bow in a thousand whirling circlets.

Our steamer was full to overflowing with travellers of every rank, age, sex, and condition of life, who were all bound to the Eldorado of the west—the Rocky Mountains—to seek new homes and new employment. During the daytime, the gaudy but commodious cabin presented a curious sight. At the after part of the saloon, which is styled the ladies' cabin, sat groups of "muchly" crinolined farmers' wives and daughters, frowsy dowagers, and laughing maidens. Some ladies sat singly (doubtless old maids), who rocked their chairs in a very melancholy manner, or appeared absorbed in some novel. At the gentlemen's end was a motley assemblage of characters—divines, dominies, philanthropists, misanthropists, innocent youth, old sinners, ubiquitous "drummers," or commercial travellers, which last are the omnipresent agents for everything under the sun, from the newly invented shawl pin to the pill that cures every mortal disease in one-twentieth part of a second, and from the lately patented, self-acting tweezer, to the magic double-performing, self-adjust-

ing, anti-freezing force pump, which has been pronounced the "greatest wonder of the nineteenth
century." All seem to be dragging a miserable
existence, and constantly smoking, or indulging in
agonising yawns. With their feet elevated to the
level and altitude of their heads, these unfortunates
contrive to pass the intervals between meals. At the
first welcome sound of the bell, all unite in a grand
rush to the table, gorge themselves with two dozen
different viands, from fish, fowl, flesh, to pudding,
cake and molasses, and in ten minutes and five
seconds, they will be found around the stove, smoking away as energetically as ever. At night they
stretch their dyspeptic bodies in two tiers the whole
length of the cabin, and thus the passengers pass
their days on board a western steamer.

On the lower deck, looking expectantly up the river,
are some dozen German emigrants lately arrived from
Faderland, as can plainly be seen by glancing at their
quaint old Dutch costumes. The females of the party
are solid, substantial-looking beings, with very rosy
cheeks. They need neither paint nor cosmetics. Hanging to their skirts are a dozen or so chips of the old
Dutch blocks, perfect resemblance to their sires. They
are bound for Colorado. The women will aid with their
healthy, pure, fresh blood in peopling the Occidental
portion of the country with energetic humanity, thereby performing the only function properly belonging to
them, according to Napoleon.

We arrived at Omaha lyesterday, and according to

our instructions, proceeded to the fountain head, where reliable information of intended operations against the Indians might be obtained.

General Augur has organised a force of two thousand men with a view of proceeding against the hostile tribes north of the head waters of the Yellowstone. But, as late despatches prove, the line of the Union Pacific is in danger. Depredations on a small scale are being daily committed by those two tribes, after whom General Custer was lately in pursuit, and who are now in the neighbourhood of the Platte River.

The Union Pacific Railroad—The Platte Valley Route— Comparisons—North Platte—Waggon Trains—Express Coaches—Emigrants—From Bishop's Ranche to Douglas Ranche by Stage—The terrible Scenes on the Route— Murder, Scalping, and infamous Outrages.

NORTH PLATTE, *May 25th*, 1867.

WE left Omaha soon after the receipt of a batch of telegrams announcing that the Indians were murdering the settlers and burning the ranches. We were curious to compare the Union Pacific railroad along the Platte, with that which runs through the Smoky Hill valley. It is true that an immense energy has been expended on the part of the road now open to the public; and it is expected that by the first of July, 410 miles of railroad along the Platte will be completed. Some twelve thousand hands, who display an astonishing amount of enthusiasm, are engaged in the great work. Passengers are forwarded regularly to North Platte, a town situated at the confluence of the two forks of the Platte, and distant 290 miles from Omaha. The railroad, however, is not so substantially built as that of the Smoky Hill, nor is the scenery so interesting, or the climate so genial as in the valley of the Smoky. In the spring, we should suppose, there would be some danger from inundation. At the time we passed over the road it only needed three inches more of water in the Platte to overflow the whole country ; and even at this high stage the river was steadily rising. The scenery along the whole route to Fort Laramie is monotonous, and most of it is wearisomely flat. The Platte valley is about twenty miles in width, and parallel on both sides are ranges of broken sand bluffs, which prevent us from seeing anything like the grand and extensive prospects that we obtain as we travel on the railway from Wyandotte to Salina. The country appears to afford meagre chances for the agriculturist. Cattle may be raised in some portions of the valley, but the bleached skeletons of oxen, mules and horses, with which it is so thickly strewn, tell a sad tale.

In the fall of 1865 we were curious enough to count every skeleton visible along the route, which marked unmistakably the nature of the journey which the pilgrim takes to his intended ranche in the far west. Along the broad trails from Atcheson to Denver City we counted the skeletons of 1290 oxen, 93 mules, and

145 horses.   This loss of animal life was caused by
the alkaline water of the Platte valley.   The poor
beasts, tortured by thirst, drank eagerly, and left their
carcasses on the prairie in the immediate neighbourhood of the poisoned district.   It is a notorious fact
to all travellers on the plains that this water is fatal
to animals.

We reached this place after a fifteen hours' journey
from Omaha, by which we averaged a little over nine-
teen miles an hour.   The town of North Platte,
which is the present terminus of the line, is of but
eight months' growth, and deserves mention.   Piled
up, and covered over with sailcloth, and lying in
every direction, are large quantities of Government
freight.   Some officials state the amount awaiting
transportation at 15,000 tons.   Encamped in the
immediate vicinity of this town were 1236 waggons,
divided into trains of 27 waggons, each train officered
by 29 men and a superintendent.   There were Mormon
emigrants bound to Utah, settlers for far Idaho, and
pilgrims to mountainous Montana, who were emi-
grating with their wives, children, and worldly substance.   The prairie around seemed turned into a
canvas city.

Wells, Fargo, & Co.'s express coaches takes the
intending traveller to Denver from the terminus of
the railroad in forty-eight hours.   To meet the
demands for seats, two coaches are put on the line.
Good stations are found at intervals of ten miles,
where a " square meal " can be had for $1·50.

Every gambler in the Union seems to have steered his course for North Platte, and every known game under the sun is played here. The days of Pike's Peak and California are revived. Every house is a saloon, and every saloon is a gambling den. Revolvers are in great requisition. Beardless youths imitate to the life the peculiar swagger of the devil-may-care bull-whacker and blackleg, and here, for the first time, they try their hands at the " Mexican monte," "high-low-jack," " strap," "*rouge-et-noir*," "three-card monte," and that satanic game, "chuck-a-luck," and lose their all. "Try again, my buck ; nothing like 'sperience ; you are cuttin' your eye-teeth now ; by-and-by you will be a pioneer." Such are the encouraging words shouted to an unfortunate young man by the sympathising bystanders. On account of the immense freighting done to Idaho, Montana, Utah, Dacotah, and Colorada, hundreds of bull-whackers walk about, and turn the one street into a perfect Babel. Old gamblers who revelled in the glorious days of "flush times" in the gold districts, declare that this town outstrips all yet.

After an interview with General Augur, we determined to proceed personally to the scene of hostilities. On our arrival at Bishop's Ranche we commenced to hear of the actions of the ubiquitous Indians. The great highway of the gold regions was strewn with emigrants thitherward bound, who were well-armed with the best and most effective arms, and on the *qui vive* against any sudden attack of the

redskins. Along the bluffs are Indian videttes,
patiently watching weak posts and helpless emigrant
trains. When the opportune moment arrives, from
every sandhill and ravine the hawks of the desert
swoop down with unrivalled impetuosity, and in a
few seconds the post or camp is carried, the tent or
ranche is burnt, and the emigrants are murdered.
It is generally believed here that, if the present
suicidal policy of the Government is carried on
much longer, the plains' settlers must succumb to
the unequal conflict, or unite in bands to carry on
the war after the manner of the Indians, which
means to kill, burn, destroy Indian villages, innocent
papooses and squaws, scalp the warriors, and muti-
late the dead ; in fact, follow in the same course as
the red men, that their name may be rendered a
terror to all Indians. From conversations with the
ranche men and freighters on the prairie, we are
of opinion that the time is not far distant when we
may hear of such confederation of whites organised
for such purposes. It is a desperate remedy, and yet
it seems the only one likely to affect the sanguinary
savage.

At Fort Kearney, there are twelve soldiers and a
band of musicians under the command of a lieutenant.
The fort is situated 490 miles east of Denver, within
half a mile of the Platte River. It is a forlorn-looking
place at present, for its prestige has departed with
the troops that were lately quartered there. It has
now become little better than a habitation for owls

and prairie dogs. The lovely parade ground that once re-echoed with the tread of many companies of soldiers is now silent. Grass grows on the walks and entangles the wheels of the howitzers. Its small garrison is at present engaged in building a strong stockade merely for the sake of employment.

The next post is Fort McPherson, so named after Brigadier-General McPherson, who fell on one of the battle-fields of the South, deeply deplored by his loyal countrymen. The garrison at Fort McPherson, which is strongly fortified, is composed of Company B, 2nd Cavalry, and Battery C, 3rd Artillery, and a small squad of Infantry. The post is commanded by General Carrington, and is situated about 350 miles east of Denver, and within one mile of the Platte.

Fort Sedgwick, called after Major-General Sedgwick, the New York hero, has a garrison composed of Companies K, F, G, B, of the 4th Infantry, two companies of the 30th Infantry, one company of cavalry, and a small squad of artillerymen. General Hunt, who is camped on the north side of the South Platte, commands the post. It is fortified in an admirable manner, and would withstand any force the hostile tribes could bring to bear against it. The fort is about 100 miles west of Fort McPherson, and is situate on a commanding eminence.

About four miles to the eastward stands a very enterprising little burg called Julesburg, which is well known because of the massacre of its citizens in the early part of 1865.

The above-mentioned posts contain all the troops between Omaha and Denver. As they are about one hundred miles apart, it is easy for the wily Indian to commit any depredation, and depart to his hiding-places unpunished. The company of cavalry commanded by Captain Mix is kept always on the move. From hill to hill, ravine to ravine, over prairie and over creeks they chase the red man, but all to no purpose. They have not succeeded in bringing one prisoner in yet. A comical tale is told of this captain by a citizen of Fort Sedgwick, which goes far to prove how these man-pursuits are conducted. "News is brought to the headquarters of General Hunt of the killing of three herders in Morgan Cañon, four miles from Julesburg. Instantly Captain Mix and his cavalry are despatched after the red-skins, and away they scour many miles of the country, until they begin to feel a "leetle" tired and hungry. To their dismay they find that they have forgotten their rations, and of course are obliged to return in haste. On their arrival in camp they are accosted by anxious inquiries, "What news of the Indians? Did you see any?" The answer is returned by the crestfallen captain, ' Nary a one. I'm durned if I believe there are any Indians in the country !' In the meantime, while the captain was away, another report has come in informing the General of the murder of two more men nine miles above Julesburg, on the north side of the Platte. This time the troopers take sufficient rations along to last a day or two. They start again in the direction where the affair occurred ; but towards night they are seen coming over the bluffs to camp. Again they are surrounded by eager questioners. 'What news ? What success?' To which they answer : 'Nary an Indian !' " If these sarcastic civilians may be relied on, such is the manner and method that regular cavalry adopt to fight Indians.

On our trip across the plains we saw enough to satisfy us that, unless the Government pursues different measures, the people will take the law into their own hands. Between Bishop's Ranche and Alkali Station there are three fresh graves visible. These were filled by persons killed about three or four weeks ago. There were three ranches burnt, and the ashes remain, tell-tale evidence of the mode of Indian warfare.

While riding from Alkali to Julesburg, we happened to turn our eyes towards the bluffs, when we saw a black object resembling a head. Calling the attention of the stage driver to the fact, he declared on oath 'twas an " Injun." The driver's rifle was placed in our hands, with an injunction to use it upon any warlike demonstrations. We also warned the inside passengers of what we saw. Thus unceremoniously awakened by the presence of Indians they got their rifles ready, and soon four bright muzzles were protruding from the coach. The Indian saw that he was discovered, and advanced more clearly to view. At the same moment we saw five others. All

were mounted, and, after an apparent consultation
with each other, they commenced to gallop rapidly in
a zigzag manner along the ridge of the bluffs. After
riding and manœvring thus, they descended a ravine,
and were soon out of sight. As they exhibited no
signs of hostilities, we did not think it necessary
to inform the post commander at Sedgwick, and
create needless alarm. The driver's opinion was that
the group of Indians we had seen thought it rather
a dangerous task to undertake the capture of a coach,
as it had been proved to them repeatedly that more
hard blows could be got than plunder.

At Old California crossing, we saw an ambulance
standing at the door. We left the stage, and proceeded to inquire the news. We were told that a
deserter had been shot by Indians and scalped.
This soldier had been seen the day before skulking
behind the bluffs, by one I. T. Nelen, formerly of
the Herndon House, Omaha, but now a resident of
Julesburg. It seems that the soldier had left with
the intention of deserting, as he was tired of a soldier's
life. He had travelled twenty-one miles due east
from Sedgwick when he was discovered by Indians.
With an exultant yell they pounced on him and trans-
fixed him with an arrow. He fell at once, and as a
matter of course was scalped. We saw the body
previous to its burial, and then for the first time
understood what scalping meant. Directly over the
bump of firmness, at least, the region designated by
learned phrenologists as such, a circular piece of skin

of about the size of a double-eagle coin is cut and snatched off. Sometimes, when in a great hurry, the savages cut a larger piece, and the remainder of the skin falls off, almost covering the eyes.

The most dangerous part of the route appears to be between Julesburg and Valley Station, where several ranches with their outbuildings lie in ashes. Each burnt ranche has in its neighbourhood from three to five graves. On the morning that we passed by, between Valley Station and Old Godfrey's ranche, about twenty-five Indians had driven the herders of some three hundred cattle across the river. The marauders are being hotly pursued by a detachment of citizens and soldiers, who have been sufferers from their operations for some months.

A Fugitive from the Indian Camp—Five Women Prisoners— A grand Attack the coming Month—Boy outraged—Female Prisoners badly used—Arms in the Indian Camp—The Indian Traders—Attack on Judge Kinney and Indian Commissioners — Interesting Accounts — War with the Indians—The Pawnees and Sioux—Augur preparing for War on an Extensive Scale.

NORTH PLATTE, *June 1st*, 1867.

A CORRESPONDENT sends me the following record of adventures undergone by a boy seventeen years old, called George Miller.

" This boy is a native of Union Village, Washington

I.   I

county, New York, and was captured by the Blackfeet
Indians between the Yellowstone and the head waters
of the Missouri, in July 1865, while engaged in herding
stock for an uncle, whom he had accompanied from
his home.   His uncle, with his wife and two children,
were killed at the time of his capture.   In June 1866
George was stolen by the Cheyenne Indians at Chimney Rock, with whom he has since lived up to the
time of the attack on Fairview Station. He states
that the Indians circled around the station, and he,
being in the rear and well mounted, thought it was a
good time to make his escape, and consequently struck
out as fast as a good horse could carry him for Wis-
consin Ranche, which he succeeded in reaching in
safety, although pursued and shot at repeatedly by
the Indians.   The Indians keep five white women
prisoners—one is the wife of a doctor at Council
Bluffs—whom they treat very roughly.   The boy
bears several scars on his person which have been
made by the Indians by stretching him over a log and
hitting him with a heavy whip.   One of the scars on
his neck we saw.   He was not allowed to exchange
a word with his fellow-prisoners, or with any traders,
of whom he saw a great many in camp last winter,
trading guns and ammunition.   At the time of the
attack on Fairview Station the women prisoners were
left under guard at or near Sand Creek. The Indians
have closely watched the forts on the Platte for
several months, and have had reports daily of the
construction of earthworks at Fort Sedgwick and

other places that were being fortified. They are armed with Spencer rifles, and their first attempts to use them appear to have resulted in several of them getting their hands injured by the explosion of the metallic cartridges, while they attempted to force them into the muzzle by pounding, not being posted in the breech-loading business. He thinks they contemplate a general and simultaneous attack along the Platte route some time about the first of June. We have given his story as he told it to us. Sergeant Furness, with whom he came part of the way from below, thinks, from circumstances that he is familiar with, that he is telling the truth. He is a bright and intelligent young man, and appears honest. He has obtained employment from Theron W. Johnson, the grocery-man, corner of Larimer and F. Streets. George estimates the Cheyenne tribe to number about fifteen hundred ; and says that the Indians are well posted in what is going on, by their spies, and that they learn much from the traders that come among them."

The following are the officers selected by General Grant to conduct the operations in the department of the Platte :—

Major-General Christopher C. Augur is a courtly gentleman of the old school, who distinguished himself at Cedar Mountain and Port Hudson. He was seriously wounded at Cedar Mountain, and for a long time he was unable to perform military duty. He has had great experience in Indian warfare in New Mexico and Utah. He is a man of rare ability, and in one respect has the advantage of General Hancock, for he is not hampered in any way by Indian agents continually dinning into his ear, " Take care, general, take care ; don't do that, for God's sake." Upon his staff are also officers, who, like Colonels Merrill, Chambers, and Alexander, are of the old military class, and have had fifteen years' rough experience of border life. They will be competent to assist the general by their advice and experience should he require it.

General Junius N. Palmer first drew the attention of the public by his brilliant deeds at the well-fought battles of Stone River and Chickamauga. He is inured to fatigue, has had two or three rough scrapes with Indians, and will prove a valuable officer on the expedition.

General John Gibbon, lately commanding the 36th Infantry at Fort Kearney, is one of the most brilliant officers in the army. South Mountain, Vicksburg, Chancellorsville, Gettysburg, Wilderness, and Cold Harbour, are a few of the fields wherein he took a prominent part. As an artillery officer he has also seen much service with the Indians.

General Henry W. Wessels, of Fair Oaks fame, has hunted and chased Indians when they were in their full strength, and when the territories were regarded as a vast Sahara.

General J. H. Potter, another officer of distinguished reputation, has had long experiences in the territories of Colorado, Dakota, Arizona, and New Mexico.

Acquainted with every creek, cañon, and eminence in the Indian country, he will prove a most efficient officer. He commands the 30th Infantry.

General Henry I. Hunt, General Meyers, and Colonel Dodge, 30th Infantry, have had years of campaigning on the plains of the Rio Colorado against the Apaches and Comanches. Major Van Voast, of the 27th, has served several years in Utah and along the Pacific slope.

Captains Morris, Gordon, Mix, Green, Mizner, Derrus, and Ball, of the 2nd, and many other officers of regiments composing the expedition, have lingered in exile, while guarding solitary outposts against the wily savage in far-off Oregon, and the most southerly points of Arizona.

It is a thankless life fighting Indians, and we heartily sympathise with the military. They fight while fat citizens sleep ; they are obliged to be constantly on the alert against the bold marauders, and are responsible for keeping open the thoroughfare across the continent.

The war correspondents begin to flock to the west to report the struggle now approaching between Sherman and his legion and the warriors of " Pawnee Killer, Tall Bull, and White Horse."

No plan has as yet been divulged. It has been discussed between men versed in the intricate ways of the Indian. Sherman's knowledge of Indian tactics is by no means small. Before he gained those brilliant stars which designate the Lieutenant-

General, he served many years of apprenticeship on the border. We have a slight inkling of what is to happen from the following orders and despatches :—

"No escort shall be provided for Wells, Fargo & Co.'s coach east of Fort Sedgwick. All passengers and freight must be sent to the end of the track, from whence sufficient escort shall be provided for all coaches westward." "Major Frank North will divide his command" (Pawnees) "into small detachments to scour the bluffs immediately contiguous to the Platte."

" *To Governor A. C. Hunt of Colorado—*

"There is no law to pay volunteers, but you ought to raise a regiment of five hundred men, and have them ready in case I call for them. I will be at Fort Sedgwick, and I don't believe you will have trouble with the Indians if your people are arduously prudent.

"W. T. SHERMAN,

" *Lieutenant-General.*"

The Cheyennes, impatient at the slow process of decorating their wigwams with the scalps of the pale-faces, have plunged hot and heavy into a war with the famous Ogallallas. A party of them have already proceeded north with the evident determination of punishing this famous tribe for their delay in not confederating with them in a war against the perfidious pale-faces. What would you more ? It is a demonstration in the pale-faces' favour. If Red Cloud, whose name alone is a host, is roused up, the Cheyennes will have more than they bargained for "Pawnee Killer" will have to cry "enough."

Murders are getting to be so tame from their plurality, that no one pays any attention to them, though reports come to headquarters every day. The following is a brief summary of the occurrences of a week :—

June 1st.—A coach was attacked at Bijou Station ; the driver fell pierced by five bullets, and a passenger was shot in the thigh.

June 2nd.—Coach attacked ; the passengers were C. C. Caldwell, E. W. Bullock, Alex. Benham, division agent of Wells, Fargo & Co., S. W. Phelps, Hiram Facht, Major Talbot. These gentlemen drove the Indians off, and killed one Indian, it is supposed.

June 4th.—Coach attacked ; Rev. W. A. Fuller, an Episcopal clergyman, the only passenger, escaped by jumping into the Platte. Ed. Kilbourne, driver, John Williams, an *employé*, from Battle Creek, Michigan, were killed but not scalped.

June 5th.—Coach attacked near Moore's Ranche. Stage supernumerary killed, and Captain Davis, of the Post-office department, *en route* to Montana, and a son of General Davies, mortally wounded in the groin.

June 2nd.—Joseph Boyd, who lost twenty mules, gave chase to the Indians, and captured twenty-three head.

June 2nd.—Turner and Paxton, of Pole Creek, lost twenty-five mules, which have not been recovered. While chasing them, he picked up a white woman's scalp.

June 5th.—Taujoin's Ranche, at O'Fallon's Bluffs, attacked ; one clerk and one herder killed. Tommy Taujoin, aged fourteen, a half-breed, had a narrow escape. He brought the information to headquarters.

Such is the position of affairs at present in the Platte valley.

Stringent Martial Law at Sedgwick—A Soldier flogged—Another bucked and gagged—A Citizen receives One Hundred Lashes—A Battle with Indians at O'Fallon's Station—Volunteering in Colorado.

FORT SEDGWICK, C. T., *June 16th*, 1867.

FLOGGING appears to be revived in the army on the plains, and citizens are shocked at some un-American scenes which have been witnessed here, and it is said that we are drifting to the time-hallowed institutions of Russia and Egypt, where the lash, the knout, the bastinado are still in vogue. On or about the 12th instant, within the limits of the military reservation of Fort Sedgwick, and within one mile of the fort, a soldier received twenty-five lashes for stealing a gun, the property of one Mart Code, a trader living at Julesburg. In the same week a soldier of the 30th Infantry, by orders, was laid out on the ground under a hot broiling sun, and a stake fastened at each limb, to which he was firmly bound, thus laying him out according to a mode well known to military officers, and which is entitled "spread-eagle fashion." He was left in that position for two hours; in the meantime the buffalo gnats covered his face by thousands, causing intense suffering to the unfortunate fellow. "For two hours he screamed, cried, begged, entreated for the love of God to be let loose. For two hours he roared; I couldn't stand it any longer; I tell you, sir, his face was perfectly bunged up." Such were the words of his lieutenant to a group of officers, who expressed deep commiseration for the man's sufferings.

While visiting headquarters on the morning of the 15th we heard that a white citizen was to receive one hundred lashes some time during the day, for giving a bottle of whisky to soldiers. There was neither trial nor court-martial, merely a summary dismissal after the manner of a Pasha. "Let him have one hundred lashes." What a fuss is kicked up all over the country if a child is switched by its teacher or parent; but here is an instance of a citizen, who, while sick of a disease which, like a cancer, had eaten up his very features, was stripped and flogged before two hundred soldiers.

Some days ago, according to reliable authority, a stranger, giving his name as Hendriks, made his appearance at Pole Creek in the vicinity of Wilson's Ranche. He was incapacitated by illness from performing manual labour. He loitered around the ranche until the night of the 14th, when he was accosted by two men dressed in citizen's garb, who politely requested him to buy them some whisky, at the same time furnishing him with the requisite funds. He willingly acceded to the request, and in a few moments delivered to them the bottle of whisky. In about an hour afterward he was arrested and brought into the guard-house of the 30th Infantry. At 9 A.M. of the 15th his case was reported by Lieutenant Lantz of Company F, 30th Infantry. About twelve o'clock the offender was brought forth escorted by two soldiers. Complete preparations had already been made for the punishment. A scantling with a board nailed transversely was planted in the ground. About two hundred soldiers and a small squad of citizens gathered to witness the proceedings. Two soldiers with plaited thongs in their hands stood on the right and left of the cross. On the soldiers, with their instruments of torture, and the cross, the unfortunate fellow gazed in dismay. Lieutenant Lantz informed the sergeant that he did not order his punishment, but that he "would like to see him flogged." On hearing this, the orderly sergeant of Company F, assisted by the two soldiers, divested him of almost every article of clothing. They then bound him to the cross, and when all was ready the sergeant gave the signal to proceed. The men detailed to strike raised their arms aloft, and, swinging the ropes over their shoulders, the one on the right

brought the hissing lash full on the naked hips of
the man, who sprang convulsively upward as if shot.

Before sixteen strokes had been administered blood
was welling in streams down his legs and pouring into
his shoes. Blood was splashed over some of the spec-
tators. After the fiftieth stroke the body assumed a
livid colour, and the skin hung in strips and flakes.
Men stopped their ears, and turned away from the
horrid sight. A respectable citizen, named F. L.
Seward, who witnessed the whole affair, turned to
Lieutenant Lantz, and said, "For God's sake, stop
that ; you will kill him." Lantz, supposing the
bleeding wretch had received enough, motioned the
executioners to desist. After the flogging had ceased
the poor fellow was ordered by Lantz from the reservation. He managed with some difficulty to put on
his nether garments, sighing and groaning deeply.
After being dressed he turned to the lieutenant, and
said : " I did not sell the whisky to soldiers, nor did
I know they were soldiers, as they wore civilian
clothes." Having uttered this, he turned from the
camp, dragging his mangled limbs painfully along
toward the sand bluffs. We have heard since that he
hailed from the State of New York. Some soldiers
state that they counted one hundred and eight strokes,
but the sergeant states eighty-two to have been the
number delivered.

Lieutenant Lantz has only been lately appointed
through the influence of Senator Coon, of Pennsylvania. He donned his new uniform, and commenced

his duties as a second lieutenant about fifteen days ago.

A fight occurred between sixty-seven white men belonging to Wilson and Claigit's train, bound for Phil Kearney with Government stores, and about one hundred and twenty-five Indians, at O'Fallon's Bluffs, on the night of the 12th instant. We arrived at the scene of the hostilities three-quarters of an hour after the battle had taken place. It seems from the information given by the waggon-master that they had driven their mules, of which there were about three hundred and forty, to water. Eight herders, armed with Spencer rifles, were guarding the stock when the Indians came dashing down the bluffs, yelling and shouting like fiends. The men instantly threw themselves down on the ground, and commenced firing. Attracted by the sound of the rifles and the confusion which was apparent in the herd, the waggon-master, with the remainder of his men, made a *sortie* out of the corral on the band of Indians, and in a few moments cleared the field. Our informant stated that he saw about nine bodies hanging down, as if lifeless, upon the ponies. The camp lost but one horse.

New Julesburg—The Navvy at Work—Grandeur of the Tornado
—Mexican Teamsters—A Model Cabin—The Indian
Question and its Solution—The Right Policy—State of
Affairs in the West—What some People say—General
Hancock—Prairie Forts—Distribution of the Troops—
Indian Troubles and their Causes—Our Missionaries—
The Indians and their Classification.

NEW JULESBURG, COLORADO, *June 25th*, 1867.

THE town we are now in (for if by a stretch of courtesy I denominate four tents and a half-finished
eating-house a town, it is nobody's business) is
situate at the base of a ridge of greyish sandy
bluffs, about two miles north of Fort Sedgwick. The
graders of the Union Pacific have long since left New
Julesburg behind. A long straight line running
parallel with the Platte River and through the streets
of New Julesburg marks the course of the great
thoroughfare. The song and jest of the Irish navvy
has long since died away in this vicinity. Forty
miles beyond, eastward, the careless fellow may be
seen shovelling his contract, little thinking of the
consequences resulting from his work. Step by step
towards the Occident he throws the earth into a
straight line over which will be placed the iron rails
for the million travellers who will roll by without a
thought of the navvies who toiled for them. The
Irishman heaves his spadeful on the common heap,
smokes his dudeen, eats his cooked rations at the

"shebang," takes "a smile," has his petty quarrels, is reckless of the future, sanguine of the present, trolls out his carol day by day, and feels himself superlatively happy.

But not to digress. New Julesburg was settled by Messrs. Allen and Seward. Although it has only a population as yet of forty men and one woman, in six months it will have a population of 2500 souls, at the rate immigrants are coming here. North Platte intends a general exodus to New Julesburg, and next week the new town will have a newspaper, which is to be called the *Frontier Index.* In two weeks the town will be a city ; then the city will elect a mayor. In three weeks we predict that it will have a theatre. In four weeks the citizens will have a branch railroad to Denver and St. Louis. In six weeks New Julesburg may be the capital of Colorado, and statesmen will gather from the east and west to see this prodigy of modern times. Such is a brief sketch of the present position and future destiny of this western "town," according to the enthusiasts.

In these distant parts of the west we meet several strange characters. Ruined merchants, unfortunate lawyers, clergymen, and men of all classes are seen pursuing humble avocations. In a train of Mexican waggons corraled close to the Platte, in the vicinity of Elbow station, we saw a son of one Kentucky's famous governors dandling the long whip with the air of an experienced bull-whacker. It would be too long a story to relate how he came to be in that position ;

suffice it he was there. With this train there were forty-three men, mostly Mexicans. They looked, taken all together, like some hybrid species, with their soiled clothes, long, tangled hair, bronzed features, cracking their long whips, shouting their "Wo, ha, ha, ha, wo, ha." In the centre of the corral were others, evidently Mexicans, amusing themselves with dance and song.

The teamsters lead a hard life, as they are exposed to all sorts of weathers. Herding animals is a dangerous, as well as an unpleasant task, when we think how they are forced to watch and follow the cattle about all night, exposed to the chilly winds, fogs of night, and the wily savage, who is continually on the prowl. They sleep in the waggons during the day, and their pay is poor compared to the fatigue they undergo. Three of this train were killed by Indians three days after we left them. One large grave was dug, and all three were put into it without any ceremony; their shrouds were the clothing they wore during life. At the head of the grave was a board, on which a comrade had carved with a knife, " In memory of Hank C. Wade, Snowdon Wade, and Andrew Small, all of Iowa, killed by Indians."

Before crossing the Platte River to Fort Sedgwick we stopped at a small shanty, built level with the river, and on its bank. Inside of the hut was an old man, who recalled to our mind the classic ferryman of the Styx. He ferries people over the shallow Platte, and his cabin was one of the most miserable ever seen by man. Its walls were lined with gunny bags, and plastered over with a composition made of sand and buffalo dung. The floor was about six feet by eight, and we narrowly escaped immersion when we stumbled indoors to make inquiries of the proprietor concerning the departure of his scow over the river. Rumour, ever busy, gave out reports that this misanthrope and apology for a man was extremely wealthy, but his hut gave no hint of an estimate of his fortune.

The body of the clerk and herder of Taujoin, a mere youth of twenty-two, presented a most ghastly sight. Without a moment's warning the Indians rushed on the cabin and murdered its defenders. There was whisky in the ranche, and, after imbibing copious draughts of the "fire water," they fell a-dancing, and celebrated its capture with drunken revelry. One more furious than the rest hurled his tomahawk at the inanimate body of the young clerk behind the counter, and split the head open. This was but a signal for the rest; they stuck arrows in the dead body, dragged it out, stripped it naked, tore the entrails out, and committed other enormities which we have not the heart to describe. The body was found about two hours afterwards by a gang of armed men, lying near the half-emptied whisky keg, and was almost unrecognisable. Two days before his death, as we were passing by on the stage, he came out to receive the mail. During our brief stay he had treated us passengers to cigars, and our

Jehu to a "drink." This driver afterwards told us it was impossible to "scare up a better boy."

Between Bishop's Ranche and Junction Cut Off, eighty miles from Denver, there are no less than ninety-three graves ; twenty-seven of which contain the bodies of settlers killed within the last six weeks. Dead bodies have been seen floating down the Platte, and still men say there is nothing in it (see Senator Trumbull's report), although Mr. Trumbull was afraid to trust himself very far on the plains. Persons have been known to travel fifty times between Denver and Kearney without being attacked, but those who betrayed carelessness have invariably been killed. The Indians, undistinguishable from the earth they lie on, continue to watch patiently from behind the hills, or from the sage brush that screens them from view. As soon as they perceive a chance to get scalps or plunder they dart down, and the deed is done.

Three modes of settling this Indian war and of keeping the great thoroughfares clear present themselves to our mind. The first is by allowing volunteer cavalry from the territories to be sent under competent commanders against the Indians. The second is extermination. And the third is one which we wish most ardently would be carried out—viz., set apart a sufficient territory, drive all the tribes within its limits, surround it with garrisons that none may leave it, and into which no white may enter without a special pass. Then, and not till then, may we hope

I.   K

for peace or a solution of the Indian question. It will take years to do it, perhaps, but when done we shall have secured a permanent peace. It is far more effective than the present policy of the Government which is to send men trained in West Point who never saw Indians, with thousands of eastern soldiers just as inexperienced as themselves, to catch savages who are always on the gallop.

Since the commencement of this Indian war we have scarcely heard of a single instance where a soldier has shot an Indian, or even secured a prisoner, excepting the party of cavalry men who killed those six Indians at Cinmarron Crossing, on the Arkansas river, but at every attack made upon emigrant trains two or three Indians have fallen. When an attack is made upon them, these western men lose no time in useless parades, but throw themselves into the first buffalo wallow, or take instant advantage of every rising ground, and shoot. Trained to the use of firearms and manœuvres of Indians, they are not liable to become excited, and demoralised; they are not likely to stand off a mile or two within the entrenchments of a fort, or within the limits of a corral.

Forming something resembling a right angle are ten forts built by the Government, which are filled with valuable stores, and garrisoned by some 3,000 men; their names are Kearney, McPherson, Sedgwick, Morgan, Mitchell, Sanders, Laramie, Reno, Phil Kearney, and Buford. These forts, built at intervals of from fifty to one hundred miles, are garrisoned by infantry. Two of the principal forts have a small detachment of cavalry, and these few horsemen are expected to protect the wide plains from the incursions of the savages. In peaceful times these forts are most valuable to emigrant trains and travellers who are driven to cross the uninhabited plains of the west, but in war time they are worthless as regards any protection derived from them. They are serviceable as depôts where cavalry can obtain supplies during operations against hostile tribes. It is an universal complaint that, managed as they are, they afford no security to the overland waggon trains. By the time intelligence is transmitted to the commanders of posts the attacking party have risen up unexpectedly in some other distant quarter, so that even the dullest must perceive that they offer but little security to moving emigrants.

A Senatorial party and a host of other eminent men lately visited these parts. During their stay they saw enough to convince them that an Indian war had really broken out and that it was carried on in an atrocious manner. They saw and deplored its evil effects. The Indian commissioners, after holding indifferent "pow-wows" with superannuated Indian chiefs, run post-haste to Washington, and lay their reports with assumed importance before the Government, and declare that there is no Indian war—that it is a *myth* conjured up by designing persons !

General Hancock, on his recent expedition, received convincing proofs that an Indian war was about to

K 2

commence. His appearance in the country severed the hostile confederation of tribes, and thwarted the designs of the ambitious and warlike young Indians of the South from joining those of the North. The expeditionary force did not create the evil, but performed most excellent service. Designing men misrepresented him and his purposes ; predicted an interminable war as the inevitable consequence ; and compared him to a firebrand. But the war, such as it is, had already commenced, and Major-General Hancock could not exceed the orders received from Lieutenant-General Sherman, his superior officer. On receiving his orders from Sherman, Hancock said : General, you have got to give me those orders in writing, if you expect me to follow them." Hancock's instructions were limited to separating the Sioux and Cheyennes, who were eager for war, from the still vacillating Kiowas and Comanches south of the Arkansas.

In flagrant violation of treaties solemnly entered into in 1866 with the Government, the chiefs of the hostile tribes have commenced their depredations on the settlers in the Platte valley and all through the western part of Dacotah. The Indians must be compelled to learn that treaties are not to be trampled upon with impunity. Some people lament and are sorrowful over the idea that a vast expenditure will necessarily arise out of this war. If the territories be permitted to defend their own frontier we will wager that before two months the Indian war will have become a thing of the past. Regular officers, though brave and able men, cannot adapt themselves to the nomadic life and the wily manœuvres of the wild Centaurs of the desert; it requires men qualified by experience and active life to become equal antagonists to these marauding savages.

At present we have at Fort McPherson six companies, Fort Sedgwick four companies, Fort Morgan one company, Fort Sanders six companies, Fort Laramie ten companies, Fort Caspar one company, a new fort established on the La Prete three companies, a new fort to be permanently established at the Black Hills fourteen companies, Fort Reno four companies, Fort Phil Kearney five companies, and Fort C. F. Smith four companies.

All these soldiers stationed at the above posts do not appear to be able to preserve the peace or to afford protection to the emigrant. The Indian question is regarded by different persons from different standpoints. All agree that we must have peace, but in the manner of preserving peace there is great diversity of opinions expressed. It appears to me that this Indian war may be easily quelled. If we adopt war, it ought to be met in a sharp, short, and decisive manner, and volunteer cavalry in numbers equivalent to the task undertaken, are the cheapest and most efficient.

The regular troops can fight Indians when they get a chance, but the difficulty with them is to find the Indians.

Extermination is a long word, but a longer task, and civilisation cannot sanction it. It has frequently been suggested by people rendered desperate by Indian atrocities. It was formerly believed that the Cherokees were untamable. As early as 1760 they manifested their hostility to the whites by the massacring of the back settlers in Virginia. In the years 1776 and 1782 they were at war with the colonists in Georgia. The general government at last allowed the Indians to reside in the country now known as the States of Tennessee, Alabama, and Mississippi. But the whites encroached on their lands, and continually annoyed them, and then it was decided to remove the Cherokees west of the Mississippi. This removal was effected in 1837, since which time they have increased in population, advanced in intelligence, and have acquired wealth. They possess a newspaper and printing press, the Bible in their own language, almanacks, hymns, and other books of instruction. They have written laws, an organised government, a head chief, elected every four years, and a judiciary, consisting of a supreme court, circuit and district courts. So, also, the Delaware nation, or, as it calls itself, the Lenape, now living on the Delaware reservation in the south-western part of Kansas, which was formerly the most powerful and ancient nation, and often called by the Indians the " Grandfather Nation." The Lenapes now possess schools, and conduct themselves as civilised people. Beautiful farms, neat cottages, commodious schools, and churches adorn their reservation. The Choctaws, Chickasaws, Shawnees, Wyandottes, Pawnees, Pottawattomies, Kickapoos, Omahas, and Kaws, are rapidly following in the train of civilised nations. Pleasing evidences of their industrious habits and natural intelligence meet the eye as the traveller journeys through their country. Through the exertions of our indefatigable missionaries these Indian nations have become Christians, and instead of revelling in slaughter and blood are engaged in the arts of peace. Even some of the barbarous Sioux, whose voices have always been for war, have changed, and now adopt the customs of civilised life. They are hooted and scorned by the wild Sioux, and their willingness to adopt the ways of the pale-face is construed as degeneracy. But encouraged by the zealous missionaries, they steadily persevere in their praiseworthy endeavours. It appears to me to be about time to try the reservation plan on these present savages of the plains on a grand scale, and after a complete system.

The present numerical strength of the Indians is estimated at 350,000 ; out of this number 70,000 are semi-civilised. According to statistics furnished us by an officer qualified by long experience and intercourse with Indians, they may be classed according to their tribal organisations as follows :—

Cheyenne and Blackfeet Sioux, 9,100 ; Arapahoes, 1,200 ; Brule Sioux under "Red Cloud," 3,000 ; Ogallalla Sioux, 3,600 ; Minneconjos, 2,400 ; Unkpapas,

2,400 ; Yanktonnais, 4,200 ; Arickaries, Assinaboines, Gros Ventres, Mundans, 9,000.*

In the northern part of Montana are the Flatheads, 600 ; Kootennais, 300 ; Pend d'Oreilles, 900. In the Indian country lying north of Texas, and west of Kansas, may be found the following peaceful tribes, which are semi-civilised : Choctaw nation, 15,000 ; Chickasaws, 5,000 ; Quapaws, Senecas, and Shawnees, 670 ; Osages and Neoshos, 3,200, and the Wichitas 2,800. In Kansas and Nebraska are the Pawnees, 2800 ; Winnebagoes, 1,900 ; Omahas, 1000 ; Iowas, 300 ; Ottoes and Missourias, 700 ; Sacs and Foxes 800. These Indians are all friendly. There are also the Chippewas, Ottawas, and Pottawatomies, numbering 7,924.

In Oregon, Washington, Arizona, New Mexico, and Texas are the Tulalips, Skokamish, Lumnis, 1,900 ; Sklallans, 1,500 ; Makahs, 1,400 ; Puyallups, Niscuallys, Squakskins, and Chehalis, 2,000 ; Quinairlt, Quillehutes, 600 ; Yakamas, 3,000 ; Spokanes, 1,200 ; Colvilles, 500 ; Cayuses, Walla - Wallahs, 1,200 ; Wascoes, Klamaths, and Modocs, 3,500 ; Snakes, or Shoshones, 1,000 ; small bands scattered, 1,250 ; Pimos and Maricopas, 7,500 ; Papagos, 5,000 ; Cocopas, Yumas, Majaves, Yavapais, Hualopais, and Chemihuevis, 9,500 ; and lastly, the most warlike tribes on the American continent, the Kiowas, Comanches, Apaches, and Navajoes 15,100.

* In the spelling of these names I am obliged to copy my informant.

In Nevada, Utah, and the Indian country east of
the Rocky Mountains, are found the following : The
Pah-utes and other tribes, 8,500 ; Bannacks and
Shoshones, 4,000 ; Gosha-utes, 800 ; Weber-utes, 800 ;
Timpanoag, 300 ; Unitah-utes, 3,000 ; Pah-vauts,
1,500 ; San Pitches, 500 ; Utahs, 3,000 ; Pueblos or
Village Indians, 7,000 ; Tahequache-utes, 4,500 ; and
the Creeks, civilised, 14,500.

From St. Louis to Fort Harker—Bachelor Bohemian in the
Ladies' Car—Indian " on the Brain "—Night at the Fort—
Social Characteristics of the Plains—How Ranche Folks
go to bed—Tarantula Bitten—Osages on the Warpath.

FORT HARKER, KANSAS, *July 12th*, 1867.

ON this our second journey from St. Louis to Fort
Harker we met some interesting adventures. Through
one unfortunate circumstance, we were ushered into
what is called out West the "ladies' car." A young
lady dressed in black took it into her head to take
our arm as we were about entering the ladies' car
through an error. The brakesman accosted us civilly
enough with the rather startling interrogatory, "Your
wife, sir ? Ah ! I see. Pass on, sir ; pass on, ma'am."
Now to be addressed thus, placed us in an equivocal
position. We discovered soon after that this young
lady was a *lunatic,* and was bound for Fulton, under
the charge of Marshal Laibold of St. Louis, and the
poor unfortunate being had unwittingly been taken

for our wife, hence we were allowed free access to the sacred precincts of a "ladies' car." There was nothing very remarkable about the car, nothing essentially different from other cars, except the hallowing name "ladies' car." It was filled with cheerful married couples bound to the interior. On our arrival at Fulton, our lunatic wife and ourself were separated for ever, with one-sided protestations of eternal sympathy.

We arrived at Lawrence in due time, where we took aboard a lot of Kansas volunteers, who conducted themselves after a style becoming the inmates of Fulton Asylum. They suffered from Indians "on the brain." They were going to hunt scalps, and to manufacture fancy knickknacks out of Indian skulls, They hallooed, whooped, and yelled in true lunatic style at everything, from a telegraph post to a little calf. We actually saw them waving a parting adieu to a superannuated old cow, which frantically lashed her tail, and made threatening demonstrations with her head.

Twelve o'clock on the night of the 10th instant we arrived at Fort Harker, and were landed on the bleak, dismal, forlorn "outside of all creation," the volunteers indulging in the bitterest invectives against everybody and everything more especially on their "foolish hearts." The scene outside of the cars was indeed one well calculated to sharpen one's acrimony. Thunder and lightning, hail and rain, a splashy prairie, the blackness of night, minus tents, shelter, and food—such were our troubles of that night, never to be forgotten, eighteen hours without food, and no prospect of getting any. We were absolutely famishing ; the fort was half a mile off, and everybody was in bed, and it was too dark to distinguish the direction it lay. There was also a chance of stumbling against a vidette, whose fears, excited by the figure of a man, might mistake us for an Indian.

Two volunteers wished to know where "Mr. Injun" was, and forthwith instituted a search for him, and bravely entered the great illimitable darkness beyond. The two courageous volunteers soon found "Mr. Injun" in the shape of a telegraph pole. In the contest the pole was victorious, for it still stood upright, notwithstanding the vigorous attack made upon it by the two valiants. After a search the two braves lay collapsed at its foot—one having a severe contusion over the orbital bone, and the other was knocked out of breath into a pool of water.

Your correspondent managed, after infinite trouble, to secure a seat in a waggon bound to the new city of Ellsworth, and for the round sum of $1 was conveyed half a mile. The sutler's house stood grim and huge as it loomed up from the great darkness around, but an authoritative knock soon roused up our quondam friend, George Snyder, who hastened in his unmentionables to unbar the door. We quickly stepped in out of the driving rain ; and after the usual preliminaries of first meeting were over, Mr.

Snyder furnished us with some blankets, and in spite of the cholera reported to be raging, the loud thunderclaps, and the lightning, we soon were at rest.

The sixty volunteers who accompanied us found their way in a miraculous manner to their comrades' camp. In anticipation of their arrival, with the aid of a few *bois de vaches*, they had contrived to keep a few gallons of coffee hot, and this beverage, freely distributed to the starving, chilled volunteers, with the generous addition of a hard cracker or two, soon restored them to equanimity ; and thus revived, they made the air resound with gleeful songs, until the "wee sma' hours" of the morning had far advanced.

A few months ago, in our ignorance of the social characteristics and distinctions in the west, we should have said that the real west commenced on the western bank of the Missouri River, but to-day, after having travelled through the Smoky Hill and Platte valleys, and having examined with attention the different traits of the western people, we should say that the genuine west commences on the western bank of the Republican River, two miles east of Junction City. From this spot, after a careful investigation, one may be able to trace the narrow line existing between east and west. At this spot begins the peculiar dialect of the west, with its accompanying characteristics—the inimitable swagger and air of the frontiersman, and the garb which is worn with a certain careless grace by a people who breathe the free, open atmosphere of the great plains.

It has been impressed on us and others many times by anxious friends, that when travelling in this wild country we should carry slung to our waists a museum of arms, such as a bowie knife, a brace of revolvers, and a Henry rifle. To carry such an armament we should be compelled to hire an esquire, which would prove sadly prejudicial to our light purse. It would also imply that we challenged every desperado we met to touch us if he dared. Such awful Quixotic responsibilities a sane man will not readily undertake. In our wanderings through the country we went armed with a pocket knife and a reporter's notebook, and our lamb-like confidence commanded the greatest respect from all, and so far we have only once been insulted by a western man, an insult that was speedily avenged by "Wild Bill," who seized the fellow, with long nervous hands, and flung him across a billiard table.

Different shades of western life have been presented to us within the last three months, and for the benefit of those who lack the means, the time, or the courage to venture out on the "great uninhabited desert," we indite these remarks. In the pages of eastern daily papers appear most minute accounts of the various styles of dress for votaries of fashion of both sexes. They even astonished the reading public lately with a novelty never before attempted, in the shape of a description of a young lady going to bed, following which came an account of a bachelor retiring to his solitary couch. As a kind of a sequel, we propose to truthfully relate how a ranche man and his wife, and his eldest son and heir, and his young wife retire. We were an unwilling spectator of the scene herein related.

Far from home, or from any civilised " diggings," we were compelled to seek shelter at a ranche. In this ranche, built of adobes, with a mud roof, lived an old grey-headed man and his " ole 'oman." It must not be supposed that this old couple were infirm, unable to move about ; far from it, they were more active and ten times more laborious than the young man and the young woman who lived under the same roof. The ranche itself consisted of a single room, eight by twelve. A stove stood in the centre, and occupying precisely one half of the ranche were two beds, one for each couple. The old woman, who was undoubtedly the mistress of the ranche, gladly consented to give us a lodging. On taking a sweeping look round this humble abode we doubted her ability to make good her word, for it appeared inconveniently crowded already.

There was a large table ; there were large tin pans brimful of milk (for the ranche man had nine cows), piled one upon another on a strong shelf ; there was a cupboard plentifully supplied with loaves of bread, yellow butter, and pitchers of genuine cream, besides loads of dishes and crockery, knives and forks ; there was also a chest of drawers, or bureau, which contained the family linen and household apparel. Under the table were three tame fawns ; under the stove

was a cat ; under the old lady's bed was a huge
mastiff ; about everybody's feet were chickens chirping incessantly, while around them moved the mother
hen cackling continually, and strutting before the
door, with a lordly mien, was a magnificent Shanghai
cock.

We have thus far been careful to give a correct
idea of the families that lived in the ranche in
which the old woman said we should find a lodging.
Ten o'clock at night arrived, and we began to
observe symptoms of uneasiness in the old lady.
We had been chatting continually from the hour the
chickens went to roost overhead among the branches
that supported the mud roof, from the time the dog
and cat and the fawns had laid to rest for the night,
and it was now time for the family to retire. The
young woman had been sitting in a corner, listening attentively to our entertaining stories, but on
observing the weariness of her mother-in-law, she rose,
and retreated towards her bed. After a preliminary
haw, and a slight hem, she turned her back to us,
and first loosed her apron. She then took off her
calico dress, which was, I think, fit for the wash-
tub, and dropped it on the top of the apron lying
at her feet. Then, sitting down on an empty soap
box, which stood at the head of the bed, she lifted
one lusty leg over the other, and in a short space
of time her shoes fell with a thump on the floor. She
rolled her black woollen stockings off, and disclosed
feet white as snow, and after softly rubbing her toes,

stood up and doffed her skirt and gown with remarkable celerity. For an instant, as she stood in the
centre of her heap of clothing, she resembled a
Venus rising from the foam. Then putting a frilled
nightcap on, she stepped into the bed, lay down and
covered herself, and after two or three uneasy turns,
finally turned her back to us, and went calmly to
sleep.

It must not be supposed for one instant that we
looked at her. We maintained a more eager conversation—if anything—than before with the old lady
and the two men, but we could not avoid being
conscious of the proceedings. We now rose and
left the room, followed by the two men, while the
old lady disrobed herself. On hearing a voice from
the inside asking a question about some cows we
re-entered the house. That question was a signal
which the old man perfectly understood. The
old lady lay nightcapped in bed, with her face
turned to the brown adobe wall. On the floor near
the stove our bed had been made. A solitary lamp
lit the apartment. In a short time we were in bed.

The old lady asked, " How do you find yourself,
Mister Man?" We replied, "Perfectly easy, ma'am."

We now watched the men undressing. Standing
at their respective beds, they first took off their boots,
then coats and vests. At this stage of the proceedings the young man blew the lamp out, and in a
second we heard the pantaloons thrown off, a creak-
ing of the beds followed, and the household was at

rest. Altogether we were three men, two women, one dog, one cat, three young antelopes, and a dozen chickens in one small room, only lighted and ventilated by two small loopholes. That is my experience of a small Western ranche.

Next day, before departing east, the old lady commissioned us to bring her a pair of shoes for herself (No. 8), seven yards of "domestic," and a romance called the "Prairie Flower," which commission we executed to her entire satisfaction.

Frank Schermerhorn, a descendant of one of the old Knickerbockers, now a resident at Fort Harker, while attending to a lot of customers at Osborne & Snyder's store, suddenly felt something crawl up his right leg, and striking his leg where he thought the insect was, received at the same moment a bite from it. This insect was a large spider, called a tarantula, one of the most poisonous insects known. In about half an hour Mr. Schermerhorn's body was swollen terribly; his leg measured about two feet around. He also felt nausea about the stomach, and commenced to vomit violently. His body assumed a perfectly livid hue, while he experienced a difficulty of breathing. A surgeon was called in, who bled him profusely, and in about six days he was enabled to be "around"; but in the immediate neighbourhood of the bitten part the cuticle appears raw, and, it is believed, will always remain black.

I.   L

Pacific Road—The Hotels—Fire-brick Biscuits—Fat Stewards
—Exorbitant Kansas City—St. Louis Drummers—Leaven-
worth and its People — Leavenworth to Weston — The
Platte Country Road—Description of Omaha.

OMAHA, *July 22nd,* 1867.

THERE are two routes, which lead through some of
the finest portions of this continent, from St. Louis to
Omaha. Almost every man and child knows that,
but many have not experienced the delightful
sensations of travelling to Omaha *viâ* the Pacific
railroad. From the time the *avant courrier* of the
omnibus bellowed up the steps of our hotel, " Passengers for the Pacific railroad," we have been wild
with pleasure. The courtesy and extreme politeness
of the conductor, the brakesmen, and even the train
boy, take away our breath ; and the fidelity and
courage of the engineer command our admiration.
Twenty-two miles an hour, a splendid road, magnificent scenery—in fact, everything tip-top, save the
hotels. If you except the McKissock House at
Sedalia, which is really a first-class hotel—the hotels
on the Pacific railroad are literally whitewashed Mugby
Junctions, built after the prevailing American style of
hotel architecture, which has been denominated by
a surly bachelor friend of ours, as " long barn style."

The proprietors of these establishments vie with
each other for exorbitant charges and poor fare,

Their peculiar characteristics may be catalogued as follows : lengthy buildings ; well-dressed proprietors, generally called "colonels," of aldermanic rotundity ; clerks who invariably hold gold pens between their teeth, and are licensed by their position to stare at people in a very unbecoming manner ; pages with well-brushed hair, acting the part of energetic gong-beaters ; fat stewards, with immense gold chains ; charming, but extravagantly becrinolined waiting girls, with gigantic chignons ; splendid apartments, newly furnished ; clean plates, snowy napkins, bright knives and forks, and shining ware, but alas ! with little that is eatable. They are in the main varnished mockeries, which we beg to assure you (and all travellers will endorse our remarks) offer few substantial comforts to hungry Nomads. The traveller enters with a voracious appetite, and expectant of good things, but departs unsatisfied and grumbling. The *servants*, or rather employees, have a pleasant, natty way of taking one's orders and departing with alacrity, but returning at leisure with very weak coffee, heavy fire-brick biscuits, and an apology for a beefsteak. It is useless attempting to masticate the leathery beef, for we have only twenty minutes. The bell rings ; the clerk with the stare is impatient, and with a feeling of compulsion you sidle up to the gentleman and demand your bill, and you are rather astonished to find it is not more than seventy-five cents ! Seventy-five cents for sitting down to the task of testing the strength of your teeth on

L 2

fire-brick biscuits and being served by pretty girls
with chignons !

The proprietor scans the passengers as they enter
the cars, and comments upon the universal gloom
on their features, and a grim smile mounts to his
face, as he mutters, "I must have money to pay for
that building before the year is out." The man is
right ; he will get it, and double. The importation
of the girls from the Eastern cities, costs him a
handsome sum, but as they are for the sole use
and benefit of the public, why, the public, like good-
natured beings, should pay.

Not long since a friend of ours was charged at one
of these hotels four dollars and fifty cents for two
meals, and was accosted by an Irish drummer, who
was a bit of a wag, with " How do you like that for
low (Lowe) ? " and then in a philosophical manner
added, " The heavier the bill the lighter the purse,
you know."

St. Louis seems at last to have awakened to the
fact that her ubiquitous "drummers" are valuable
agents for extending her commercial interests.
Chicago, until lately, monopolised almost all the
trade west and north of Kansas City, but, through
the indefatigable exertions of these drummers, the
trade that rightfully belonged to St. Louis has
returned to its proper channel. In every western
city and town that we have visited we have seen
them, sometimes, for the sake of business, hob-
nobbing with gamblers and keepers of groggery

shops, and then again sanctimoniously conversing on theology with members of the church. Their elastic consciences enable them to hold forth upon all subjects with all manner of persons ; and if they but get an order for goods they consider themselves amply repaid for their fatiguing efforts. Kansas city merchants, who formerly sent orders to Cincinnati, have learned that it is cheaper to get their goods from St. Louis. This is as it should be. Every hotel swarms with the drummers—Washington, Hermann, Independence, Sedalia, Warrensburg, Kansas City, Wyandotte, Lawrence, Topeka, and the towns of the far west, are full of them.

Kansas City is in Missouri, one mile from the State line, two hundred and eighty miles north-west of St. Louis. It is the most religious city in the State ; it is the Boston of the west. Her churches are legion ; they embrace all the denominations. The family and general reading book of the people is the Holy Bible. The streets of this religious city are huge furrows in the hills, and are sunk to the depth of fifty feet and over. The cliff-like walls rise frowningly above the street pedestrians. Behind them, on the river bank, stands the city, stretching its skeleton arms even into Kansas State. The houses appear to be built without regard to order ; some are built on stilts, others on rocks, others are situated on perpendicular bluffs —this latter class probably from a desire for views. The city possesses a public square. To-day it is most forlorn, planted with scraggy-looking shrubs,

Ten years hence it will have undergone a magical transformation. There will be shade trees, grass plats, and parterres of flowers. So they say, though to-day it seems doubtful.

Leavenworth is about thirty miles north-west of Kansas City, and is considered the metropolis of Kansas. There is a solidity about this city which strikes the new-comer at a glance. It has wide, well-paved streets, square blocks of elegant stores, magnificent hotels, and an orthodox activity pervades the whole. The citizens claim a population of twenty thousand. Taking a ride through its streets we are struck at their unusual length for such a young city. Many of the private houses are of palatial proportion. At dusk the streets are covered with well-dressed pedestrians proceeding to various places of amusement. Elegant teams, harnessed to showy carriages, and horsemen, splendidly mounted, exhibit themselves at this hour, and attract a great deal of attention.

Leavenworth, like New York, commences its second life at dusk ; and it is a treat to see this young Western town enjoy itself. There are six daily papers published here, at the head of which stands the *Leavenworth Conservative*, which is most ably edited. This paper has undertaken lately to imitate the journals of the larger cities in sending out special correspondents.

From Leavenworth we took passage for Weston on the favourite steamer *Hensley*, commanded by Captain

John A. Nicely. From Weston we tooĸ the Platte country road, which seems to have been dragged through the mire of Chancery by the very dilapidated state of the carriages used on it. The president is greatly scandalised at the terrible slander invented by JENKS; and feels grieved that your reporter should have asserted the monstrous fib that the "Platte country road had no family ties."

The grasshoppers have vanished from this region, and the whole country appears resuscitated. The wheat harvest seemed to be over. In our journey to St. Joseph through this part of Missouri we saw one of the most beautiful forest glades we ever beheld. Versailles and aristocratic Vienna might well be proud of it. A king would have bartered a ducal coronet for its possession, if it were possible to transfer it to his possessions in Europe.

We arrived at Omaha late in the evening; but late as it was, the depôt was crowded with runners, yelling out the names of the hotels they represented. It was a perfect Babel wherein cries, oaths, and screams, mingled. Several of the timid passengers preferred to steal away to the other side of the cars, rather than encounter such a desperate multitude.

The Republicans and Democrats of this State, Nebraska, living north of the Platte have been at loggerheads with the Republicans and Democrats south of the Platte, on account of the capitol question. The people south of the Platte are envious of their northern neighbours, because the capitol

was built at Omaha. The south Platte party succeeded in getting the capitol removed on their side
of the river. All northern Nebraska is aghast, as
this vast expenditure is about to be incurred. The
Republicans and Democrats north of the Platte,
though bitter opponents in politics, have made common cause against their southern neighbours. The
party north proclaims loudly, and with a show of
good sense, that for many reasons it would be wise to
leave the capitol in Omaha, the commercial capital
of the State. The party south answer: "Equitable
division of influence, of wealth and business. Let it
be in the centre of the State, so that business, intelligence, and wealth may radiate to its four corners.
It is too long a journey to Omaha."

The Union Pacific railroad cuts through the centre
of Nebraska, and if the representatives of the State
lived at the end of the railroad they could reach
Omaha in nineteen hours, whereas it may take days
and weeks to reach the future capitol, located as
it is about to be, far away from the iron road.
However, commissioners were appointed to locate the
capitol and public buildings of Nebraska at some
suitable point, but before they could be qualified for
the office they were to file a bond in the sum of
$60,000 each, payable to the State of Nebraska within
ten days, as a surety for the faithful performance of
their duties. Sixty days ago they started on their
perilous journey; they travelled north, south, east,
and west, and at last a suitable location was found;

whereon a city was to be built forthwith, which was to be named Lincoln, after the martyr of America. The southern party were in raptures, and predicted prosperity to the State ; in short, all was joy. But the *Omaha Republican* found a flaw in the scheme— the commissioners had not filed their bonds within ten days, as the law had required ; they had not filed them within sixty days ; they never filed them.

The Indian Peace Commission, consisting of Generals Sherman, Harney, Terry, Colonel Lewis Tappan, N. G. Taylor, etc., is daily expected at Omaha. Harney is reverenced ; old western men remember his frequent victories over the Indians. Terry is respected for his brilliant capture of Fort Fisher ; the civilians are Indian Bureau men, but Sherman, in the coming peace conference, will be the soul of the party. His views will probably have controlling weight. Cautious, calculating, with a dash of statesmanship in him, he is a valuable acquisition to the West at this time. He is perfectly aware of the responsibility attached to his present commission, and that all the people desire peace, and the results of the conference will be looked for with unusual interest. We earnestly hope that peace may be secured, although we have grave doubts that anything lasting will come of treaties of peace between a civilised nation and bands of savages.

Particulars of the Plum Creek Massacre—The Dead brought
to Omaha for Burial—A missing Man turns up, but
Minus his Scalp—His thrilling Story and Marvellous
Escape—Statement of One of the Brakemen—Who committed the Deed?—Views of General Augur and Superintendent Denman—Generals Parker and Sully, the Commissioners—They report the Indians Ready for War—
The Demands of the Indians—Captive Females.

OMAHA, NEBRASKA, *August 8th*, 1867.

DISPATCHES forwarded early in the afternoon to the
office of the superintendent of the Union Pacific railroad announced that the dead bodies of the engineer,
Brookes Bowers, and the fireman, Gregory Henshaw,
would be brought to this city, and would probably
arrive at four o'clock P.M. The news spread like
wildfire through the city, and as the hour of their
arrival approached, a large crowd of men and boys
assembled to witness the spectacle, and, if possible,
to catch a glimpse of the remains of the unfortunate
men who but a few hours previous had left Omaha in
the prime of their manhood on their usual duties.
The train arrived punctual to its time, and a general
rush was made for the baggage car.

Two small boxes, thirty by twelve inches, contained
all that was left of the bodies, and both together
would weigh about thirty pounds. These were taken
out carefully and reverentially, with uncovered heads,
by men who wished to pay the last sad tribute to

murdered friends. We confess to have been curious to see the remains. Men whispered to each other that the bodies had been burnt. What did they look like? How were they burnt? Coffins had already been provided, one metallic, the other an elegant mahogany, finely carved, and covered with black silk velvet, ornamented with silver fringe.

One of the boxes was opened, and every spectator involuntarily stepped back, for, exposed to view, surrounded by cotton, lay a charred trunk about two feet in length, resembling a half-burnt log of the same size. The remains were soon transferred to the caskets, and were then borne away towards the cemetery, followed, on account of the popularity of the poor fellows, and the exceptional circumstances, by hundreds of sympathetic people.

On the same train was a man named William Thompson, a native of England, who turned out to be one of the telegraph repairers, and was reported killed. He attracted a great deal of attention from the very extraordinary fact that he had been scalped, and lived to travel and tell his tale in Omaha. People flocked from all parts to view the gory baldness which had come upon him so suddenly. The man was evidently suffering tortures, and appeared weak from loss of blood. He showed a gaping wound in the neck, and a bullet-hole in the muscle of his right arm. In a pail of water by his side, was his scalp, about nine inches in length and four in width, somewhat resembling a drowned rat, as it floated, curled up, on the water. He was taken to the Hamilton House, and a physician was sent for, who attended to his wounds.

His statement is as follows :—

"About nine o'clock Tuesday night, myself and five others left Plum Creek station, and started up the track on a hand car, to find the place where the break in the telegraph was. When we came to it, we saw a lot of ties piled on the track, but at that same moment Indians jumped up from the grass all around and fired on us. We fired two or three shots in return, and then, as the Indians pressed on us, we ran away. An Indian on a pony singled me out, and galloped up to me. After coming to within ten feet of me he fired, the bullet passed through my right arm ; but seeing me still run, he rushed up and clubbed me down with his rifle. He then took out his knife, stabbed me in the neck, and making a twirl round his fingers with my hair, he commenced sawing and hacking away at my scalp. Though the pain was awful, and I felt dizzy and sick, I knew enough to keep quiet. After what seemed to be half an hour, he gave the last finishing cut to the scalp on my left temple, and as it still hung a little, he gave it a jerk. I just thought then that I could have screamed my life out. I can't describe it to you. It just felt as if the whole head was taken right off. The Indian then mounted and galloped away, but as he went he dropped my scalp within a few feet of me, which I managed to get and hide. The Indians were

thick in the vicinity, or I might then have made my
escape. While lying down I could hear the Indians
moving around whispering to each other, and then
shortly after placing obstructions on the track. After
lying down about an hour and a half I heard the low
rumbling of the train as it came tearing along, and
I might have been able to flag it off had I dared."

The rest of the story we have given in our first
letter. The engineer and firemen were shot and
scalped, but before the Indians burnt the train they
plundered the box-cars of everything that might prove
of the least value, or what attracted their fickle fancy,
—bales of calicoes, cottons, boxes of tobacco, sacks of
flour, sugar, coffee, boots, shoes, bonnets, hats, saddles,
ribbons, and velvets. They decorated their persons
by the light of the bonfire which they made of the
rifled boxes ; their ponies were caparisoned with
gaudy pieces of muslin, and the ponies' tails were
adorned with ribbons of variegated colours. The
scalp locks of the Indians were also set off with
ribbons, while hanging over their shoulders were rich
pieces of velvet.

Some of them came across a barrel of old Bourbon
whisky. They quickly stove the head, and quaffed
huge draughts of the fire-water, which rendered them
still more ferocious. A violent war-song was chanted
with furious gesticulations in honour of the victory
achieved over the pale-faces. At daybreak they set
fire to the wreck, taking fire from the furnace and
throwing it into the box-cars, and while the flames

roared and crackled the Indians danced and held a carnival. The dead bodies were thrown into the fire, and a terrible yell announced to the scalped and trembling man the fate of the engineer and fireman.

By and by, Thompson managed to crawl away, and found refuge at Willow Island station, until he was taken care of by a rescue party, who brought him to this city.

Doctors Pecke and Moore, of this city, will endeavour to reset the scalp on his head, and they express themselves as confident they can do it well. As he is a sturdy man, it is expected that he will soon recover from the effects of his terrible experience.

From Charles Ratcliffe, a supernumerary brakeman, who was in the caboose of the freight train when the attack took place, we had the following :—

When the train ran off the track he was asleep on the bench in the caboose, and was suddenly thrown to the floor by the concussion. At the same time he heard the yells of the Indians, and a smart volley was fired upon the people in the caboose. In the cars with him were William Kinney, conductor ; Fred Lewis, brakeman ; and a man who had been a fireman. The locomotive was thrown off the track by a pile of railroad ties across it, and fell into a hollow about four feet deep ; the tender and the first five cars were jerked on top of one another, as the train had been running at the rate of twenty-five miles an hour. Looking out of the window of the car they could see the Indians in strong force on the south side of the track, shouting and yelling at something at the foremost end—probably the engineer and the fireman. They closed the door, but in a few moments came out, and the conductor told the brakeman to go and flag off the train which was coming about three miles behind. The brakeman replied, "I dare not—the Indians are all around here." To which the conductor replied, "D—n the Indians. Go and flag off that train, or by G—d she'll be into us." Still the man hesitated, and the conductor rushed down the track himself, and the brakeman, Lewis, and the fireman went after him. Ratcliffe hid himself on the track under the car. He had laid there for five minutes when he saw an Indian cautiously approaching, drawn thither by the light that still hung in the caboose.

This obliged him to crawl away, and on reaching a safe distance, he rose to his feet and struck for the sand bluffs with the speed of a startled deer. He thought he heard some one pursuing him, from the crackling of the dry prairie stalks behind. The fear of an enemy drove him to increased speed, but the footsteps of the pursuer still sounded ominously near. He was yet a mile off from the train, so he started directly towards it, and never did Persian gaze upon the sun with a more loving look than Ratcliffe, the pursued, looked upon the welcome face of the reflector. It was to him an omen of safety, the pledge of guidance, the face of a deliverer. On casting a glance behind him—he now saw that two forms were bounding after him, and fresh impetus was given to his limbs.   Nearer came the engine ; he could see the engineer ; heard the whistle of " down brakes," saw the figures of three men hurrying up to the locomotive ; a few more bounds, and he could hear their voices.   He now shouted out with all his power ; a welcome shout was returned.   In a few seconds he was saved.   The engine was immediately reversed, and when it had gathered, as it retreated, increased speed, he laughed and cried by turns, and committed all sorts of extravagances.

The engine returned to Plum Creek station.   On their arrival they switched off and telegraphed to Mr. Beam, the director of transportation, for orders. The answer came to " Get out of the way as soon as possible."   They therefore continued the retreat as far as Elm Creek, eighteen miles from Plum Creek, bringing with them all the people at the latter place, except one man who obstinately declined to leave.

Next morning they all returned to Plum Creek, whence with the aid of a spy-glass they could see that the cars were on fire, and some Indians galloping around, while others were conveying their plunder to the Platte River.   A party of twelve Indians could be distinguished on a bluff evidently watching the train.   Towards evening they advanced as far as the wreck with a company of soldiers from Lone Tree station, where they found a mass of embers, bones, and congealed blood. All the Indians had disappeared.

General Augur holds to the opinion that Spotted Tail's band had nothing to do with this attack. Both he and Superintendent Denman believe that the guilty Indians are Cheyennes and Sioux. Many believe that it was an act of the Cheyennes and Ogallallas, who were returning north from the Smoky Hill and Republican Forks. Plum Creek has always been notorious for massacre, and is a favourite place to the Indians for crossing. Others again assert that whites led the Indians, but this idea is rejected, as no white man was ever seen leading them except Charley Bent, who is an educated half-breed.

Generals Sully and Parker, who have just returned from the Northern Indian country, report that the Indians are defiant and warlike, and that they demand the exclusive possession of, what they are pleased to term, their country, the withdrawal of troops, and the suspension of railroads. They also decline to co-operate with the generals for the purpose of inducing their countrymen, who are at open war, to return to their allegiance, but tell them in emphatic terms to go themselves to the Indian camps.

General Augur has received an urgent call for assistance from South-west Nebraska. Permission has also been asked by the people there to raise a company of volunteers for defence. The excitement in that direction is on account of the late attack made by Indians in the vicinity of Beatrice, on the

I. M

Blue River, eighty miles east of Kearney, during which two girls were made captive. General Augur has telegraphed to Sherman, requesting to know if he may buy horses for the purpose of mounting them.

News was received this morning from Fort Phil Kearney, of an attack upon a train engaged in the transportation of army supplies, by a very large force of Indians, on the second day of this month. The despatch containing this news was sent from the commander of Fort Fetterman to General Augur. An ox train of thirty waggons, owned by J. R. Porter, of Plattsmouth, and protected by an escort commanded by Brevet Major Powell, 27th Infantry, and Lieutenant Jennep, was attacked about five miles from Fort Phil Kearney by a large force of Indians, estimated at from 2000 to 5000 in number. Major Powell, behaved with conspicuous coolness and gallantry in the emergency, instantly corraled the waggons, and made breastworks of the waggon beds and ox yokes, from behind which he fought a desperate battle, which lasted fully three hours, until Major Smith, with two companies of troops and a howitzer, came to their rescue. The Indians were at last driven from the field, taking away all their dead but five. The Indians drove off all the stock. Major Powell reports sixty Indians killed, and his own loss five men, besides Lieutenant Jennep, killed.

Intelligence has also reached headquarters that Indians were hovering in the neighbourhood of Plum Creek Ranche, on the south side of the Platte.

Orders were despatched to Major Frank North to send a force of Pawnee scouts to drive them off. Major North, on receipt of his instructions, detailed Lieutenant Davis, with twenty enlisted Pawnee Indians, to proceed to the telegraph office at Plum Creek, and assist in repairing the telegraph line which had been cut in the morning.

About 2 P.M. a messenger returned, with a request from Lieutenant Davis to assist him with a reinforcement, as he was overpowered, and obliged to retreat. Major North, with his well-known promptitude, despatched Captain Music, commanding Company A, with thirty men, well mounted, to the rescue. In fifteen minutes they were in the saddle, and on their way to the assistance of their comrades.

Captain Music advanced with the command to the point where Lieutenant Davis had fallen back. Together they recrossed the river, and from the other bank took an easterly direction, heading direct for Plum Creek Ranche, where they found the enemy ready to receive them.

Music formed his men in line, crossed a bridge and advanced upon them—carbines ready.

The Cheyennes, one hundred in number, on seeing the Pawnees approach, gave a loud whoop, and discharged a perfect cloud of arrows at the little band, who kept steadily advancing on the double trot.

When they were within one hundred yards of each other Music gave the order to charge, which the Pawnees gallantly obeyed, using their Spencer rifles in the meantime with terrible execution. The triumphant whoops and yells of the Cheyennes were soon turned to groans, as the Pawnees, who are fatally expert with their rifles, shot them down without mercy. The Cheyennes soon became demoralised, and did their utmost to escape, but the Pawnees pursued them for fifteen miles, shooting them right and left, and scalping the fallen.

Captain Music and Lieutenant Davis did their utmost to prevent the mutilating of the dead, but it was impossible, for when the Indian blood is heated, they seldom listen to orders of that nature. Fifteen scalps, two prisoners, one squaw, and a boy of thirteen years, thirty head of stock, and a large number of blankets, were taken.

The Pawnees came off without a scratch, save some injuries a few of them sustained by being thrown from their horses.

Arrival at Julesburg—Its Peculiarities—Transformation of the Far West—A Stage Ride over the Plains—Approach to Denver—How it appears—Its Growth, Drawbacks, Traits, and Prospects—Its Hotels, its Newspapers and Editors.

DENVER, *August 23rd*, 1867.

I ARRIVED at Julesburg by stage from the east. A mixed crowd, composed of gamblers, teamsters, and soldiers, greeted us, all of whom were eager and

anxious for news. Bustling through them, I found
my way to the very comfortable quarters at the
Julesburg House, and was fortunate enough to find a
feast composed of various styles of soups, *fricandeaus*,
vegetables, game in abundance, pies, puddings, raisins,
apples, nuts, wine, and bread *at discretion*, for the
moderate sum of twelve bits. I was astonished to
find such company as then and there sat at table.
Everybody had gold watches attached to expensive
chains, and were dressed in well-made clothes, and
several wore patent leather boots. I vow I thought
these were great capitalists, but was astonished to
find they were only clerks, ticket agents, conductors,
engineers, and "sich like." These *habitués* of the
Julesburg House were the upper-tendom of sinful
Julesburg. Dinner over, I took a stroll through
its streets, and was really astonished at the extraordinary growth of the town, and the energy of the
people. It was unmistakable go-ahead-it-ative-ness,
illustrated by substantial warehouses, stores, saloons,
piled with goods of all sorts, and of the newest
fashion. As might be expected, gambling was
carried on extensively, and the saloons were full.

I walked on till I came to a dance-house, bearing
the euphonious title of " King of the Hills," gorgeously
decorated and brilliantly lighted. Coming suddenly
from the dimly lighted street to the kerosene-lighted
restaurant, I was almost blinded by the glare and
stunned 'by the clatter. The ground floor was as
crowded as it could well be, and all were talking loud

and fast, and mostly every one seemed bent on
debauchery, and dissipation. The women appeared
to be the most reckless, and the men seemed nothing
loth to enter a whirlpool of sin. Several of the
women had what they called " husbands," and these
occasional wives bore their husbands' names with
as much ease as if both mayor and priest had
given them a legal title. The managers of the
saloons rake in greenbacks by hundreds every night ;
there appears to be plenty of money here, and plenty
of fools to squander it.

These women are expensive articles, and come in
for a large share of the money wasted. In broad
daylight they may be seen gliding through the sandy
streets in Black Crook dresses, carrying fancy
derringers slung to their waists, with which tools
they are dangerously expert. Should they get into
a fuss, western chivalry will not allow them to be
abused by any man whom they may have robbed.

At night new aspects are presented in this city of
premature growth. Watch-fires gleam over the sea-
like expanse of ground outside of the city, while
inside soldiers, herdsmen, teamsters, women, railroad
men, are dancing, singing, or gambling. I verily
believe that there are men here who would murder a
fellow-creature for five dollars. Nay, there are men
who have already done it, and who stalk abroad
in daylight unwhipped of justice. Not a day
passes but a dead body is found somewhere in the
vicinity with pockets rifled of their contents. But

the people generally are strangely indifferent to what is going on.

The only sure preventive of these murderous scenes is martial law, or the ready strong arm of the *vigilantes*. The civil law is as yet too new to be an impediment to the unwashed *canaille*, and it certainly offers no terrors to the women who travel about undressed in the light of day. The females are monstrous creatures undeserving the name of women, and their male followers are a disgrace to manhood.

The population of Julesburg is rapidly growing ; and the town, like its predecessor of North Platte, may be epitomised as a jumble of commencements, always shifting, never ending.

The advent, to the west, of those engines of civilisation, railroads and telegraphs, has given a new impetus, which was entirely unfelt when the slow, weary, and laborious journey from the Missouri River to the mountains occupied weeks and months two years ago. The wonderful improvement in the means of travelling has given rise to a no less remarkable transformation in the effects of western emigration. The new territories are rapidly becoming developed ; towns and cities spring up with marvellous rapidity, and the great disorder of the western world is showing signs of being moulded into the form it will take eventually.

Let me introduce each novelty found west of Julesburg in due form.

The passengers are all on the south side of the

Platte, sleeping soundly in the small station just two miles east of Fort Sedgwick. It is three o'clock in the morning, and the mail coach bound for Denver City is driven to the door. The Jehu, clad in thick overcoat, sits on his box, reins in his hands, and sings out, " All aboard ? " The passengers, having finished their very early breakfast, hasten to occupy their seats, and I take mine on the top of the coach alongside of the driver. The doors are closed, a few instructions are given, the driver whispers to his horses, " Pick it up, ladies," and we are off to Denver City, the capital of Colorado.

Away we go through and past the fort, catching a glimpse in the early dawn of two or three sentinels who are leisurely pacing their beats ; of a few houses arranged in the form of a square, with one or two howitzers placed in the centre, and we are gone out on to the prairie, which spreads out before us wide, open and bare. The weather is perfect, the air cool and bracing, and I fall back into a sitting posture, but wide awake. The coach chuckles to itself as it rolls along the level road, giving one an idea that it enjoyed its own easy, swaying, rapid motion. The driver and horses appear to be smart. A word from me, and the driver becomes loquacious, and until we reach the next station he speaks incessantly of his border experiences and " Injuns." They were entertaining, and served to while away the time. After a short pause of ten minutes, we again bowl along over the prairie at a rattling pace. Presently the swaying of the coach rocks me to sleep, and just as I commence to slide into dreamland I pick myself up with a jerk, and find myself sliding over the foot-board.

After a while the driver's stories cease to be interesting, the scenery is deadly dull, the novelty of stage-riding has already been worn away, and the dreadful monotony of earth and sky becomes distressing. Hour after hour the same eternal outline and vast expanse of level plain are seen, graced here and there with abortive, sickly-looking shrubs, and clumps of sere grass. Thirty hours of imprisonment on a stage roof before me—it is horrible! And now the sun has risen; it is high in the heavens, and the stage appears to be a powerful focus to draw the entire heat upon me; buffalo gnats add to my torments, stinging and buzzing, determined to draw blood-toll. An adobe cabin is in the distance; it is the dinner station. An ablution and a substantial dinner will prove an immense benefit, after which a mild cigar, and life will again be bearable.

A few energetic spasmodic gallops, and we arrive at the ranche, and hasten to alight for another breakfast. The passengers congratulate each other, and arm-in-arm we walk in with glorious appetites. On a table spread before the crowd are abundant viands, with which the most fastidious could find but little fault. Godfrey, the proprietor of old Fort Wicked, has a fellow-feeling for travellers, and never stints them. His bountiful table is celebrated,

In excellent good humour I mount my high throne, and we are whirled away from Fort Wicked, rocking and swaying as before. Thirty hours more of such driving brought us at last within five miles of our destination. As we approach Denver the country continually improves in appearance, but retains the same general features, a regular succession of rolling hills, though we have been rising into a higher altitude at every stage. It is now drawing near the close of day, and we commence the ascent of a long hill. The cool, balmy air, the magnificent mountains, with their array of peaks covered with snow, made doubly glorious by the setting sun ; the sight of the rich and extensive champaigns, covered with tall grass, which gaily rustles before the gentle breeze ; the singing of the birds, the mournful note of the wild plover, the amatory croaking of frogs, and the everlasting whirr of the grasshopper,—all these are soothing to the nerves. But see! our driver is divesting himself of his overcoat, and by this dumb show gives notice that he intends to drive us to Denver in traditional style.

The summit of the hill is gained, and our eager eyes sweep over the view from the soaring peaks of the grand old " Rockies," which impress us as being impassable to further travel, down to their very base, where we see a gleaming stretch of river, and the scattered beginnings of a city lying widely spread. From the confused masses of red and white houses, the smoke of their fires lazily curls upward to form a thin, hazy cloud which lingers about the highest spires, whose gilded vanes glitter in the mellow light of the sun.

This city is Denver, the queen of the plains. In appearance it is puritanical enough, with its trim and neat villas and cottages, and embryonic suburbs. It is situate on the western confines of the great plains. But onward, downward we go, thundering along the smooth road, down the gently sloping hill, our swiftly-revolving wheels grinding through the gravel and hissing through the sand, leaving behind us for many rods a long, trailing cloud of glittering dust. The outskirts of Denver are soon reached, the pattering of the horses' feet becomes more and more animated ; the rumbling coach follows, and after winding through two or three wide streets lined with elegant stores with gilded and ornate signs, we halt at a large commodious hotel, the " Pacific House "—and our journey over the prairie is at an end.

There is a well-known saying, that " tall oaks from little acorns grow." Never was this saying more fully exemplified than in the extraordinary rise and progress of Denver, the emporium of the gold mines.

A few years ago a party of hunters found shining particles of gold near the base of one of the loftiest peaks of the Rocky Mountains. The story got wind, and men came streaming in multitudes from the

eastern States to secure a share of the fabulous
quantities of gold reported to have been discovered.
New discoveries were made in placers and in lodes.
Gold was found in every creek and stream. People
became delirious at the glowing accounts of the
nuggets found in the new El Dorado. Men of all
classes flocked thither, ruined merchants, young
clerks, mechanics, miners, and labourers, and in the
van and rear of these were the gamblers, thieves,
ruffians, murderers, and the scum of society, in such
numbers as to shortly turn the mines and the new
settlements into hells. No man's life was safe ; and
Denver became notorious for the frequency of its
murders. Still men continued to come to the gold
mines of Colorado, bringing with them, paradoxical
as it may seem, religion and sin. Many had left
their farms, and embarking with their all on board
the faithful " prairie schooner," had commenced their
weary journey towards the setting sun. To the right
and left of Denver they scattered, and built houses
and cultivated the ground. They brought their
garden and field produce to the western Babylon,
and received so much gold dust in exchange, that
in time they became rich.

Gradually the gold excitement wore off.

A different class of people came, the capitalist
and the honest miner. These two classes effected
a thorough transformation in the country. The
capitalist constructed stamp mills, and the miners
dug out the precious quartz. The farmers settled in

perfect security in the valley of Cherry Creek, on the fertile plateaus at the base of the mountains, and in the cañons. Merchants built large, commodious stores of brick. Each passing day witnessed the progressive growth of trade, and Denver became a city.

Then order-loving people organised themselves into a vigilance committee—the most powerful antidote for rapine and violence. During the first days of this American institution trees were frequently found close by the city, with men hanging stark and stiff, ticketed "murderer," "robber." The persevering regularity of the system, and the mysteriously-swift even-handed justice which invariably followed crime, sent a cold terror to the hearts of outlaws. The hempen rope proved to be a necessary auxiliary to justice.

Peace and law now reign in Denver. Under the protection of the law the city has continued to grow with such rapidity that it has no parallel in this age of improvement. The efflux of population from the east was so continuous and increasing for a period that city lots commanded immense prices which checked the prudent capitalist, though it did not eliminate the progressive element with which the city was imbued. To-day, broad streets flanked by stately buildings of stone, brick, and wood meet the traveller in every part of the city. An incredible amount of business is done in some of the wholesale stores, the proprietors counting their sales by hundreds of thousands. When you consider that underneath this progressive agency lay a thick *substratum* of evil, exceedingly detrimental to the west, one may well wonder at the extraordinary outcome of all this. The people have created out of an uninhabited, sterile wilderness of prairie and mountain no less than thirty cities, with an average population of about three thousand inhabitants.

That which has most retarded western advancement has been the suicidal policy of Government towards the Indians. Let any man with a *modicum* of common sense travel through the country, and he will soon perceive how much cause Colorado people have to curse the imbecility of Government. If not satisfied then, let him go east, and ask the farmer, who halts between a wish to emigrate and a terror of the journey, why he does not go to Colorado, and he will be answered in the bizarre style of the pioneer farmer, "Oh! them ere blarsted Indians are playing h—l again on the plains. I wish they were all swept into ———." You have an answer which, though over-forcible, fully explains his hesitancy, and the restlessness which chafes him, as well as it betrays his eagerness to depart.

Yet in spite of this drawback, I have been told by a gentleman that three hundred and twenty buildings, exclusive of outhouses, have been built this last year ending 31st July. Among this number were churches, banking houses, hotels, mammoth brick stores, besides many elegant private villas, which form a pleasing and refined background to the whirl of business in Denver proper.   The rising ground surrounding the city swarms with villas and neat stables, in which are housed blooded horses, able to trot a mile in 2 minutes 35 seconds any time.

The location of Denver for a commercial centre of these parts cannot be surpassed.   The neighbourhood offers superior advantages to ranche men, and the rich valley of the Platte and Cherry Creek at the base of the mountains, are fairly studded with dairy farms. It is a natural outlet to the rich minerals of the territory, for the cañon in which Golden, Black Hawk, and Central Cities are situated, opens out into the plains in view of Denver, and as a depôt for supplies for the miners and other pioneers of the mountain land, nothing could be better than this terminus of the grassy sea.   It is a pity that neither of the Union Pacific railroads runs direct to this point.   The trade of an immense and rich territory would have been permanently secured could the wise capitalists have foreseen the result.   As it is, Denver is left in the cold, but a branch railroad must eventually be built from one or both the great lines.   A vast trade like that of auriferous Colorado cannot go long a-begging for a market, and the company which first guides the iron horse Denver-ward will reap a deserved profit.

The hotels are very numerous, and their appointments are equal to those of any second-class hotel in the Eastern States, and the charges for board are most reasonable.   The best are the Tremont, Pacific, and Planter's.   The first is mostly frequented by families.

In the Rocky Mountain newspapers we gain many valuable hints as to the temper of the editors, and other eccentricities which mark these dwellers of the mountains.   The editors appear to be strange fellows, and to delight in shooting at each other salvoes of satire, and to rake one another fore and aft with their hard-hitting personalities.   The people are divided, like the rest of American humanity, into two distinct classes, Republican and Democrat, the former being largely in the majority.   Among the most enterprising of Colorado newspapers is the *Denver News* (Republican), characterised by boldness of speech and extreme partisanship ; the *Denver Gazette*, a spicy little sheet, and as fiercely Democratic as the other is the reverse.   The *Golden City Transcript*, an ably-written journal, dealing largely in geology, mines and ores.   The *Central City Register*, of the orthodox "Out-west" type, full of queer mountainisms, radical in politics, and for the development of Colorado, and the *Colorado Times* (formerly the *Black Hawk Mining Journal*, edited by O. J. Hollister, author of the "Mines of Colorado").

I rather admire these plain-speaking journalists, because they are very useful in throwing a blazing light on public matters.   I considered it a duty to call upon each editor in succession, having been told by some of my class that they were most amiable people, but Hepworth Dixon's libel upon Denver and its people positively frightened me, and forbade my entering within the sancta of the formidable editors ; and then again, the short time I had before me prevented my visit. I had heard that the editors were savage fellows, ever ready with the pistol and bowie-knife to fight anybody who differed with them ; but such stories are pure slanders I think, and the next time I visit Colorado territory I shall try to see more of them.

From Denver to Golden City—Through the Golden Gate—The Mountain Scenery—Mythic Gold Lodes—Quartz Mills—The Gold Mines—Black Hawk—The Mountain Mines—Loafers—Wages, etc.—Smelting Works—Iron Pyrites—Processes—On the Mountains.

DENVER, *August 23rd.*

EARLY next morning the passengers bound for the mountains took their seats in a comfortable coach, to which were harnessed six splendid horses. "Get up!" shouted the driver, with a scientific play of his whip, and away we went, whirling towards the mountains which loomed up like an immense barrier in front of us. Though they appeared near, a good hour's drive lay between us and them.

Meanwhile, as we rode, the passengers enlivened the hour by pointing out the various localities renowned in the brief history of Denver, and by giving graphic descriptions of the incidents which rendered such places notorious. "See here !" cried one, "there is

I.   N a tree on which fifteen men have been hung ; just beyond is the tree on which D. M. and C. I. were strung up for murdering poor L——n ; here is a hollow where the d—dest fight took place you ever saw between, etc. ; and there, just round that bluff, some lucky chaps picked up a nugget weighing fifty-six ounces."

Conversation was maintained in this style until we arrived at Golden City, which is situated at the very base of the mountains. The foreground presented an impressive variety of bluffs, massive boulders, crags, and bold plateaus.

Crossing Clear Creek, we enter the most wonderful portion of America, the great mountains, by the " Golden Gate," their natural portal. The scenery is inexpressibly wild and majestic. On each side of the cañon rise dizzy heights, the slopes of which are covered by shrubs and plants, luxuriant creepers, where grape vines, wild raspberry and strawberry grow in profusion. Almost under the horses' feet is Clear Creek, foaming and shooting up into little billows as it rushes down towards the Platte —its eternity. Crystal-like springs issue from the earth in all directions, which form little arrowy rivulets, and empty into Clear Creek. Ahead is the long winding road, up which the six horses go panting and struggling with the lumbering coach. Above our heads is a narrow line of ethereal blue, and behind, looking down, we see the apparently interminable plains and Denver City like a patch on them.

The voice of the driver echoes in the cañon, the rumbling of the coach resembles crashing artillery, and the pattering of the horses' feet on the rock may be likened to continued volleys of musketry.

We have entered the heart of the mountains and are enclosed on all sides by threatening crags and lofty hills crowned by dark pineries, above which soar the ravens, their romantic " caw ca-aw " sounding shrill and clear in the rocky solitude around. Feathered songsters hop from bush to bush, and delight our ears with their cheering notes ; strange insects go buzzing and humming gaily in the air. Beautifully minute, humble flowers of unknown name bloom sweetly and refreshingly under the shade of the birch, along the margin of the creek. Here we come to a large moss-covered boulder, which appears to invite the " weary toiler up the rugged steep " to a seat, while a sparkling streamlet issuing from underneath forms a slight cascade as it falls over a bed of quartz of snowy whiteness. We permit our delighted eyes to wander over a nature fresh in its vernal bloom, and to admire its richness, to which the streaming sunshine gives a varying and animated complexion. We are led to think

> " Of April buds and showers,
> Of charming songs in July bowers,"

as we go tugging up the hill. After a short walk we step again into the stage ; and as we rattle down a hill with lightning speed, some new beauty, some new phase, some more surprising charm is constantly

N 2

developed to the eye. At the foot of another hill we see a stage station, where we are to stop for the noon dinner.

The station is quite a romantic place, situated in a kind of hermit's glen, or poet's retreat, which equals in its wild solitude and loveliness any Alpine valley ever seen. A circling range of stupendous mountains shelters it from rude windy blasts, and imparts to it an aspect of deep seclusion and repose. The humble station possesses every requisite for our animal wants, from the maccaroni soup to an exquisite dessert. My fellow-travellers are satisfied, and join with me in thinking that the world is not so bad as it is represented by slanderers.

From the wooden floor of the piazza we enjoyed for a brief space the scenic beauties around ; but as the hostlers have put fresh horses to the coach, we must haste to resume the journey to Black Hawk and Central Cities. Only a fifteen-mile drive ! We shall be in Black Hawk by 5 P.M.

We have seen no gold mines yet, neither have we seen the miners who delve for " gold, glittering gold ! " We are off at full speed, curving round and round the hill. The road is level, and Clear Creek, which admirably deserves its title, chants musically as it goes hurrying by. All around us are lofty mountains and forest solitude. I have seen grand Tauran scenery, Alpine and Pyrenean mountains, about which much has been said, but they are puny in comparison with the grandeur of the Rocky Moun-

tains. Nothing can be so idyllic as the lesser hills
of Colorado, as they stand hemmed in by the weather-
beaten peaks which loom up above them in silent
majesty.   In these America is unrivalled.   While
many of the eastern States lie to-day humbled and
crushed by internal dissensions, these *great* mountains are witnessing a new creation which must act
its part in the great drama of the Republic.

But while I have been meditating upon the unexpected grandeur of Coloradian scenery, we have
been nearing Black Hawk.   Neat cottages appear in
view against the side of steep hills.   Tow-headed
youngsters troop out of a small ravine to catch a
sight of the stage, and to cheer it.   Here are great
buildings with black smoke stacks, empty and silent
—melancholy evidences of a rash speculative fever,
and warning monitors to future reckless capitalists.
Instead of endeavouring to aid good miners with
their capital in gold-producing mines, these moneyed
men purchased claims, called "gold lodes" by rascally
prospectors.   The gold lodes and valuable claims (?)
turned out to be myths *only* when the capitalist had
spent thousands in developing his claims—*i.e.*, by
employing a lazy, incompetent superintendent, who
wasted the capital in building a mammoth mill with
all its appurtenances.   Before the mill was completed
the capital had been expended, and the great boiler,
which had been sent from New York, or St. Louis,
or Chicago across the plains and half-way up the
mountains, was left perhaps within ten miles of its

intended destination. About half-a-dozen monstrous iron boilers lie scattered along the mountain road.

But here is a mill, the "New York Mill." One or two spasmodic blows resound inside, and ahead of us is a long stone building; this also is silent. I am told it is "General Fitzjohn Porter's." On the left, on the very highest mountain top, two thousand feet above the road, stands another mill, the property of Commodore French, formerly commander of the famous supply steamer *Star of the West.* But see! on our right, covering Harry's Point, where two roads converge, is a collection of buildings, covering many acres of ground. A dozen bell-mouthed smoke stacks, a tall chimney eighty feet high, and a flume running its serpentine length (225 feet) up a hill, vomit black, sulphurous smoke. The busy clang of iron and voices of command are heard from within. Big piles of galena and crushed pyrites, shining pigs of lead in rows, pyramidal heaps of washed ore, and near each a gang of men, are seen. Capital, intellect, energy, and muscle have been invested here worthily and with profit. These works belong to the "Consolidated Gregory Company," formerly to James E. Lyon, one of the pioneer miners of Colorado. We pass the toll gate, and we are in Black Hawk! But, hark! What thundering sound is that? That is the exhilarating thunder of one hundred heavy stamps as they crush the quartz with their ponderous blows. They awaken the echoes of the mountains by their deep-toned sound. The annihilators are at work day and night ; and their resonance makes the blood course faster.

We gallop through the one street of this mountain burg. The street is full of miners hurrying home from their day's work. We reach Central City, which appears to be the uppermost end of Black Hawk, though the largest portion. Clear Creek is a natural gutter for these two cities, and sweeps down to the great valley the refuse of the towns. Here is Main Street, and we halt at the O'Connor House. Awaiting our arrival is a mixed crowd of stalwart men, with huge bushy whiskers, sharp grey eyes, soiled features, lead-coloured hats, smutty blouses, and muddy boots. These people are the miners of Colorado.

*　　*　　*　　*　　*　　*

Pent within these mountains' comparatively narrow pale are men of remarkable acuteness and restless activity, pursuing their various avocations as miners, merchants, or manufacturers. Whatever may be said of them, they have not been laggard ; they have persevered in spite of prospects which have been often gloomy. The cañon, mountain slope, and sum-mit teem with evidences of their toil. The granite heart of the mountain has been pierced, and the glittering ore which men so highly value has been torn up by them. Two cities have been built in the heart of the mountains, which now contain 11,000 inhabitants. Churches, colleges, schools, theatres, and lecture halls have been raised to meet their wants. In the gulch which contains them a traveller observes

INDUSTRY in its most literal sense. By their know-ingness, their patience under difficulties, and their quick facility in applying means to ends, the in-habitants are building up a State which one day will rank with the greatest.   These hardy people are generators of future power and influence. There is not a community of men that has a more living and growing interest in whatever gives dignity and grace to humanity. They partake of the intellectual activity and moral integrity of New England as much as they do of the enterprising character of New York, and the characteristic hospitality of the south.   The edu-cation of their children is carefully attended to, a large school fund being reserved.   Neither is religion forgotten, for churches grace every hill.

Every   class   and   profession   is   represented   in Colorado.   The   lawyers   are   too   many   for   such   a narrow   compass.   They   are   an   uneasy,   restless   set of   men,   who   are   continually   exciting   the   people. Nightly   they   hold   forth   about   some   political   ques-tion,   as   if   that   bowl   in   which   Central   City   lies   com-posed   the   world.   Dickens   or   a   Thackeray   could   find new   characters   in   Colorado   lawyers.   Their   sign-boards,   bearing   the   title   of   "Attorney   and   counsellor-at-law,"   swaying   to   and   fro,   meet   you   at   every   step. Another   class   is   too   largely   represented,   composed   of the   effeminate   clerks.   Every   vacancy   is   filled,   and they   know   it   well,   yet   they   persist   in   standing   idle all   the   day,   loafing   at   the   street   corners,   impressing the   superficial   traveller   that   times   are   dull   in   Colorado.

Times are not dull in Colorado, or in any part of the west, to those who are ready to engage in manual labour.

Wages are good ; board is cheap ; work is abundant. For the benefit of the intending emigrant to Colorado, I append some information concerning the wages paid :—

Labourers	. . .	$3.50 per day.
Miners .	. . .	$4.50 to $5 per day.
Carpenters	. . .	$5 per day.
Millwrights	. . .	$6 ,,
Blacksmiths	. . .	$6 ,,
Stonemasons .	. .	$7 ,,
Bricklayers	. . .	$7 ,,
Plasterers	. . .	$7 ,,
Teamsters	. . .	$2 ,, and board.
Farm hands	. . .	$60 per month and board.
Machinists	. . .	$7 per day.
Engineers	. . .	$5 ,,

Clerks, lawyers, clergymen, and schoolmasters command from $2000 to $2500 per annum.

Good board can be had for $8 per week, and a party of miners "batching" together contrive to live on good, substantial food for $5 per week.

There is a tremendous bustle of work, attended by practical results, going on daily. I have been astonished at viewing the valuable lumps of gold and silver at Lyons' smelting works, of which Professor Frederick C. Johnson is the able superintendent. Dr. Charles Johnson's smelting works at Georgetown have turned out immense bricks of pure silver and bars of gold. New lodes and new placers containing

native gold are frequently found. Miners who work
their own placer claims very often make from $50 to
$150 each per day. Any man, taking a common
sheet-iron pan and pick, can make excellent wages
in gold. It only needs determination, industry, and
a little practice, to be able to make any day from
$8 to $10.

But there are three classes which curse Colorado—
viz., lawyers, dandies, and men who have claims, and
who refuse to work them, but stand open-mouthed,
their hands in their pockets, waiting for some silly
speculator who will pay $50,000 for some undeveloped
claim. Many of the latter class count their worldly
wealth by the number of their claims, each claim
commanding a certain stated nominal price. This is
"counting chickens before they are hatched" with a
vengeance. Ask any one in the street what his
claim is worth, and he will answer with imperturb-
able coolness, "$25,000." I have tried it simply
as an experiment, as I was told it would prove so
by a man who seemed perfectly acquainted with
Colorado.

This country strikes a person at a first glance as
being immensely rich in the precious metals. But
"All that glitters is not gold" I found a very true
proverb. In my prospecting tour over the mountains,
I saw quantities of yellow metal which I believed to
be gold. I filled my pockets with the precious stuff,
as there was so much of it. I filled a satchel with it,
and had a very good mind to fill my hat also. I

carried my treasure to the hotel, and up to my room, and, choosing a small piece, I took it down, and carelessly asked a rough-looking fellow what he thought of it. Imagine my surprise and disappointment when he pronounced it a "pretty nice specimen of pyrites of iron." All my castles in the air had vanished ; the great good I was about to do mankind had to be postponed ; and my fine house, with all its magnificent appurtenances, I was obliged to defer to some other day. " Iron pyrites," as defined in the New American Cyclopædia, "is a very common mineral of golden appearance, and is frequently mistaken by those unacquainted with minerals for the precious metal." In spite of my great disappointment, I retain a belief that Colorado is as rich in gold as any territory in the United States, though capitalists are just now shy of Colorado mining stock, and prefer to invest their money in other speculations.

The list of processes for extraction of gold from the quartz is very long. Here is the " Keith process," the best in the world ; the " Sensenderfer process," also the best ; the " Wolff process," the very best ; the " Lightning process," the most wonderful ; and scores of others, which always proved a success, though they all left in their " tailings " quite as much as they took out.

The smelting process was introduced in Colorado by Professor Johnson, who was a thoroughly practical man, having visited many of the best smelting works in the world, and had been superintendent for fifteen

years over the well-known works of Staten Island.
Under his direction, and backed by James E. Lyon,
the Milwaukee Mill, on Harry's Point, was refitted,
and the immense buildings previously referred to
were erected. This smelting process was found to
be a success for extracting the precious metal from
Colorado ores. Had there been a railroad to the
mountains it would still be a success ; but the heavy
cost of fuel and transportation, and high wages, have
caused them to labour under a great disadvantage.
Although profits were made, still they were not so
great as to satisfy bondholders, and the great smelting
works have been forced to jog along as they can until
Denver is connected by rail with the East. But if a
stranger is desirous of satisfying himself concerning
the richness of Colorado minerals, let him make a visit
to the Black Hawk smelting works.

After visiting the artificial wonders of Colorado—
the deep mines, the ponderous quartz crushers, the
capacious smelting furnaces ; and examining the specimens of coal, iron, copper, tin, zinc, lead, silver, and
gold ; the various specimens of beautiful stones found
in Clear Creek, such as crystals, moss agates, and
chalcedonies ; viewing with wonder the different kinds
of fossils such as insect, fish teeth, bones, and fish
spines, wood, and vitrified water—I determined to
devote an afternoon to a ramble over the mountains.
I travelled a road gently ascending towards Nevada
and Idaho Cities ; I then walked a mile east of
Missouri City, along the highest ridge, but continually

ascending until I stood on the topmost point. I had
been four hours walking, seeing nothing very remarkable ; but the view now stretched before me amply
compensated me for any trouble I had taken.
Looking westward, I saw the sun gradually descend
beyond the seemingly illimitable heights, each rough
peak and mountain top clearly defined, while long
dark shadows covered the eastern slopes. Away to
the northward rose peak upon peak till lost in an
infinity of snowy whiteness, the whole view rendered
beautifully distinct and brilliant by the sun. Above
all towered Long's Peak, fully one hundred miles
distant direct north, yet each ravine, fissure, and crag
seen distinctly. To the southward lay Pike's Peak,
surrounded by myriads of peaks of lesser height, and
covered with eternal snow. I was standing almost
equi-distant between the two highest mountains, while
an area of five hundred square miles was spread out
A portion of Montana was, I believe, visible ; I caught
a glimpse of future Wyoming ; and my eyes rested
upon a corner of New Mexico. Westward, behind
the convulsed mass of peaks, rose black clouds in
fantastical shapes, in whose depths brooded a hurricane. One frowning cloud resembled somewhat a
mighty Pegasus, with a dragon for its rider, which
exposed its long fangs as if in fierce mockery of some
unseen enemy. But what terrific upheaving of
America must there have been when rock was heaved
upon rock, and mountain reared upon mountain, when
the inland sea rushed affrighted from its immense

bed carrying with it the waters that laved the mountain's base !

Standing upon the mountain top in the red evening sunlight, which sheds a golden lustre upon earth and sky, I predict, that this country will be acknowledged in the coming future as no mean State. Time is flying, the iron horse is upon the plain, impatient to rush through the heart of the mountain towards the Pacific. Two years hence the dwellers upon the Atlantic slopes will unite hands with their brothers of the Pacific shores, and then—and then will the desert rejoice, and the wilderness be made glad.*

Notorious Julesburg—Omaha—Off by Special Train to the end of the Track—The Treacherous Platte—A German Author's costly luxury—General Casement and his Masterly Railway Construction—16½ Miles of New Track in a day.

JULESBURG, *September 17th,* 1867.

FROM Omaha I passed over the great continental highway, the Union Pacific railroad, one of the most wonderful enterprises of this most prolific nineteenth century, out to the " end of the track," marked by the four hundred and sixtieth milestone west of the

* Twenty-one months after this letter was written, that is in May, 1869, the Great Trans-Continental Railway was completed by the junction of the Union Pacific from the East, with the Central Pacific R. R. from the West.

Missouri River to Denver, then back again to this place where my letter is dated. Julesburg is now an overdone town, a played-out place. It was built in a single month. I forgot to tell you that it was named after an old French trader and freighter named Jule, who was murdered by his partner in business. It is now about to be abandoned by the transient sojourners, and many of them are shifting their portable shanties to some prospective city west —Cheyenne, or some "prairie-dog town," where cash can be made without work, and by any means that will not subject the operator to an indictment before a Grand Jury for obtaining money under false pretences.

While at Omaha information was obtained that the Indian Council at Laramie would not come off at the time appointed, but that some of the Cheyennes and Ogallallas on the Republican would come in and meet us at North Platte on the 21st instant. Therefore it became a question whether to go on, or to remain at Omaha until the council would meet. A majority of the Commissioners, with most of the correspondents, decided to remain. Those who had swallowed enough of Omaha dust to satisfy their appetite for this kind of luxury decided to push on ; for be it known that Omaha, notwithstanding its beautiful location, its enterprise, its George Francis Train, and its desire to become connected with St Louis by rail at the earliest possible period, yet truth compels me to say, and John Finn will back the

assertion, that no town on the Missouri River is more
annoyed, even afflicted, by moving clouds of dust
and sand—when the wind is up—than Omaha. It
is absolutely terrific. The lower terrace along the
river is a waste of fine sand, which is blown about
in drifts, and banked up against the houses, like
snow in a wintry storm. For two or three days
people have been obliged to shut themselves up in
their houses for protection from the sand. But
Omaha is a wide-awake, energetic town, and is
beautifully located, on the second high terrace from
the river, with a cordon of hills which are mantled
with country residences, among which the State
capitol, with its small cupola, is the most conspicuous
building.

On Saturday, Generals Sherman and Terry, and
Senator Henderson, with your correspondent, took a
special train for the "end of the track," a point which
constantly changes. Fred Gerstaecker, of the *Cologne
Gazette*, the celebrated author of a four years' tour
around the globe and "Sketches of Things that I
have Seen," also accompanied us. The German
traveller proved to be a most original character in
his way. He crossed the "frozen Missouri" afoot
from Bloody Island to St. Louis on Christmas Eve,
1837, took a daguerreotype of that frontier post, went
on board of a Mississippi steamboat as fireman,
hunted bears four years in Arkansas, bought a plantation in South America, and married his second wife
in India. He turned out to be a most genial com-

panion. Our party were placed in charge of Major Bent, a gentleman of rare qualities for the position assigned to him.

We travelled around the southern side of Omaha, and made our exit out of Train Town, a suburb which is filled with numerous cottages, erected by the "Credit Foncier" of America, of which George Francis Train is the President. At dusk we entered upon the unbounded prairies, passing Elkhorn, Fremont, North Bend, Shell Creek, Columbus, another mushroom town, created under the auspices of the "Credit Foncier" of America ; next we swept by Silver Creek, Lone Tree, Grand Island, shot across Wood River, passed Kearney, Elm Creek, and Plum Creek, where Turkey Foot threw the train off the track, the wreck of which is still to be seen, and then on by Willow Island, Bradley Island, and tenderly across the North Fork of the Platte, over a low bridge thirteen hundred feet long, which rests on cedar piles, and then we stopped at North Platte, where we halted for dinner. These places were mainly mere railway buildings erected by the company, with a few adobe dwellings for the accommodation of railroad *employés* and traders. After dinner the party again embarked on the special car.

On our left was truly a beautiful stream, notwithstanding the bad repute given to it by emigrants. Its shifting shoals and treacherous quicksands may render fording in many places dangerous and impracticable, but they do not detract from the view.

I.   O

The surface of the river appeared nearly on a level with the meadow lands, and glistened like a tin roof in the noonday sun.   The stream is choked with myriads of small islets, tufted with wild grass and tall weeds, that lie basking in the sunshine like huge bouquets tossed by some wandering Peri into the stream.   Over one hundred of these little islets were counted within a short distance.

Beyond the little railroad stations of O'Fallon, Alkali, Ogallalla, and Big Springs, which we next passed, the herbage on the prairies is of a dusty yellow colour, while the bluffs appear to be still more sterile.   We saw numerous herds of antelopes galloping away as the train sped along.   The elevation of the country has attained an altitude of over 1,800 feet above Omaha, on the Missouri, and about 4,000 feet above the ocean.   No rain has fallen here of any consequence since the 3rd of June last, consequently the agriculturalist is inclined to despair about his crops.   Taking a hasty dinner at Julesburg, we again took the car and rolled past Sidney, Antelope, and one or two other places, and reached the end of the track about dusk.   The German traveller made his bed under a pile of railroad ties.   This was a costly luxury, as these ties were brought from near Fort Sully on the Missouri River, and cost about $1.25 each.   The next morning General Sherman and the military gentlemen breakfasted at General Augur's camp, while the German traveller was left behind to feed on sugared suppositions.

As for your correspondent, he had a most excellent breakfast on the boarding car of General Casement, who, with his two brothers, has the contract for laying down the rails. Before he undertook the work it had progressed very slowly on the old system, but, bringing to bear on it all his energy and ability for organisation, and the discipline of military life, he quickly revolutionised affairs. By running his boarding cars to the end of the track he is able to keep his 250 men close to their work. Behind them are cars laden with a certain number of rails, all of the same length, with the exact number of chairs and spikes to secure them.

The boarding cars having been pushed as far as possible toward the end of the track, the material is thrown off behind them ; then the boarding cars are shoved back, and the smaller cars loaded with the rails are brought up. The small loaded car is drawn forward to the end of the track by horse power. A couple of feet from the end of the rails checks are placed under the wheels. Before it has stopped, four men on each side grasp a rail, run it beyond the cars, lay it down in its chairs, gauge it, and, ere its clang has ceased to reverberate, the car is run over it, and another pair of rails laid down. This process is continued as rapidly as a man can walk. Behind the car follow two boys on each side, who drop the spikes, others set the ties well under the ends of the rails, then come thirty or forty men driving in the spikes and stamping the earth under the ties. All this work

O 2

is executed with great rapidity and with mechanical regularity, and Captain D. B. Clayton, superintendent of laying the track, showed your reporter a specimen of what could be done.   He gave his men the hint, and in the space of exactly five minutes, as timed by the watch, they laid down the rails and spiked them, for the distance of seven hundred feet.   The rails are twenty-eight feet in length.   There were fifty rails laid down, of course one on each side of the track. At that rate sixteen miles and a half of track could be laid down in one day.

We were then invited into Captain Clayton's car, and introduced to Major North, who commands the Pawnees, who invited us to accompany him to his camp, where he would show us a lot of Cheyenne scalps obtained by his men.   But presently the Major-General's carriage came thundering back from Augur's camp, in a cloud of sand, and it was seen at once that the special car would start, without regard to absent reporters or any other characters.

The Commissioners at the Council Ground—Arrival of the
Indians—White Captives restored to liberty—Night Scenes
and Incidents—A German Bohemian and a Veteran—The
Grand Council—" Swift Bear's " Oration—Commissioner
Taylor's Address—Sharp Speeches of " Spotted Tail,"
" Man-afraid-of-his-Horses," " Pawnee Killer," " Turkey
Foot," and " Big Mouth."

NORTH PLATTE, NEBRASKA, *September 18th,* 1867.

THE Commissioners intend to hold a grand pow-wow
to-morrow with the Brule and Ogallalla Sioux and
Cheyennes.

In the latter part of the month of July your readers
may remember the account sent you of the capture of
three women and two boys from a settlement near
Fort Kearney. Through the runners sent to the
camps of the hostile Cheyennes, by Mr. Patrick, the
Indian agent, word was conveyed to the captive
females that negotiations were pending for their de-
liverance from captivity. Invitations were also sent
to the chiefs of Cheyennes, Ogallallas, and Brule
Sioux to come to the Grand Council at North Platte,
and bring their captives with them to exchange for a
squaw and a male child who were taken in the late
affair at Plum Creek. Spotted Tail, the chief of the
Brules, used his influence to draw the Indians to the
pow-wow. All went on satisfactorily. The Commissioners in due time arrived at Omaha ; they
started west, arrived at North Platte. The Indians

had not come.   The Commissioners, having an eye
to pleasure as well as business, took the train for the
end of the track, where they had an opportunity of
admiring the method of railroad construction on the
Union Pacific, and then returned back to North
Platte, where we are at present.

The Indians and their white captives arrived here
last night.   There were two hundred warriors, fresh
from bloody exploits, and with their hands dyed with
the blood of the unfortunates at Plum Creek.

Foremost among the whites, who stood between
the village and the advancing Indians, were Sherman,
the hero of many battles, Alfred H. Terry, of Fort
Fisher fame, and Senator Henderson, ready to greet
the red men, and to give them welcome by a shake of
the hand.   In the rear of these were ladies and
gentlemen, members of the press, and others, who
crowded up, and gazed curiously at the meeting.
The Indians, on being greeted so kindly by the long-
suffering pale-face, soon became more jovial, and
laughed with a reckless glee as they threw themselves
on the ground.

Among our party was Mr. Fred. Gerstaecker, the
German author and traveller, who entertained us with
comparisons between the tribes dwelling on the South
American Pampas with the Indians of North America,
and gave us several interesting reminiscences of his
life among the Ashantees in Africa.

Another notable was Colonel W. H. Wolcott, of
the 17th U.S. Infantry, a one-legged hero, and a

Radical. Said he, "Boil Horace Greeley, Wendell Phillips, W. Lloyd Garrison, and all the leading Radicals together in a pot, and I am a stronger Radical to-day, and have been, than the essence of those three would produce." He served at Bull Run and scores of other battles ; he has suffered three separate amputations, and has risen simply by merit from a sergeant to a colonel in the regular army. He has lately been dispatched on the plains for active service, though the possessor of but one leg. He exhibited his artificial leg to the chiefs, and the wonder manifested was very great. Spotted Tail and Big Mouth, with becoming reverence for this extraordinary soldier, inserted a finger within the hollow of the leg, and for all future time they are likely to declare to the rising generation that they have seen the veritable " Big Medicine Man."

Thursday—the day that was to witness the Grand Council held between the Red warriors of the Ogallallas, Brules, Cheyennes, and pale-faces, dawned gloomily enough, and a drizzling rain set in. But the Indians were impatient, and, rain or no rain, the council must be convened.

The Indians had been dissipating the night previous. Some reckless white had supplied them with whisky, which had plunged many of them into forgetfulness of the scenes about to be enacted. Two hundred dollars reward was offered for the name of the man who had supplied the liquor. No informer could be found, but martial law was established over the denizens of this town, and each saloon and bar had a guard placed over it, and neither white, red, nor black man could get liquor of any kind. Sherman is a man who can act promptly on occasion.

At noon the council was convened. Two large wigwams converted into one were to hold the hostile chiefs of the Brules, Ogallallas, and Cheyennes, and the Peace Commissioners.

On one side sat Spotted Tail, Man-afraid-of-his-Horses, Man-that-walks-under-the-Ground, Pawnee Killer, Standing Elk, Swift Bear, Black Bear, Turkey Foot, Cut Nose, Whistler, Big Mouth, Cold Face, Crazy Lodge, and several other minor chiefs. Facing them were Generals Sherman, Harney, Terry, and Sanborn, Commissioner Taylor, Colonels Tappan, Dodge, and Wolcott, Senator Henderson, and several representatives of the press.

The chiefs formed separate circles, and smoked the tribal "pipes of peace." Big Mouth and another chief handed their pipes around to the Peace Commissioners, who inhaled with befitting gravity three distinct whiffs from each. This important ceremony over, Leon Fallardy, interpreter, announced that the chiefs were ready.

Then Swift Bear commenced his oration as follows :—

"My friends and all you chiefs that are here to-day, whatever you say shall be made known all over the country. It makes my heart glad to see you here to-day. We have a mode of making peace different from the whites. When we make peace we pray to the Great Spirit. We have no witness, but keep our treaties faithfully, by praying to the Great Spirit."

Then the Chief Indian Commissioner, N. G. Taylor, through the aid of the interpreter, delivered the following :—

"My friends, your Great Grandfather, whose heart is right, has heard of the troubles of his red children on the plains, and he has sent us to you to see what is the matter. [Cries of "Ugh! ugh!"] He has heard that there is war, and that blood has been shed. He is opposed to war, and loves peace, and his heart is sad. He has sent all these great white chiefs to ascertain what is wrong.

"You see here the great war chief of old times" (General Harney). "There is the great warrior" (Sherman) "who leads all the white soldiers on the plains, and here are other great chiefs. Here is a great peace chief" (Senator Henderson), "who helps to make laws in the great council chamber at Washington, and last of all, here is your friend who speaks to you now, the Commissioner of Indian Affairs, and the Superintendent of all Indian Agents and Traders. [Loud cries of "Ugh! Helo!"]

"If the Great Father did not love you, he would not have sent us to you. We are sent out here to inquire and find out what has been the trouble. We want to hear from your own lips your grievances and complaints.

"My friends, speak fully, speak freely, and speak

the whole truth. If you have been wronged, we wish to have you righted, and if you have done wrong you will make it right. All that you say we will have written in a book, and will not forget it. We will think it all over, and will then speak our minds to you. War is bad, peace is good. We must choose the good and not the bad. Therefore we are to bury the tomahawk, and live in peace like brothers of one family. [Cries of "Ugh! Ha-ow!"] I await what you have to say."

Then one of the Indian chiefs rose and said: "You chiefs that are here to-day, and all you soldiers, listen unto me, for there is no fun in what I have to say to you. My Great Father did not send you here for nothing, therefore we will listen unto you. The Great Father has made roads stretching east and west. Those roads are the cause of all our troubles. We have no objection to this road" (U. P. R. R.), "but we object to those on the Powder River and the Smoky Hill. The country where we live is overrun by whites. All our game is gone. This is the cause of great trouble.

"I have been a friend to the whites, and am now One of these roads runs by Powder River, the other up the Smoky Hill. I object to those—we all object to them. Let my Great Father know this; you can read and write; be sure and let him know. The country across the river" (Platte) "belongs to the whites; this belongs to us" (north of the Platte). "When we see game there, we want to have the privilege of going after game. I want these roads stopped just where they are, or turned in some other direction. We will then live peacefully together.

"Last spring I told that man" (General Sanborn) "there was plenty of game in this country yet. The time has not come for us yet to go a-farming. When the game is all gone, I will let him know that we are willing.

"If you stop your roads we can get our game. That Powder River country belongs to us" (Brule Sioux), "the Smoky Hill belongs to the other tribe" (Cheyennes). "When we make peace we will stick together. Give these men something. They have travelled far ; make their hearts glad. Give them something to wear, give them ammunition to kill game ; by doing this you will make all the tribes feel glad. I hope that you will let these men trade with us as before, and that you will let the trader come to our camps as formerly.

"My friends, help us ; take pity on us. If you intend to make us presents, give them to us, and we will thank you. I have spoken."

Another Indian chief then stood up and said: "My friends, you see this coat I have on. It is my best. You have also fine coats on. Last summer you gave me this paper" (producing a permit) ; "all my people know what is written on it. I have listened to what you have said. If you are true I will listen again. By holding this paper in my possession, my children and myself have suffered.

"Ever since I've been born I have eaten wild meat. My father and grandfather ate wild meat before me. *We cannot give up quickly the customs of our fathers.*

"My arms are not long, but I can reach over my head. I am listening to what you have to say for peace.

"These roads, even before you made iron roads, scared all our game away. I want you to stop all these roads just where they are, the Smoky Hill and the Powder River.

"Tell your Great Father that our arms are long and our shoulders are broad, and we can almost reach to where he is.

"All the nations were brought up here, but the white men are numerous, yet if we can all live together in it we will abide by what you say.

"Let our game alone. Don't disturb it, and then you will have life. [Loud cries of "Holo, Ha-ow, How!"]

"You asked me to-day what was the cause of all this trouble. I have told you. Tell the Father this, and then let us know his plan.

"I am small, but I am a married man, and have children. The game of this country is going away, and we lack ammunition. I hope you will give it to us. Look at me; I am small. You have told me the truth, and I have told you the truth. I have said it."

This warrior was succeeded by Pawnee Killer, the leader of the Cheyennes on their Smoky Hill depredations, the antagonist of Hancock and Custer, and the one who measured his strength against A. J. Smith's cavalry.

"Who is our Great Father? What is he? Is it true that he sent you here to settle our troubles? The cause of our troubles is the Powder River road running north, and the Smoky Hill road on the south. In that little space of country between the Smoky Hill and Platte River there is game. That is what we have to live upon. By stopping these roads I know you can get peace. If the Great Father stops the Powder River road, I know that your people can travel this road" (U. P. R. R.) "without being molested. There is not many of us here, but what there is of us we are not guilty of these troubles alone.

"If you tell the truth you ought to be able to furnish us with ammunition. I have seen you. I hope to be able to go back and sleep in peace.

"Take pity upon us and the traders. We want to get our trade back."

Following him came Turkey Foot, the leader of the Plum Creek raiders.

"My friends, you that are here, are you chiefs? Is it true that the Great Father sent you here? Will the white people that travel this road" (U. P. R. R.) "and the Arkansas road listen to what you say? If so, then listen unto me. Tell the Great Father to *stop* these roads—the one on the Smoky Hill, and the Powder River road. All the tribes around this country are our relations. They have intermarried with each other. They are all one flesh. Let the traders come back ; they are our friends. I have spoken."

After this warrior came Big Mouth, a jovial, jolly Indian, who loves good living, and fire-water. Next to Satanta, he is the best Indian orator living. Big Mouth is an appropriate name, for that very useful part of the human body is in him of extraordinary capacity. His remarks were listened to with great attention.

"My friends, and you, my people, open wide your ears and listen. Towards the north there are a great many Ogallallas, south there are Ogallallas, and I with my people stand between. But I am strong and bold. I wish to succeed in establishing peace between my people and the pale-faces. This day, you General Harney tell me, did the Great Father send you here ? Do you tell the truth ? You are a great chief. I am a big chief, also. I hope that the Great Father sent you to us. All you" (to the Indians) "that are sitting here in the council, I want to advise you. Be quiet. Behave yourselves. Leave the whites alone. Who and what are you ? The whites are as numerous as the years. You are few and weak. What do you amount to ? If the whites kill one of your number, you weep and feel sorry. But if you kill one of the whites, who is it that weeps for them ? [Loud laughter, and applause from all hands.] I am saying this for your good. And now, you whites, I speak to you. *Stop* that Powder River road ; that is the cause of our troubles. The great evil grows daily. It is just like setting fire to prairie grass. The evil is spreading among all the nations.

"Red Cloud and the Man-afraid-of-his-Horses had a talk with General Sanborn last spring at Laramie. Did you" (Sanborn) "tell the Great Father what we said? Here are the Sioux on one side and the Cheyennes on the other side. I stand between two fires ; and you, after talking and talking, and making treaties, and after we have listened to you, go and make the great evil larger. You set the prairie on fire. My Great Father told me through men like you that he would give twenty years' annuities for these two roads—the Powder River road and the Smoky Hill road. Where are those annuities? I stand between the pale-faces and the Indians.

"My people have come from afar. Give them presents and make their hearts glad. ["Bastak-telo, Bastak-telo!" Loud and enthusiastic cries of "Ha-How, Ha-How!"] Ah, I forgot something. I have a country up by Bear Creek, where a lone tree stands. It has my name carved on it. That is my country. I am going there as soon as the council is over. I am going to keep it. I have spoken, and if you have anything to say I will listen, and my people here will listen."

The council then adjourned till noon to-morrow. I send you these speeches condensed and stripped of useless repetitions. The reply of the Commission will be forwarded as early as possible.

General Sherman's Speech—Speech of Senator Henderson—
   Reply of the Indian Chiefs, "Swift Bear," "Man-that-
   walks-under-the-Ground," "Pawnee Killer," and "Big
   Mouth"—Commissioners deliberate—Pawnee-Killer departs in Anger—A Decision.

NORTH PLATTE, NEBRASKA, *September* 20*th*, 1867.

THE Grand Council, according to agreement, met
again to-day.   The reply of the Commission was
delivered by General Sherman in his own peculiar
and pointed manner.

"Friends, we have heard your words, and have
thought of them all night, and now give you our
answer.   You say that the Smoky Hill and Powder
River roads are the principal causes of your troubles.
The Government supposed that the Cheyennes and
Arapahoes agreed to give up that road four years ago,
and it has been travelled by the whites ever since.
Military posts and mail stations were built along it
two years ago, and they were not then considered to
be a cause for war.   Government thought that to
build an iron road would be nothing more to you.
To us it was more convenient and rapid, and it was
necessary to our people in Colorado and New Mexico,
and the road will be built.

"We are to meet the Cheyennes next month, in
October, on the Arkansas, and if we find that the road
is damaging to them, we will make them compensation.

But the roads will be built, and you must not interfere with them.

" The Powder River road was built to furnish our men with provisions. No white settlements have been made along the road, nor does travel destroy the buffalo, nor the elk, nor the antelope. The Indians are permitted to hunt the buffalo as usual. The Great Father thought that you consented to give up that road at Laramie last spring ; but it seems that some of the Indians were not there, and have gone to war. While the Indians continue to make war upon the road it will not be given up. But if, on examination at Laramie in November, we find that the road hurts you, we will give it up or pay for it. If you have any claims present them to us at Laramie.

"You also ask of us presents, more especially powder and lead to hunt buffalo. We will give you some presents because you have come up here to see us. But we will not give you much till we come to a satisfactory agreement. We cannot give you now powder and ball, because very recently you killed white people, innocent immigrants ; some of you attacked a train, and killed people who were carrying provisions to whites and Indians. To Spotted Tail, Standing Elk, Two Strike, Swift Bear, and bands, we are willing to give them almost anything they want, because they have remained at peace all the spring and summer. But the rest of you must work with your bows and arrows till you satisfy us

I.   P

you will not kill our people. This answers all that question.

"We now give you advice. We know well that the red and white men were not brought up alike. You depend upon game for a living, and you get hats and clothes from the whites. All that you see white men wear they have to work for. But you see they have plenty to eat, that they have fine houses and fine clothes. You can have the same, and we believe the time has come when you should begin to own these things, and we will give you assistance. You can own herds of cattle and horses like the Cherokees and Choctaws. You can have cornfields like the Poncas, Yanktons, and Pottawatomies. You see for yourself that the white men are collecting in all directions, in spite of all you can do. The white men are taking all the good land. If you don't choose your homes now, it will be too late next year. This railroad up the Platte and the Smoky Hill railroad will be built, and if you are damaged we must pay you in full, and if your young men will interfere, the Great Father, who, out of love for you, withheld his soldiers, will let loose his young men, and you will be swept away. We therefore propose to let the whole Sioux nation select their country up the Missouri River, embracing the White Earth and Cheyenne Rivers, to have their lands, like the white people, for ever, and we propose to keep all white men away except such agents and traders as you may choose. We want you to cultivate your land, build houses, and raise cattle. We propose to help you there as long as you need help. We will also teach your children to read and write like the whites.

" The Cheyennes and all southern Indians shall have similar homes in the country on the Arkansas and if the Sioux Indians prefer to go down there, they can enjoy the same privileges. A great many agreements have been made by people gone before us. We propose to stand by them, but I am afraid they did not make allowances for the rapid growth of the white race, and you can see for yourselves that travel across the country has increased so much that the slow ox waggon will not answer the white man. We build iron roads, and you cannot stop the locomotive any more than you can stop the sun or moon, and you must submit, and do the best you can, and if any of you want to travel east to see the wealth and power of the whites you can do so, and we will pay your expenses. Our people east hardly think of what you call war here, but if they make up their minds to fight you they will come out as thick as a herd of buffalo, and if you continue fighting you will all be killed. We advise you for the best. We now offer you this, choose your own homes, and live like white men, and we will help you all you want. We are doing more for you than we do for white men coming from over the sea. This Commission is not only a Peace Commission, but it is a War Commission also. We will be kind to you if you keep the peace, but if you won't listen to reason, we are ordered to make war upon you in a different manner from what we have done before.

"We shall be here again in November, until which time you can hunt on the Republican, then you must meet us here again. Then we shall want to know whether you are willing to go up next spring to White Earth or down on the Arkansas. We will feed you till spring, on Brady Island. We advise you to go as near as possible to the Missouri River, as you can get your provisions much cheaper than you can get them a long distance from the river. Think of these things. Now we want to hear your reply, but we don't propose to make final agreement till the 1st of November. That's all."

Commissioner Taylor also made a speech, which lasted about an hour. It was a fervid production, and in true Indian style, very much to the same purpose as Sherman's.

Mr. Taylor was followed by Senator Henderson, who made a few remarks, as follows:—

"We meet at Medicine Lodge Creek next Full Moon, October 13th, south of Fort Larned, and at Laramie on the 1st day of November. We want you to appoint chiefs to appear before us at either of these places. If you want to treat by yourselves, you can do so. If the Ogallallas wish to treat, they can do so here at this place. If the Brules wish a joint treaty with the Brules of the north, they can make it. Between this time and till we meet again we want you to keep the peace. You must not attack the

roads nor the cattle trains. If you want to go to hunt
you can do so.

"We have no powder and lead with us. We did not
bring any, nor shall we bring any till we make a full
peace. The council has talked plainly. What we
do will be more pleasant than our talk. We will look
into your grievances, and will do perfect justice to
you. That is all."

Perfect silence reigned throughout the council
wigwam. The inhaling of the calumet as it passed
around was plainly audible. The features of the
Indians exhibited no emotion ; they were grave and
taciturn throughout, though it was evident that the
refusal of the Peace Commissioners to accede to their
wishes had displeased them. The pipe was finished,
a few words were whispered, and from the circle rose
"Swift Bear," always pleasant of speech, and advanced
towards the Commissioners. He addressed them in
the following manner :—

"My friends, you have been talking with me the
last two days. You have said not one bad word in all
your speeches. All you spoke to me was good. You
told me your Great Grandfather sent you here to fix
up all that was bad. You have told me so. You see
me standing here as a Sioux. All the red men talk
straight.

"I was here, and camped here, and was friendly to
the whites. I thought I brought the red men here to
make peace. I told them what you told me. You
have made me tell a lie. I understood there were six

Peace Commissioners come here to make peace. I made these men lay down their arms, and come to the council to make peace. I told them so. They are here. After doing all this work, I thought you would take pity upon them, and give them powder and ball.

"My friends, take pity upon me this day. I have been friendly. Give these men some ammunition. They don't want much. We won't kill you; we want powder and ball to kill game as we go to our villages. I am an Indian, but I believe what the pale-face tells me. That's all I have to say."

"Man-that-walks-under-the-Ground," a chief of the Ogallalla Sioux adorned with eagles' feathers, and dressed in a fancy deer-skin coat, ornamented with beads and fringed with horsehair, then said, as he approached the Commissioners:—

"The white man takes off his hat, I will do so also, as I am going to speak. [Saying which he dashed his hat and plumes on the ground.] Look at me well. [Whispers of "Good."] I am an Ogallalla. I was born and raised on this ground.

"Now I am getting to be a big man. I am married. My heart beats strong, but I will do nothing out of the way. My Great Father has sent you here. We have come here to meet you to-day as invited by Spotted Tail and Swift Bear. I am a red-skinned man. I am poor. You are rich. When you come to our villages we always share with you. Where is the living" (present) "I am to get? What

am I to do? This day I ramble around with
nowhere to go. I cannot make powder nor can I
make ball.

"I am not a chief, but I am a warrior. My Great
Grandfather may have some ideas in his head, but I
am a warrior; I may have some also. I am not alone
here. I have plenty of braves with me. When we
meet in large councils we always do something.
Those people from whom I came have been doing
very wrong this summer, but we heard that you were
going to make peace. I came here. I was raised
upon buffalo meat. I want to live upon it. After a
battle, when two nations meet and they shake hands,
they ought to be at peace. I have said it."

It will be seen by the above speeches that the cry
is for ammunition and for peace.

Pawnee Killer had a good idea when he said:
"After a battle, when two nations meet and shake
hands, they ought to be at peace." And now the
council proposes to wait till the first of November
before they will make peace. The Indian chiefs have
humiliated themselves already; they have begged in
an abject manner, and they feel it. Frowns are seen
upon their features, and still the Commissioners
deliberate. Harney proposes to give them powder
and lead; the others demur. Look at the Indians.
Pawnee Killer creeps away, and disappears under the
flaps of the wigwam. He hurries to his tent. He
comes out, his face painted a fiery red. His faithful
horse stands near, the lariat is cut, and with one

spring Pawnee Killer is mounted, heading directly for the bluffs north of North Platte.

In the council tent I find the interpreter looking eagerly around for Pawnee Killer. His place is vacant in the circle. The Commissioners have arrived at a decision. But three or four chiefs have followed the example of Pawnee Killer.

However, the decision is given, and peace is declared with the Brules, Ogallallas, and Cheyennes. Powder and ball will be given the chiefs to-morow. It is rather dubious whether the Cheyennes will keep the peace, as the head chief absented himself.

The Commissioners now go to Fort Larned to meet the Southern Indians.

————————

The Members of the Peace Commission, and the Press Gang—Report from the Indian Superintendent—Our Camp—The Gathering of Indian Tribes.

FORT LARNED, *October* 13*th*, 1867.

ABOUT 2 P.M. the train of two ambulances, containing the Commissioners and the press gang, a battery of Gatling guns of the 4th Artillery, and thirty waggons, containing stores, roll off westward, escorted by three companies of the 7th Cavalry, commanded by Major Allen.

In the ambulance are Generals Terry, Harney, J. R.

Hardie, Senator Henderson, Commissioner Taylor, Colonel Tappan, Governor Crawford, ex-Lieutenant Governor Root, Senator Ross, A. S. H. White, Secretary Commission ; John D. Howland, *Harper's Weekly* ; Bulkeley, *New York Herald* ; S. F. Hall, *Chicago Tribune* ; George Center Brown, *Cincinnati Commercial* ; H. I. Budd, *Cincinnati Gazette* ; William Fayel, *St. Louis Republican* ; George Willis, phonographer ; Reynolds, editor *Kansas State Journal*, correspondent *Chicago Times*, one from the *Chicago Republican*, one from the *Leavenworth Bulletin*, and your own correspondent.

A march of one mile, across the Smoky River, and we camp. The reason that we have such an escort may be seen by the subjoined letter :—

" MEDICINE LODGE CREEK, *October 5th*, 1867.

" SIR,—I have the honour to inform you, that as far as I am concerned, I feel perfectly safe among these Indians without soldiers, yet, if the honourable Commissioners feel otherwise, it might be better to have an escort with them, and in this event I would suggest that you bring regulars, and in number not exceeding two hundred. I make this suggestion for the reason that the strictest military discipline will have to be enforced while these soldiers are among the Indians. This discipline is not often found outside the regular army. It would be wiser to come without any soldiers, than to come with a few ; hence

I name two hundred as a sufficient number for an escort, and few enough not to alarm the Indians. I will meet you at Fort Larned, and will have some of the chiefs of each tribe with me. Do not leave that post until I get there.

" Your obedient servant,

" THOMAS MURPHY,

" *Superintendent of Indian Affairs.*

" HONOURABLE N. G. TAYLOR,
 " *Commissioner of Indian Affairs.*"

Just one mile away to the northward across the river stands Fort Harker. A tall flagstaff towers above all the buildings, and even from here the American flag can be seen waving from its peak. Our camp is situated on the brow of the hill looking across the river, and into the old fort, now dilapidated, and only distinguishable from where we stand by two solitary adobe chimneys, which last winter saw a group of exiled soldiers hugging them for the friendly warmth of their hearths. At the west end of our camp are the tents of three companies of the 7th Cavalry under the command of Major Allen. The waggons of their regiment are clustered near, and are loaded with green, red, and blue blankets, gaudy calico, blue cloth, hats, beads, and silver medals for the friendly chiefs that we intend to visit. Then comes the artillery, two Gatling guns belonging to Battery B, 4th Artillery. The tents of the artillerists flank the north side of the battery. Eastward are ranged the ambulances, ten in number. At the eastern end are the tents of the Commissioners. Those exposed to the shrieking wind are swayed wildly by the fierce gusts. Like the Levanter, the gale comes down upon this exposed spot without a warning, sometimes levelling every object to the ground. It is the first thing the residents at Fort Harker complain of.

Fronting their tents in a social circle, even while the wind is making such a terrible racket, sit the Commissioners, now composed of Henderson, Taylor, Harney, Tappan, Terry, and J. B. Hardie, are discussing the Indian question. Though their efforts may fail to perfect a peace between the white and the red men, no person catching a glance at this extemporaneous council could but see that they had their duties at heart. When General Harney stands erect he towers above his associates like another Saul. Underneath his venerable exterior there remains still a wonderful power of vitality and passion despite his old age.

Opposite Harney is John B. Henderson, known here as Senator Henderson. He is the business man of the Commission, doggedly perseverant in the cause of western interests.

On the Senator's right sits Sanborn, a general who has served on many a hard field—a good-natured and jovial gentleman, pleasant to converse with, free of access, and pretty thoroughly posted on Indian matters.   The general has been selected to superintend the movements of the Commission.

On the Senator's left sits Colonel Tappan, of Colorado, an agreeable companion, but of few words. He is also very well acquainted with Indian affairs.

And there is Commissioner N. G. Taylor, the president of the Commission, full of philanthropic ideas respecting the poor Indian.   He is undoubtedly earnest in his opinions.   Formerly a Methodist minister, he has turned his attention to secular matters, and devotes his life to an improvement of the social *status* of the American aboriginal.

And lastly, there is Terry, the captor of Fort Fisher ; but as his praises and his good deeds have been recorded by nobler pens than mine, I will not essay the task.   The country cannot forget him.

The following letter has just been received by the council :—

" MEDICINE LODGE CREEK, *October 5th*, 1867.

" SIR,—Having been selected by the Hon. Peace Commission to proceed to the Indian country and put myself in communication with the Indians of the plains, Cheyennes, Arapahoes, and Apaches, with a view of assembling them at some point near, at south of Fort Larned, there to await the arrival of the Commissioners at Full Moon in October, and, if possible, have the Indians, now on the warpath, come in and cease fighting, I have the honour to report that

I have assembled at this place the following number
of Indians :—

Arapahoes, number of lodges	..		..		..	171
Apaches	..	..	..	..	..	..	85
Cheyennes	..	..	..	..	..	..	25
Kiowas	..	..	..	..	..	..	150
	Making in all		..	..	..	431

"Little Big Mouth, of the Arapahoes, who has 21
lodges, is far away south, and will not be here with
his lodges, but is represented. The Cheyennes sent
in word last night that they were moving their whole
village, numbering some 200 lodges, and would be
here in a few days. The Comanches who, I am
informed, number 100 lodges, are in camp about
thirty miles below here, and would be present now,
but that they have made some arrangements with
Colonel Leavenworth, and were waiting to see him.
They sent me word to that effect yesterday, and also
that they would be here in two days.

"We count now on the ground 431 lodges ; those
coming in and who will be represented, 421 lodges ;
making in all 852. Averaging each lodge at six
persons, we have over five thousand Indians.

"In the performance of this service both myself
and those with me have taken considerable risk so far
as our persons and lives were concerned. We were
compelled to go into their country in order to gather
the Indians together, or go home and abandon the
whole project ; and, in order to make our mission a

success, were obliged to come without soldiers. These Indians have been so often deceived by whites and sought by soldiers, that they are very suspicious of the former, and cannot see why people calling themselves friends of the Indians cannot come among them without bringing their enemies, the soldiers, with them. So far our mission has been a perfect success, and I hope the honourable Commission will crown our efforts by making with the Indians such a treaty as will insure peace in the future to the Indians, and security to the frontiersman and pioneer. Everything now looks well.

> " Respectfully,
> " THOMAS MURPHY."

We arrived at Fort Larned on the 12th instant, and we now strike for Medicine Lodge Creek, 80 miles south-west from this spot.

The change at Larned—" Bummers "—An Indian Agent is relieved of his duties—The train of the Peace Commission —Buffalo herds—The encampment of the Tribes—Multitudes of Olive-Skinned Warriors—The Muster of the Indians.

MEDICINE LODGE CAMP, *October 16th*, 1867.

A COMPLETE change has been effected at Fort Larned since Hancock's army swept by in pursuit of " Roman Nose " and " Tall Bull's " tribes. The shabby, vermin-breeding adobe and wooden houses have been torn down, and new and stately buildings of hewn sandstone stand in their stead. The comfort of the troops has been taken into consideration by the architect and builder. The fort is now garrisoned by six companies of infantry and one company of cavalry. Major Kidd is the commandant.

Generals Harney and Sanborn paid a visit to the fort, accompanied by the correspondents. Like many other institutions, this place has also a whole squad of "bummers," who seemingly do nothing but imbibe a wretched infusion of rye, and smoke "Virginia" and "Birds-eye" tobacco.

While we were in the private room of the sutler, a number of Indians, among whom were the redoubtable Satanta ; Little Raven, head sachem of the Arapahoes; Stumbling Bear, and two fine-looking Apache chiefs, walked in.

Satanta, or White Bear, gave me a *bear's* hug as his greeting. He was introduced to the other members of the press, who looked upon him with some awe, having heard so much of his ferocity and boldness. By his defiant and independent bearing he attracted all eyes. He would certainly be a formidable enemy to encounter alone on the prairie. It is said that he has "killed more white men than any other Indian on the plains."

Little Raven is a fat, good-natured sachem ; one who loves to smoke his pipe peacefully in his lodge, surrounded by dusky concubines. There was one

Apache chief, a tall, wiry fellow, and, if I may trust to my knowledge of physiognomy, cunning and unprincipled.

A little fire-water was given to them, which opened their hearts. For the nonce White Bear, ever ready with his tomahawk, allowed his enmity of the paleface to sleep, and laughed gleefully like a child.

Three of the reporters were introduced to Major Wynkoop, the agent for the Cheyennes and Sioux. The Major narrowly escaped with his life two or three days ago at the camps of the Indians now on Medicine Lodge Creek. Roman Nose, with ten warriors, rode up to the lodge in which Wynkoop was then staying. Wynkoop heard that Roman Nose, a Sioux sachem, had threatened his life, and was even then hurrying to his lodge for that purpose. Though there were then at the camp three or four thousand warriors kindly disposed towards Wynkoop, still it was evident that Roman Nose, with his fierce eloquence, could command aid, and carry his point. Behind the lodge was a fast horse, which he quickly mounted, and, putting spurs to him, left the village at the very moment Roman Nose had a revolver drawn on him. The animosity of this chief towards Wynkoop originated from a suspicion that he was the person who informed Hancock of the whereabouts of his people's lodges, and thus became the cause of their destruction.

After a brief examination of the fort we started for camp, and, for the first time, crossed the celebrated

Arkansas River, three miles south of Fort Larned. At this point the river was very shallow, at no place over two feet in depth. The southern bank of the river was covered with luxuriant grass, into which the pedestrian sunk to his waist.

Here our train was increased by sixty waggons, containing stores and presents. The number of waggons and ambulances with the expedition is now one hundred and sixty-five. Six mules to each waggon, and two hundred cavalry horses, make the number of animals twelve hundred and fifty. The number of men on this trip, including the camp followers, is six hundred. When on the march we present quite a formidable appearance.

In our company are the Indian agents, Colonel Leavenworth, Major Wynkoop, Superintendent Murphy, Colonel Rankin, Captain John W. Smith, interpreter, with a host of camp followers, who pretend to have special commissions, but who really follow out of mere curiosity, and to live on the bountiful rations doled out by the Peace Commission.

Until to-day we were not prepared to accept all the statements we heard about the numbers of buffalo on the plains, for prairie folk are like sailors, fond of embellishing the truth. When we were told that the prairie has been seen so packed with them, that one might walk on their backs for ten miles, we set it down to the narrator's desire to express a countless number, rather than as a literal fact. When they swore that, not many years ago, military expeditions were compelled to mow a passage through them with grape shot from their howitzers, we thought they were taking advantage of the credulity of youth, and inwardly lamented their depravity. We are becoming wiser every day, however. We think of all the bales of buffalo robes annually exported East, of the many thousands of hides required by the 150,000 Indians of the plains for their wigwams, of the thousands of robes in use among the military and civilians out West ; and we are not so sceptical as formerly.

We have seen many herds at various times, but to-day we had the pleasure of seeing ten great herds, of about a thousand head each, guarded by their sentries and videttes, which suspiciously watched our advance, and continually snorted the alarm to the respective hosts.   It was to me a thrilling sight.

At night we fared on buffalo steak and hump. Jack Howland, *Harper's* artist, mounted on a bay nag, brought down a fine buffalo expressly for the special's mess.

The next day we came to a place where the prairie was on fire.   But we travelled through the smoke and fire, lost for a short time to each other, but our advent from the cloud was hailed with gratitude.

General Augur caught up with us at night. He was ordered by the President to join the Indian Commission *vice* General Sherman, the latter having received a telegram to return to Washington.   The press has already conceived an opinion as to the reasons of his recall, and all doubts upon this subject have been satisfied by this time.

The country south of the Arkansas, through which we now travel, has been selected by the Commissioners for the Indian reservation. There promises, however, to be a difficulty about this. The State of Kansas stretches away over one hundred miles to the southward of Medicine Lodge Creek, and this portion south of the Arkansas is about as fertile a country as the State can boast of. The representatives, now with the Commissioners, object to the division of their State. The proposed Indian reservation, they say, must be selected somewhere in the neighbourhood of the salt plain, so that no collision between the Indians and the State authorities can take place.

Monday morning, about ten o'clock, we came in sight of the great encampment of the Southern Indians. A natural basin, through which meandered Medicine Lodge Creek, between gracefully wooded banks, was the place selected for their winter camp. On the extreme right was the Arapahoe camp, consisting of 171 lodges. Next to this, and almost buried in a dense grove of fine timber, was the camp of the Comanches, numbering 100 lodges; adjoining which was the Kiowa camp, 150 lodges. At the western extremity of the basin were the camps of the Apaches, numbering 85 lodges, and the Cheyennes, 250 lodges.

Thousands of ponies covered the adjacent hills,

while in the valley grazed the cattle. The camps resembled a cluster of villages. All these camps were pitched so as to form a circle, in the centre of which sported the boys and girls, and little papooses in a complete state of nudity.

Quite a multitude of olive-skinned warriors, braves, young bucks, papooses, damsels, and squaws, from the different villages, hurried up to see the Commissioners. The escorts were left to come on after us in an hour or so. This was a wise plan, as so many treacherous deeds have been done whenever the troops have come up, that the Indians are extremely suspicious. By this seeming confidence, we found all the Indians quite willing to see us.

During the march several little things occurred which many feared would disturb the peace. The vagabondish followers, who insisted on joining the expedition at Fort Larned, on the pretence that they had special commissions for some business not down on the list issued, shot down buffaloes in the most reckless manner. This multitude of bummers not only entailed expense upon the Government at the rate of a good round sum, but by their indiscriminate shooting of game foster ill-will between the Indians and the whites at a time when so much tact and diplomacy are needed to reconcile both parties.

Satanta, never backward of speech to assert his rights, burst forth at last, and said :—

" Have the white men become children, that they

should kill meat and not eat? When the red men kill, they do so that they may live."

This speech produced the desired result. Two or three of the bummers were put under arrest, and the Major commanding the battalion was also arrested for not preventing the shooting. Satanta is a plain-speaking chief.

When we arrived at the camp the Indians were engaged in the important ceremony of "making medicine." Shields of tanned buffalo hides were slung on poles facing the sun, with the view of propitiating it. The unsophisticated aboriginals believe that the sun will aid them if they turn their shields towards it while it shines, and cover them by night from dew. The medicine man, whom they revere so much, and regard as priest, is absent, engaged in his incantations.

There are five thousand Indians in the encampment, and their chiefs are named as follows :—

Parry-wah-sahmer, or Young Bear, head Chief of the Comanches ; Tip-pah-pen-nov-aly, or Painted Lips ; Ponen-e-weh-tone-you, or Iron Mountain ; Para-er-ehve, or Wise Shield ; Za-nah-weah, or Without Wealth—100 lodges.

Satanta, or White Bear, head sachem ; Black Eagle, Sitemgear, Stumbling Bear, Satank, or Sitting Bear, Ton-a-enko (Kicking Bird), Sitting Man—150 lodges.

Little Raven, head sachem ; Spotted Wolf, Stone, Yellow Bear, Powder Face, Ice—171 lodges.

Wolf Sleeve, head sachem ; Poor Bear, Iron Shirt, Crow—85 lodges.

Black Kettle, head sachem of the Cheyenne nation; Big Jake, Bull Bear, chief of the Dog Soldiers, Tall Bull, Heap of Birds, Slim Face, Black White Man, Grey Head — 250 lodges. Medicine Arrow, their peace chief, is absent.

We are camped within half a mile of the Indian villages.

At this point the departure of the courier makes it necessary to break off short. Will resume in my next.

Another Council—Four Tribes represented—Distribution of
  Clothing—Incidents of the Council—Wynkoop's Testimony
  —The Cause of the War—More about Hancock's Expedi-
  tion—Comments.

MEDICINE LODGE, *October 17th.*

A COUNCIL was held this morning at which the Peace Commissioners, Colonel Leavenworth, Colonel Wynkoop, Dr. Root, A. S. H. White, and the reporters were present, with twenty-five chiefs of the Kiowas, Arapahoes, Cheyennes, Apaches, and Comanches. In the front row sat Kicking Bird, Little Raven, Spotted Wolf, Fishermore, Heap of Birds, Black Kettle, Elk, Poor Bear, Satanta, Satank, and Mrs. Adams, interpretress for the Arapahoes.

This woman came in dressed in a crimson petti-coat, black cloth cloak, and a small coquettish velvet hat, decorated with a white ostrich feather. She appears intelligent, and speaks fluently the English, Kiowa, and Arapahoe languages.

Before the council commenced, the village crier, in a loud voice, gave command to the nations sitting around " to be good, and to behave themselves."

At this period Fishermore, the Kiowas' council orator, stepped up, his dirty face beaming with joy, and loudly shouting out " A-how, a-how!" insisted upon shaking hands with all. Fishermore is a stout Indian of ponderous proportions, and speaks five languages. He is a favourite with all the tribes. When the calumet came to him he directed the stem north, south, east, and west, and then took three deliberate whiffs, and passed it to his neighbour.

When all were ready, Commissioner Taylor said that he had distributed twenty suits of clothes to the Arapahoe runners ; he was ready to distribute twenty suits to each of the different tribes ; and if they could agree upon terms of peace at the general council, he had many more presents to give away.

The clothes were immediately brought in to the Council and distributed around.

The meeting having been called to order, Commissioner Taylor said :—

" We understand that you are tired of staying here, and in the talk yesterday you requested us to defer the council for eight sleeps. To that proposition we assented, supposing that you would all be willing to wait. We have found, however, that delay does not please some, the Arapahoes, Apaches, Comanches, and Kiowas, having waited here so long; therefore we have agreed to hold the general council at your village, when the council circle is prepared."

At this juncture McCloskey said that if the Commission excused him, he would go and bring the Comanches to the council, that they might also hear the proposition of the Commission.

Ten Bears, head chief of the Comanches, Iron Mountain, Little Horn, son of Ten Bears, were introduced to the Commission. When I saw these powerfully built warriors I thought of the wonderful stories of Mayne Reid and other authors, and the various battles said to have taken place between this warlike nation and the Texan Rangers. When they were seated, McCloskey, their interpreter, related the late talk to them. They were all well pleased.

Mr. Taylor again spoke: "My friends, these Commissioners have come from Washington to make peace with all of you. We desire to make treaties with you all together. Now, we are anxious, therefore, that all you chiefs should agree together upon what day the grand council takes place. We are also anxious to have it over as soon as possible, that we may do justice to the northern Indians. If you can agree among yourselves upon what day you will hold the council, we will be willing to treat with you, but if not, we must treat with each tribe as they are ready. We are done, and we hope the chiefs will let us know upon what they agree."

Black Eagle rose and said: "I know Generals Sanborn and Harney of old—when there was no blood on the path; when the whole country was all white. I speak for the Kiowas now. We should like to stop until four sleeps have passed before we speak."

A good-natured old warrior, who had the honour of once being introduced to President Lincoln, said: "I had a talk with the Great Father himself when I was at Washington. I am willing to repeat it here. Since I have made peace with the white men I have received many presents, and my heart has been made glad. My young men look upon you with gladness. I have not much to say, except it be to say that we are willing to travel any road you lay out for us."

Then the Kiowa chief said: "We would like to hold the council to-morrow, and then wait four days before receiving the goods."

Satanta said: "I don't want to say anything at this talk. I will say what I have to say at the grand council."

Ten Bears, angry at this vacillation of the Kiowas, here made the remark: "What I say is law for the Comanches, but it takes half-a-dozen to speak for the Kiowas."

After a few more retorts of this kind, it was finally agreed that the Comanches and Kiowas should meet in grand council later.

Poor Bear, an Apache chief, stepped up, and after a long pause said: "When the grass was green I was on the Ouachita, and I heard that the Commissioners wanted to see me. I am glad. The Apaches, though few, are all here. I have been here some time. I would like to get my annuity goods as soon as possible, as I understood they were here. I will wait four days for the talk. I have spoken."

After this speech Satanta stood up before the warriors, of whom there were fully five hundred dressed in the barbaric Indian costume. His remarks were universally applauded, judging from the frequent bursts of gratified "Ugh! ugh!"

His style of delivery is well calculated to please a savage multitude. Of formidable and striking appearance, and gifted with native eloquence, he compels attention. His name is a thing to swear by.

A portion of his remarks we took down phonetically, of which the following is a true copy :—

"*Anitate y ben antema, usebah ghis elek men a yu tah durpua cabelah inst ma den y cat ah damht ahu echan arabeuyshtabelunyau.*" (Loud "Ugh! ugh!") What it all means we do not know.

Black Kettle, chief of the Cheyennes, got up now, and addressed the multitude of Indians present as follows :—

"We were once friends with the whites, but you nudged us out of the way by your intrigues, and now when we are in council you keep nudging each other. Why don't you talk, and go straight, and let all be well? I am pleased with all that has been said."

Little Raven followed in the same vein, appealing to them "to behave themselves and be good."

The council was then adjourned, to meet again on the morning of the fifth day in solemn council at the place which is to be specially prepared for the occasion.

Senator Henderson, remarkable for his business aptitude, urged upon Taylor to make the "talks" as short as possible.

While the talk was being interpreted, the honourable gentlemen were engaged in different things. Harney, with head erect, watched with interest each dusky and painted face of the Indians around the tent. Sanborn picked his teeth and laughed jollily. Tappan read Indian reports about the destruction of the Indian village. Henderson, with eyeglass in his hand, seemed buried in deep study. Terry busied himself in printing alphabetical letters, and Augur whittled away with energy. Leavenworth examined his children, and made by-signals to old Satank, the oldest chief of the Kiowa nation. Under the table sat Commissioner Taylor's papoose, making wry faces at some pretty squaws sitting astride, behind some aspiring youths on ponies, in the background. The correspondents sat *à la Turque* on the ground, their pencils flying over the paper.

At dusk Gray-Head came to camp from the war-

path with fifty Dog Soldiers. His band looked as
ferocious as though they were going to begin fighting.

Gray-Head presented the following time-honoured
credentials to General Harney :—

> "HEADQUARTERS, COTTONWOOD SPRINGS,
> *July 15th,* 1858.

"This is to show that the bearer, Gray-Head,
a chief of the Cheyennes, has voluntarily visited my
camp, and made promises of peace towards the
whites. And believing that these promises are made
in good faith, I commend him to the friendship of
our people and the troops.

"W. S. HARNEY, *Brigadier-General, U.S.A.*"

Black Kettle lately received a message from Medicine Arrow's band, saying that if he did not make his
appearance at their camp on a certain day, they
would come in and kill all his horses.

Towards night Colonel Wynkoop was called up
before the Commission to testify as to the cause
of this Indian war, which he gave in the following
manner :—

Wynkoop said that Governor Evans of Colorado
had blamed him for bringing the Indians to Sand
Creek ; but as the Cheyennes were desirous of peace
he had resolved to see them, and he had brought
them to Sand Creek for that purpose. The massacre
of the Indians at Sand Creek by Colonel Chivington's
force took place two days after he had left Fort

Lyon, of which he was in command. Directly after the massacre, two hundred Sioux Indians went on the warpath, attacked Mexican trains, killing every one they came across, and since that event the Indians have been burning with resentment.

In answer to a question which Henderson asked, Wynkoop said Chivington's reply at the council in Denver was, that his business was to kill Indians, and not to make peace with them.

After Sand Creek the Indians were at war everywhere, mostly on the Platte. Property was destroyed, horses were stolen, emigrants were killed, etc., etc.

"Some annuity goods which Commissioner Goodall bought in New York, three-point blankets, which are used as wrappers, and which are charged in the bill at $13 per pair, were the most worthless things that I ever saw. The Indians told me that they would not have taken those goods from anybody else but myself. It was a most shameless affair. They were not only killed, but the friendliest were cheated, etc., etc.

"Concerning the disposition of the Sioux, I will state that they were under the impression, previous to the destruction of that Cheyenne village by General Hancock, that as the Cheyennes had made peace, they ought to do the same thing. I asked Pawnee-killer, a Sioux chief, and he said the same.

"The Mexican killed at Fort Zarah was killed by an Indian who was under the influence of liquor. But the Indians generally were satisfied with keeping the peace, and except that solitary murder at Zarah they had kept it. They had certainly done nothing after the treaty was made, in '65, until Hancock made his appearance with his army. There was a report that the Indians had run off stock near Fort Wallace. General Hancock heard various statements from his officers of several depredations, but these could not be fixed upon any particular band. I know of one affair,—viz., a young chief attempted to run off some stage horses, but he did not succeed.

"Concerning Hancock's Expedition, the first I knew of it, was when I received a communication from him dated at Leavenworth, stating that he was coming with a large body of troops. He intended to make peace, but at the same time was prepared for war. He also wished me to accompany him. He stated that he was going to make a demand for the parties who committed the depredations on the Smoky Hill, and also for the Indian who killed the New Mexicans at Zarah. I received another letter, stating that his orders from General Sherman were not to make demands.

"As soon as I received this communication I sent out runners to gather in the chiefs. When Hancock arrived at Larned they had not reached there. But two days afterwards seven arrived. Amongst them were Tall Bull, White Horse, and Bull Bear, chiefs of the Dog Band. The night of their arrival a council was held, and General Hancock made a speech."

(You have already received and published it.) "After him Tall Bull spoke, and said that his tribe were at peace, and he wished to remain so; they hoped he would not go to their village, as he could not have any more to say to them there than where he was. General Hancock answered that he was going to see them at their village on the morrow.

"The next day he started for the village. That night we camped twenty-three miles from the fort. The day after we met a body of Indians on the plains. As soon as they saw us they started to run away, but Edward Guerrier made signs with his horse that we were peaceable. So they came back. Hancock told them he wished to see them at the village that night and talk with them, to which they agreed.

"Roman Nose and his party started back towards their village. The troops took up the line of march for it. Bull Bear remained behind with the column, and he then told me that it would produce no good to march up to the village; that the women and children would be afraid. This I communicated to General Hancock; but he did not agree with that view of it.

"They still marched on, and at last camped within three hundred yards east of the village. About five P.M. Hancock sent interpreters to fetch the chiefs to the council. They returned immediately, and informed Hancock that the women and children had fled. He then sent them back, and ordered them to

send the head men to him.   Bull Bear and Tall Bull
came accordingly.   General Hancock appeared very
angry, and asked them why they had acted so meanly
towards him.

"About eleven o'clock that night Guerrier returned
from the camp, and stated that the chiefs had come
back from the pursuit of their women.

" Hancock sent for me, and told me when I reached
his tent that he had ordered General Custer to surround the camp, and detain all who would be found
in it.   He asked me my opinion upon the order.   I
told him that if there were only ten men found there,
when they saw the cavalry they would have a fight.
Hancock said it mattered not.   The cavalry marched
up and surrounded the camp.   A little while after
that, General Hancock ordered General Custer to
pursue the Indians and bring them back.   Custer
immediately started in pursuit.

"About two A.M. Hancock stated in my presence
that he intended to burn the village next morning,
as he considered that they had acted treacherously
towards him, and they deserved punishment.   Upon
hearing this, I wrote him a letter urging him to do
nothing rash, but to ponder well on what he was
about to do.   Hancock did not burn that village,
however, next morning, as he had promised.   I also
urged General Smith to endeavour to show the
General that it would be unwise to burn the village.
General Smith did so.

" The night of the 16th a courier came from General

Custer, bearing a letter, stating that two men had been killed and burned, and Lookout Station destroyed, on the Smoky Hill. That same night General Hancock gave orders to General Smith to burn the village next morning.

" The next day, as the troops were leaving Pawnee Fork, the order of General Hancock was obeyed. The village was set on fire, and everything in it was burned.

" A courier was dispatched to the commandants of Forts Larned and Dodge, ordering them to prevent the Indians from crossing the Arkansas River. Two days after that a party of Indians were intercepted at Cimmaron crossing, and ten were killed.

" The old Indian and young girl who had been in the deserted village, and who had been taken to Fort Dodge by General Hancock, died a few days after the expedition left, at that post."

In answer to a question by General Sanborn, as to whether he (Wynkoop) had any idea who had committed the outrage upon her, Wynkoop said : " I firmly believe that the soldiers ravished the child. It was the conclusion I arrived at when I heard that she was ravished. It is my belief now." *

" The Cheyennes whom I have seen lately gave me to understand that the war this summer was in retaliation for the destruction of their village by General Hancock."

---

* This is an instance of the jealousy existing between the Military and Indian Agents.

I.   R

There are several little inaccuracies in Colonel Wynkoop's testimony.

First. War was already declared when Hancock appeared with his force.

Second. He did not burn the village until the 19th, four days after his arrival at Pawnee Fork, and not until he had received positive proofs that the Indians were at war. Nor did he then burn it until he had taken counsel with his officers.

Third. The soldiers were not the persons who violated the young girl found at the Cheyenne village.

Your readers cannot have forgotten the facts. It appears to us that the Indian Agent is somewhat prejudiced against the military.

Major Henry Douglass, formerly commandant of Fort Dodge, was examined relative to what he knew of the origin of the Kiowa troubles. Being sworn, he testified as follows :—

" The information which I sent to the War Department concerning Indian raids and their dissatisfaction with Colonel Leavenworth, I received from traders and interpreters. All the leading chiefs were dissatisfied with him. They have affixed their names to a letter sent to me, containing a list of their grievances.

" I held several councils with Satanta, the great Chief of the Kiowas, and Tonaenko, the second in importance, in which they stated over and over that their agent did not treat them well, that he refused to give them annuity goods when due, as per treaty.

" Colonel David Butterfield and Charley Rath, a trader at Zarah, have issued guns, pistols, and ammunition, the consequence of which was that before Hancock appeared with his army, Satanta openly boasted that they had plenty of arms and ammunition, and were not afraid of the whites.

" The accounts of the depredations committed by the Kiowas, before Hancock came along, were based upon affidavits, and I believed them to be true, and therefore transmitted them to General Hancock. The Kiowas brought three women — the Misses Box, daughters of Farmer John Box, of Texas—to me at Fort Dodge, and upon payment of money and provisions, they were given up."

Question by Sanborn: "Do you not think that these Indians made that boast of cleaning out the whites as a joke?"

Before an answer could be given old General Harney said: "I never knew the Indians to jest. In their boasts there is always a meaning."

"According to information received by me, the Kiowas scalped seventeen coloured soldiers and stole two hundred head of horses early in February, 1867. They also abused Major Page, an officer of the United States regular army, in the month of March."

It seems that these statements of Major Douglass, which he sent to General Hancock, were the main causes of the expedition being sent to the west.

An Amphitheatre in a Grove—The Council Personages—
Senator Henderson's Speech to the Indians—Replies of
the Chiefs Gray-Head, Satanta, Ten Bears, Toosh-a-way,
and Poor Bear—A Present for A. J.—Adjournment.

MEDICINE LODGE CREEK, *October 19th,* 1867.

A GREAT clearing had been made in the centre of a
grove of tall elms for the convenience of the grand
council.   Logs had been arranged so as to seat the
principal chiefs of the Southern nations, and tables
had been erected for the accommodation of the
various correspondents.   In front of these tables were
the seats ranged in a semicircle for the Commissioners.   Facing the Commissioners were a few of
the most select chiefs of the different tribes.   Beyond
all were the ponies of the chiefs, forming a splendid
background to the scene.   Over the space allotted to
the Commissioners and the press were placed a few
branches as a shelter from the sun.

At ten A.M. the council was opened by Fishermore,
the lusty crier of the Kiowa nation, who with a
loud voice counselled the tribes to do right above
all things.   Satanta, their chief, sat proudly on a camp
chair, and behind him were his principal warriors.
Near him sat Mrs. Virginia Adams, dressed in a new
crimson gown, made specially for this important
occasion.   She is the interpretess for the Arapahoes.

Looking around, Commissioner Taylor perceived

that all was ready. Telling the interpreter that he was going to speak, he rose and thus addressed the assemblage of chiefs :—

"We have selected a great peace man—a member of the peace council at Washington—to tell you what we have to say. Listen to him."

Cries of "Ow-how-ugh!"

Senator John B. Henderson then rose, and addressed the chiefs in the following manner :—

"Our friends of the Cheyenne, Comanche, Apache, Kiowa, and Arapahoe nations, the Government of the United States and the Great Father has sent seven Commissioners to come here and have a talk with you. Two years ago the Government entered into a treaty with you at the mouth of the Little Arkansas. and we hoped then that there would be no war between us. We are sorry to be disappointed. During the last year we heard several times that persons belonging to your tribes were committing war against us. We heard that they were attacking peaceable persons engaged in building our railroads, that they were scalping women and children. These reports made the hearts of our people very sad. Some of our people said that you committed these deeds, others denied it. Some of our people said that you commenced the war. Some of them denied that you commenced it. Some of our people said that you and other Indians were going to wage a general war against the whites ; others denied the charge. In this conflict of opinion we could not find the truth, and therefore the Great Father has sent us here to hear from your own lips what were those wrongs that prompted you to commit those deeds, if you had committed those acts of violence. We do not like war, because it brings bloodshed to both sides ; but we do like brave men, and they should speak the truth, for it is an evidence of their courage. We now again ask you to state to us if you have at any time since the treaty committed violence.

"What has the Government done of which you complain ? If soldiers have done wrong to you, tell us when and where, and who are the guilty parties. If these agents whom we have put here to protect you have cheated and defrauded you, be not afraid to tell us. We have come to hear all your complaints and to correct all your wrongs. We have full power to do these things, and we pledge you our sacred honour to do so. For anything that you may say in this council you shall not be harmed. Before we proceed to inform you what we are authorised to do for you, we desire to hear fully from your own lips what you have done, what you have suffered, and what you want. We say, however, that we intend to do justice to the red man. If we have harmed him, we will correct it ; if the red man has harmed us, we believe he is brave and generous enough to acknowledge it, and to cease from doing any more wrong. At present we have only to say that we are greatly rejoiced to see our red brethren so well disposed towards peace. We are especially glad because we as individuals would give them all the comforts of civilisation, religion, and wealth, and now we are authorised by the Great Father to provide for them comfortable homes upon our richest agricultural lands. We are authorised to build for the Indian school-houses and churches, and provide teachers to educate his children. We can furnish him with agricultural implements to work, and domestic cattle, sheep, and hogs to stock his farm. We now cease, and shall wait to hear what you have to say, and after we have heard it we will tell you the road to go. We are now anxious to hear from you."

Gray-Head got up, and said that as there were only two of the Cheyennes present they could not speak until the rest were present.

Satanta became uneasy, buried his hands in the ground, and rubbed sand over them, after which he went round shaking hands with all, and then stood in the circle dignified and ready with his speech. He said :—

"The Commissioners have come from afar to listen to our grievances. My heart is glad, and I shall hide nothing from you. I understood that you were coming down here to see us. I moved away from those disposed to war, and I also came from afar to see you. The Kiowas and Comanches have not been fighting. We were away down south when we heard that you were coming to see us.

"The Cheyennes are those who have been fighting with you. They did it in broad daylight, so that all

could see them. If I had been fighting I would have
done so also. Two years ago I made peace with
General Harney, Sanborn, and Colonel Leavenworth
at the mouth of the Little Arkansas. That peace I
have never broken. When the grass was growing
this spring, a large body of soldiers came along on
the Santa Fé road. I had not done anything, and
therefore was not afraid.

"All the chiefs of the Kiowas, Comanches, and
Arapahoes are here to-day. They have come to listen
to the good word. We have been waiting here a long
time to see you, and we are getting tired. All the
land south of the Arkansas belongs to the Kiowas
and Comanches, and I don't want to give away any of
it. I love the land and the buffalo, and will not part
with any. I want you to understand also that the
Kiowas don't want to fight, and have not been fighting
since we made the treaty. I hear a good deal of fine
talk from these gentlemen, but they never do what
they say. I don't want any of these medicine homes
built in the country ; I want the papooses brought up
just exactly as I am. When I make peace it is a long
and lasting one ; there is no end to it. We thank you
for your presents.

"All these chiefs and head men feel happy. They
will do what you want. They know that you are
doing the best you can. I and they will do so also.
There is one big chief lately died—Jim Pockmark, of
the Caddoes—he was a great peacemaker, and we are
sorry he is dead,

"When I look upon you I know you are all big chiefs. While you are in the country we go to sleep happy, and are not afraid. I have heard that you intend to settle us on a reservation near the mountains. I don't want to settle there. I love to roam over the wide prairie, and when I do it I feel free and happy, but when we settle down, we grow pale and die.

" Hearken well to what I say. I have laid aside my lance, my bow, and my shield, and yet I feel safe in your presence. I have told you the truth. I have no little lies hid about me, but I don't know how it is with the Commissioners ; are they as clear as I am ? A long time ago this land belonged to our fathers, but when I go up to the river I see a camp of soldiers, and they are cutting my wood down, or killing my buffalo. I don't like that, and when I see it my heart feels like bursting with sorrow. I have spoken."

Satanta's speech produced a rather blank look upon the faces of the Peace Commissioners. Satanta has a knack of saying boldly what he needs, regardless of what anybody thinks. On the close of his speech he sat down, and wrapped a crimson blanket around his form.

Little Raven said that he had nothing to say, as his young men had been dispatched after the Pawnee horse thieves. "G—d d—n them mean squaws!" said he.

After Little Raven delivered himself of his wrathful speech, old Parry-wah-sah-mer, or Ten Bears, chief of the Comanches, after putting on his spectacles, commenced in a shrill voice, as follows :—

"Of myself I have no wisdom, but I expect to get some from you ; it will go right down my throat. I am willing to do what you say."

After saying which the old chief hobbled around the circle, and shook hands with the Commissioners with as much gravity and unimpressibility as a Turk.

Toosh-a-way, another Comanche chief, stood up, and in a calm, argumentative voice, said :—

"I have come from away down south to see and hear you. A long time ago the band of Penekdaty Comanches were the strongest band in the nation. The Great Father sent a big chief down to us, and promised medicines, houses, and many other things. A great, great many years have gone by, but those things have never come. My band is dwindling away fast. My young men are a scoff and a byword among the other nations. I shall wait till next spring to see if these things shall be given us ; if they are not, I and my young men will return to our wild brothers to live on the prairie. I have tried the life the Great Father told me to follow. He told me my young men would become strong, but every spring their numbers are less. I am tired of it. Do what you have promised us, and all will be well. I have said it."

Poor Bear, chief of the Apaches, a poor-looking,

superannuated warrior, next got up, and in a hurried manner said :—

"Some time ago the President sent for me. I went to see him, and heard what he had to say. I remember it well. What he told me I repeated to the Apache braves. What I promised to him I and my young men have kept, even until this hour. Many whites travel the Santa Fé road, but no Apaches have troubled them, for I am chief among the warriors, and I know what I say. My young men recognise me alone as chief, and they listen and obey. At my bidding they came with their squaws and papooses to listen to your good words. We will listen attentively to them, and will follow the straight road. I am very tired of staying here. I wish you would get through as soon as possible, and let me and my braves go to our homes south. As we have never broken any treaties I think we might get our annuity goods without delay. Since I was a child I loved the pale face, and until my departure to the happy lands I hope to follow in their footsteps. I have said it."

After delivering his speech in a very effective manner, so far as regards delivery, he said he had some presents to give the "Great Peace Chief of Washington." A shield was brought to him by a select warrior, which he presented to the Commissioner with these words : "I have slain many an enemy, this shield has saved me many a time from death. When my foe saw this shield he trembled, and I triumphed ; go you and do the same."

This ended the first day's proceedings, after which the council adjourned to meet again at the same spot, at the same hour, next day. The Arapahoes and Cheyennes could give no definite answer, as their principal chiefs were not present.

The Comanches and Apaches will doubtless accede to the wishes of the Commissioners.

Arrival of Osage Chiefs—Indian Speeches—Senator Henderson proposes the Treaty—Its favourable Reception by the Kiowas and Comanches—Presents.

MEDICINE LODGE CREEK, *October 20th,* 1867.

BEFORE the council commenced, twelve Osage chiefs made their appearance at the council ground. They had been travelling for ten days to see the Commissioners. They appeared very tired and hungry. Their ponies were also lame from excessive travelling, and had buckskin wrapped around their feet. "Little Bear," the principal chief, requested an introduction to the Commissioners. After a shake of the hand all around, he said that he had come from the Osage reservation to see the great Peace chiefs.

Ten Bears, Comanche chief, said :—

"My people do not trouble the white man at all ; but two years ago, on this road, your soldiers commenced killing my young men, and on the Canadian also. My young men returned the fire, and fought your soldiers. Your men then attacked our villages ; we retorted as well as we could, but we finally made peace, and there was an end of it. We have been at peace since.

"There is one thing which is not good in your speeches ; that is, building us medicine houses. We don't want any. I want to live and die as I was brought up. I love the open prairie, and I wish you would not insist on putting us on a reservation. We prefer to roam over the prairie when we want to do so. If the Texans were kept from our country, then we might live upon a reserve, but this country is so small we cannot live upon it. The best of my lands the Texans have taken, and I am left to shift as I can best do. If you have any good words from the Great Father I shall be happy to hear them. I love to get presents, for it reminds me that the Great Father has not forgotten his friends the Comanches. I want my country to be pure and clean."

Another shaking of the hands, and then Ten Bears sat down, and was followed by Satanta, who spoke as follows :—

"The Kiowas have no more to say. We have spoken already. When you issue goods, give all that is our due to us ; do not hide any from us. Keep none back. I want all that is mine."

After saying this he went and dragged Black Eagle up before the Commissioners, that he might speak. Black Eagle had nothing to say.

Commissioner Taylor said that the Council Chief

would reply in form to them, and that their annuity goods would be distributed to them the next morning. Upon hearing this, Satanta seemed to get sulky. Folding his blanket about him, he deliberately mounted his horse and rode off. In a short time he returned, and made another speech :—

"We need two agents—one for the Kiowas and Comanches. There are so many hearts in the two tribes that it requires two. I have no objection to Colonel Leavenworth or anybody else in the Commission, but it requires two to distribute our goods properly. For myself and my band, we will take John Tappan" (a cousin of S. F. Tappan); "the other Kiowas may take Leavenworth if they will."

Although he said that he had no objection to Leavenworth, still, his dislike to him was only too manifest.

Senator Henderson next spoke. As his speech was important, I copied it *verbatim* :—

"To our Kiowa and Comanche friends who spoke to us on yesterday through their chiefs Satanta, Ten Bears, and Toosh-a-way, the Commissioners say they have listened to your words and considered them well.

"We are glad to hear you express confidence in us, and to be assured that you will follow the good road we shall give you. We will not abuse that confidence. What we say to you may at first be unpleasant, but if you follow our advice it will bring you good, and you will soon be happy.

"Through your great chief Satanta, you say you

desire to hold this country south of the Arkansas River. By your treaty of the Little Arkansas, two years ago, you received into your country here the Cheyennes, Arapahoes, and Apaches. We agreed you might continue to hunt up to the Arkansas River. We are still willing to stand by that treaty.

"You say you do not like the medicine houses of the whites, but you prefer the buffalo and the chase, and express a wish to do as your fathers did.

"We say to you that the buffalo will not last for ever. They are now becoming few, and you must know it. When that day comes, the Indian must change the road his father trod, or he must suffer, and probably die. We tell you that to change will make you better. We wish you to live, and we will now offer you the way.

"The whites are settling up all the good lands. They have come to the Arkansas River. When they come, they drive out the buffalo. If you oppose them, war must come. They are many, and you are few. You may kill some of them, but others will come and take their places. And finally, many of the red men will have been killed, and the rest will have no homes. We are your best friends, and now, before all the good lands are taken by whites, we wish to set aside a part of them for your exclusive home. On that home we will build you a house to hold the goods we send you ; and when you become hungry and naked, you can go there and be fed and clothed. To that home we will send a physician to live with you and heal your

wounds, and take care of you when you are sick.
There we will also send you a blacksmith to shoe your
ponies, so that they will not get lame. We will send
you a farmer to show your people how to grow corn
and wheat, and we will send you a mill to make for
you meal and flour.

"Every year we will send to the warehouse a suit
of clothing for each of your men, women, and children,
so that they shall not suffer from cold. We do not
ask you to cease hunting the buffalo. You may roam
over the broad plains south of the Arkansas River,
and hunt the buffalo as you have done in years past,
but you must have a place you can call your own.
You must have a home where we can send your goods,
and where you can go and see your physician when
you are sick. You must have a home where all your
people who wish may farm, and where you may bury
your dead and have your medicine lodges. We
propose to make that home on the Red River and
around the Wichita mountains, and we have prepared
papers for that purpose. To-morrow morning, at nine
o'clock, we want your chiefs and head men to meet us
at our camp and sign the papers."

This last speech ended the proceedings for this day.
It was understood before the Council broke up that
the Kiowa and Comanche chiefs would be up at our
camps at nine o'clock to-morrow, to sign the treaty.
Thus far, so good, though the business of the Commission is not half completed yet.

The Cheyenne and Arapahoe braves will be here at

the end of three days from date. The Cheyennes are
those who have been at war. If peace is not made
with the tribe then, the Peace Commission will be a
failure, and it only remains to carry out the last
section of the Act of Congress, relating to the Peace
Commissions—viz., the raising of 4,000 additional
troops for the vigorous prosecution of the war.

We have been waiting eight days for the Cheyennes.
The Commissioners are tired, and they talk of splitting
up the party—one part to go up to Fort Laramie in
the Black Hills to give presents and make arrangements with the Indians to meet again next spring,
another to go up to North Platte to settle with the
Ogallallas and Brules, and then they go for dividing,
beyond what they have spent already for the
Government, over $250,000. Senator Henderson
uses all his influence to bind and cement together
the Commission for the settlement of the Indian
question.

The treaty with the Kiowas and Comanches cannot
be made public until the President has proclaimed it.
But to satisfy the public it may be well to state that
it contemplates no cession of any lands, except the
removal of the tribes ten miles southward of Medicine
Lodge Creek.

Over $150,000 worth of provisions have been distri-
buted to the tribes, also two thousand suits of uniform,
two thousand blankets, fifty quarter boxes tobacco,
twenty bolts of Indian cloth, three bales of domestics,
one bale linsey, twelve dozen squaw axes, one bale of

I.   S

ticking, fifty revolvers (navy size), besides an assort-
ment of beads, butcher knives, thread and needles,
brass bells, looking glasses, and sixteen silver
medals.

MEDICINE LODGE CREEK, *October 21st,* 1867.

THE treaty was signed this morning by the following
chiefs : Satanta, Satank, Black Eagle, Tonaenko,
Fishermore, Manietyn, Sitemgeah, Satpaga, Cauvois,
Satamore, Kiowa chiefs, and ten Comanche chiefs.
All the Commissioners signed it, and we reporters
subscribed our names as witnesses.

Arrival of Hostile Chiefs—Their People " Making Medicine "—
    Important Religious Rites—Time wanted—Spicy Colloquy
    between the Commissioners and Indians—Interesting An-
    nouncement—Little Raven.

MEDICINE LODGE CREEK, *October 22nd,* 1867.

LAST night Little Robe, Black Kettle, Minnick, and
Grey Beard, four chiefs of the great Cheyenne nation,
came to camp, and said they wished to talk with the
Peace chiefs.

Admitted into a special council, they gave their
excuses for their non-appearance.

They had advanced one day in their medicine-making work. They had three days more; ordinarily it takes four days to renew medicine arrows, but as this was an urgent necessity, they will only take three.

Taylor said to them : " We are glad to see you ; we have been anxiously expecting you. We would like to know how soon your people could be here."

Little Robe replied : " It may be four or five nights after this. I was requested by the Cheyenne nation to communicate their wishes to you. I came here for that purpose. If you can detain the chiefs of the other tribes we should be very well pleased, as we have something of importance to discuss in general council. The Cheyenne soldiers have all got together ; no more shall leave their village until we arrive there. It has taken us a longer time to collect the men of this nation together, as they were scattered. Do not be in too much of a hurry to leave. We want to see you very bad, and want to shake hands with you. If you have anything very particular to send back to our village, one of our men shall be a runner, and start back to-morrow."

The Commissioners consulted together about using their influence to request the other tribes to stay till the arrival of the Cheyennes.

General Harney said: "Well, I am in favour of asking the tribes to stay."

Henderson : " I suppose that asking us to stay is to test our endurance ? "

Harney : " Well, then, let us show the Cheyennes that we can endure."

Henderson: "I do not see why the Cheyennes could not be here sooner. It does not usually take five days to travel twenty-nine miles."

General Augur: "That is not the point, Senator Henderson. It is this: these tribes have engaged in certain ceremonies, and they cannot cut them short any more than a man would leave church to take a drink." (Laughter.)

Henderson: "Many a man has done it, and you know it, General. I think these men might cut short their ceremonies. I must be home by the 1st of November, and I cannot wait here five days. We have waited here eight days already, and they had promised to be here to-night."

Harney: "Well, Senator, you cannot go home. We cannot do without you, and if you go I fear I shall have to arrest you." (Great sensation.)

Sanborn: "Tell the chiefs that if they want to see us together, they must be here at the end of three days."

Taylor: "Tell them also that these other tribes have finished their business with us. We can request them to stay, but we can do no more. We can say also that it is the Cheyennes' wish."

Little Robe: "We are in as much of a hurry as yourself. We have thrown away one day to please you. You have your engagements, we have ours. We want to do all in our power to meet together. If we can't meet, then we must abide the consequences."

Black Kettle: "I give you my word I will not ask

you to stay here six or seven or eight days. When I look to my left I see you, and that you intend to do right; and when I look to my right I see my men, and know that they intend to do right. I want you both to touch and shake hands."

Henderson (to Commissioners): "Ah! I see what is the matter. They are afraid to come in. Tell them, interpreter, that they have our full pardon and forgiveness for past offences."

Harney: "Oh no! don't tell them that. I am sure they will come here. I'll bet my life on their keeping their word."

Henderson: "Bah! this medicine is all humbug."

Augur: "Oh no, it ain't; it is life and death with them. It is their religion; and they observe all the ceremonies a great deal better than the whites theirs."

Henderson: "It must be. I never knew a white man that would not put aside religion for business."

Taylor (to interpreter): "Tell them that they must send a runner to their villages; that we can wait four days, and that is all."

At this point Murphy, of the Central Superintendency, requested to make a remark. On being permitted to do so, he said that Little Raven had informed him that he was ready to go into council and sign a treaty to-morrow morning at 9 o'clock. Little Raven wished to dissolve their confederation with the Cheyennes, and go with the Apaches instead. The Cheyennes had always got them into trouble, and by that trouble had prevented them from getting their annuities.   Moreover, the Cheyennes had made threats against them, and they did not wish to be with them any more.   " Little Raven also told me to tell you that his young men would be in camp in the morning ; they had caught up with the Indians who had stolen their ponies, and had killed some of them, and when they returned to camp to-morrow not to be alarmed, as they would give some startling whoops, yell, and fire, and he hoped the soldiers would not get alarmed and fire upon them."

"Hurrah ! " said Harney.   " I hope they killed them all.   What were they, Pawnees ? "

"No, sir," said Murphy ; "they were Kaws."

"Well done," replied Harney ; "the Arapahoes ought to have killed them all, durn them ! "

Interesting Proceedings—Gathering of the Chiefs—Address of Commissioner Taylor—Chiefs angry—Sanborn propitiates —Impassioned Eloquence of the Chiefs—They proclaim their People Outraged, and demand Reparation.

FORT LARAMIE, BLACK HILLS COUNTRY,
575 MILES WEST OF THE MISSOURI RIVER,
November 12th, 1867.

IN a large room, 100 feet by 40, the Crow chiefs, to the number of sixteen, were assembled to hear the emissaries of the Great Father, who had come with propositions for peace and goodwill.   Among the most prominent of them were Bear's Foot, Black Foot,

Wolf Bull, Shot-in-the-face, Bird-in-the-Nest, White Horse, etc.

On one side sat these chiefs, a group of red-skinned athletes, their long black hair hanging down their backs in masses. In the rear of them, and filling the hall, was a crowd of soldiers, teamsters, strikers, Laramie loafers, and citizens employed in the Quarter-master's Department, who had thronged in to witness the novel ceremony of a pow-wow.

Generals Harney, Sanborn, Augur, Tappan, and Terry sat opposite. Behind these Commissioners, and towering high above their heads, was the gigantic form of Beauvais, the special Indian Commissioner, appropriately termed by the untutored savages, "Big Belly." Alongside of Beauvais sat a *redacteur* of the Paris *Moniteur*, with spectacles on nose, interested in Indian physiognomy and character. Quietness obtained, Dr. Henry M. Mathews rose up and said that he had the honour of introducing to the gentlemen composing the Peace Commission the chief of the Crow nation ; after saying which he turned round to the Crow interpreter and requested him to interpret the following :—

"Here are the gentlemen sent from Washington to make peace with you. Listen well to what they say, and you will find whether I have told you any lies or not."

His speech was greeted with uproarious shouts of "Eya-ough!"

While the chiefs deliberated upon the preliminary remarks of Dr. Mathews, the calumet was passed around with strange mysterious gestures. Then Bear's Tooth, a chief of tall stature, very deliberately got up, and taking his calumet took three deliberate whiffs, and handing it to Dr. Mathews, said :—*

"Smoke, and remember me this day, and grant what I shall ask."

To General Harney he said : "Father, smoke, and take pity on me," which request the General gladly complied with.

To Colonel Tappan he said : "Father, smoke, and remember me and my people, for we are very poor," which Tappan willingly did.

Then, after another whiff, he handed the peace hookah to Augur, repeating the same words, and did the same to each of the rest.

He then sat down, saying that he was ready to hear their talk.

Commissioner Taylor then rose up, and spoke as follows :—

"My friends, the chiefs and head warriors of the Crow nation of one blood, the Great Spirit made all people. We are therefore brethren. At our invitation you have come a great way, and with much difficulty, to see us. We have travelled a great distance to see you, and to shake hands with you. Your Great Father at Washington, though so far away from you, is well informed of your friendship. He knows your friendship to his white children. He knows, also, of the many proofs of peace you have given to the

---

* For real Indian eloquence, the Crow chiefs excelled.

Government. He knows, also, of some of the difficulties and troubles which beset you. He has sent us to see you in order that we may receive from your own lips how you stand, and that we may take all necessary actions to relieve you of your difficulties, and to make the road smooth with you. We learn that valuable mines have been found in your country, and in some instances taken possession of. We learn, also, that roads have been made through your land; that settlements have been made upon them; that your game is driven away, and is rapidly disappearing. We learn, also, that the white people are taking possession of your valuable lands and occupying them.

"We are therefore sent by the Great Father to relieve you, as far as possible, of the bad consequences of this state of things, and to protect you from future difficulties. We desire to set by a part of your country, that your people may live on it for ever, upon which the Great Father and the white council will never permit any white man to trespass. We wish you to mark out what section would best please you. When you have thus marked this tract out, we wish to buy from you the rest of your land, leaving to you, however, the right to hunt upon it as long as the game lasts. Upon the reservation you may thus select, we intend to build a home for your agent, to build a mill to saw your timber when you wish it, and a mill to grind your corn, a blacksmith's shop, and a home for your farmer, and such other buildings as may be necessary. We also propose to furnish you horses and cattle to enable you to raise for yourselves a supply of stock, with which to support your families when the game has disappeared. We also intend to supply you annually with warm clothes and farming implements. We will also send you teachers to educate your children. You have made our hearts glad by coming here to see us, and you shall not go back empty-handed. We have presents on the road.

"We wish to hear from you everything you have to say. We will consider it well, and will answer you in a friendly spirit. I am done."

The first part of this prepared speech of the Commissioner was loudly applauded, but as he drew near to the business of the council, contempt and indifference were depicted upon their swarthy countenances.

After a few moments of silence, during which the Crow chiefs stared at each other or gravely smoked their pipes, General Sanborn requested the interpreter to state to them fully what the Commissioners intended by their remarks.

The keen, dark eye of Sanborn had detected displeasure, and, wishing to dissipate all bad feeling, said in a deprecating manner that they did not wish to take all their land away, except what was already occupied by the whites in the Gallatin Valley. Besides, were the Commissioners not willing to pay well for what they bought, give them yearly presents, and what not?

Heedless of Sanborn's smooth pleading, Bear's Tooth said :—

"What you have told me I understand well. I came here to see you, and I am going to say to you just what I think." Stalking up to Taylor, he said: "I have come a long ways off to see you. Do right to me."

To Harney, he said: "Father, you have sent for me; listen to me well." Turning to Tappan, he said: "From a far country up north I have travelled at your bidding. Look at me. I am poor. Will you not do something for me? And you" (Terry), "will you not do the same, and you, father" (Augur), "do the same, and you (Sanborn) take pity upon me, and hearken to my voice?"

Three times more did Bear's Tooth walk round the circle, and in an imploring voice repeat the request to each individual. After the fourth time he took a buffalo robe from his squaw, who stood waiting.

"Father, last spring I came round the Big Horn, and one of your young men said that you were coming to see us. My father asked for me to come in. I thought deeply, and at last I concluded to come. Now this fall, when the leaves of the trees were falling, the Crows were on the Yellowstone River. Your messenger brought to me ten plugs of tobacco, and delivered your message inviting us to come to Fort Laramie. In answer I said, Yes, oh yes. I wanted my father to come to Phil Kearney, and not to Laramie, and said, that had he come, I would have said yes, yes, to everything. But the cold days have come, and I came to Laramie. I therefore want my father to say yes, oh yes, to every request of mine. I have been waiting for you a long time. I am hungry and cold. Look at me, all of you. I am a man, like each of you; I have limbs, and a head like you; we all look like one and the same people. I like my people and my children to prosper and grow rich."

He strode up to Taylor and Harney, and cried out aloud, with all his might, "Achan! achan! achan! Father, father, father, listen well. Call your young men back from the Big Horn. It would please me well. Your young men have gone on the path, and have destroyed the fine timber and green grass, and have burnt up the country. Father, your young men have gone on the road, and have killed my game and my buffalo. They did not kill them to eat; they left them to rot where they fell. Father, were I to go to your country to kill your cattle, what would you say? Would not that be wrong, and cause war? Well, the Sioux proffered me hundreds of mules and horses to go with them to war. I did not go.

"A long time ago you made a treaty with the Crow Nation, and afterwards you took the Crow chief with you to the States. He has never returned. Where is he? We have never seen him, and we are tired of waiting for him. Give us what he left. We have come for his last message.

"I have heard that you have sent messengers for

the Sioux like you did to us, but the Sioux tell me that they will not come. They say, you have cheated them once.

"The Sioux said to us, 'Ah! the white fathers have called for you; you are going to see them. Ah! they will treat you as they have treated us. Go and see them, and then come back and tell us what you have heard. The white fathers will beguile your ears with soft words and sweet promises, but they will never keep them. Go on and see them, and they will laugh at you.'

"In spite of these words of the Sioux I have come to see you. When I go back I expect to lose more than half my horses.

"Father, father, the Great Spirit made us all, but he put the red man in the centre, surrounded by the whites. Ah! my heart is full, yet sad. All the Crows, the old chiefs of bygone days, our forefathers, told us often, be friendly to the pale faces, for they are strong. We, their children, have obeyed. A long time ago, over forty years, the Crows camped on the Missouri; our chief was knocked on the head by a white chief."

Here he was interrupted by General Harney, who said: "The white chief was crazy. I was there, and saw it done."

"On the Yellowstone stream there were three waggons camped: there were three white men and a white woman there also. Four Crows went up to them and asked for a piece of bread. One of the

white men coolly took out his gun and shot 'Sorrel
Horse'" (a chief) "dead, but we passed over it.

"These things I tell you to show you that the pale-
faces have done wrong as well as the Indians."

"That's so," responded General Harney; "the
Indians are a great deal better than we are."

"Some time ago I went to Fort Benton, because
we had done some wrong also, and begged pardon
from the white chief. I gave him nine mules and
sixty robes as atonement for what we had done. I
thus paid for our wrong.

"I then went on the Big Horn to Fort Smith, and
found that there were whites there. I went up to
shake hands with the officers, but they replied by
shoving their fists in my face, and knocking me down.
That is the way we are treated by your young men.

"Father, you talk about farming, and about raising
cattle. I don't want to hear it; I was raised on
buffalo, and I love it. Since I was born I was raised,
like your chiefs, to be strong, to move my camps
when necessary, to roam over the prairie at will.

"Take pity upon us; I am tired of talking.

"You, father" (Taylor), "take these moccasins, and
keep your feet warm."

So saying, he took off his own moccasins and
handed them to Commissioner Taylor, which the
peace chief accepted with many *soft words*.

Then Blackfoot, who had been loud in applauding
the sentiments of Bear's Tooth, stood up, and, while
shaking hands with each of them, implored them

individually to be patient and listen to him, to open wide their ears, and grant their requests. He then, disrobing himself of his buffalo robe, folded it around Commissioner Taylor, saying, " Let this rest on your shoulders, for by this token I accept you as my brother."

Lifting up his hands high above his head, he said that when the Crows wanted arrows, they went and picked shovel blades, pieces of hoop iron, and with their own hands made arrows. When they wanted a fire, they picked up flints and struck them together, and thus they made a fire to warm themselves. When they wanted to butcher, they made stone knives, and it was thus they killed their game. If they went on a reserve they would not know how to drive their oxen, or plough up the land, therefore, they did not like that talk, but if the Fathers gave them horses to catch game, and guns to kill them, then that was good, and all would be well.

Years ago, a party of whites had come to buy this California road that passes by Laramie. For the road the whites were to pay fifty years' annuities, but they had received the goods only for two or three years. One of their big chiefs had gone east. Black Foot said he would like to know whether their chief had gone under the ground or ascended up to the skies.

He then closed with a peroration about his extreme love for the whites, his extreme poverty, and his extremely universal good-nature.

Black Tooth made a most logical speech. He

carefully took up the past history of his nation, and placed their general characteristics in a plain manner before the whites, and then drew his inferences from their past conduct, as to what they would do in the future. He also explained how the last treaty had been kept on both sides ; how the whites had not kept to the strict letter of their promises, which caused his nation to doubt whether it was really of any use to make any more treaties. He avowed his intention to live as he was raised, and begged the Commissioners not to talk any more about settling them upon reservations. He earnestly entreated that they would stop that Powder River road, and recall their young men that were stationed on that road, as they were the cause of all the war. As he uttered this earnest request his voice rose to the pitch of passion, his gestures rapid, his eyes flashed with excitement, and his old form trembled under his emotion. As he thundered out his righteous demands his body swayed from side to side. While he seemed struck by some sudden spasm, he frantically gathered his long hair and held it up aloft. Then again, as he described the cheats practised upon his people by the whites, his voice sunk into whispers, while every gesture was eloquence itself. Raising himself to his full height, and elevating his arm, with the air of a hero he proudly exclaimed, "But for all this, my heart is rock, and I will not complain." At times he appeared like some prophet of old about to declare the evil that would surely follow this monstrous robbery of their lands, and again his lips would wreathe with lofty scorn for the underhand work to which the pale-faces stooped, as he said, " Though I am poor, I shall not die ; my arm is strong, and I can hunt the buffalo as my father did." Suddenly, as if remembering the former insults that they had been compelled to endure, his eyes flashed like living coals of fire—and he almost demanded that the soldiers should be recalled from their country ; but finally calming down his wild passion, he implored the Commissioners to take pity upon them, and do right for once. After which, shaking hands with each Commissioner, he returned to his seat, and as if brooding over past wrongs, over his nation's utter inability to protect themselves from the whites, he smoked his calumet in silence, with bent head, never lifting his head once.

He accused Judge Kinney of having wilfully cheated them, selling and giving them most miserable flour, which caused the death of five or six of their tribe. He accused him of having told a big lie, defrauding them of their rights by bartering shoddy things for robes, etc. After this, Wolf Bull, springing up, walked to the centre of the circle with a long hickory stick, on which were cut ten notches. Each of these notches he called a generation ; how a generation had grown up, become old, and died, and was succeeded by another generation. Each died, and were followed by another. Throughout these generations his tribe had been friendly to the whites. " To secure the present generation as faithful friends, do not send any

I. T

more waggons up to the Powder River country. Send
no more young men here. Recall your soldiers from
our country, and then we shall be happy, as we have
been in times long ago."

This speech closed the proceedings, after which the
treaty was signed.

NORTH PLATTE, NOV. 24TH, HOMEWARD BOUND.

ABLE men have time and again attempted to give a
history of the Indians. So far as concerns the last
three centuries, we have many voluminous histories of
America and her aborigines, but of the prehistoric
period we know almost nothing. Some writers of
fame describe the North American Indians as a
mixture of the Mongolian, Polynesian, and Caucasian
races ; others say they are from a distinct and
separate stock, altogether American ; others again
pronounce them to be descendants of Danish Vikings ;
and still others as the descendants of the ancient
Britons, who emigrated to the far west under Dafydd
ap Llewellyn and became lost to history. But the
most reasonable conjecture is that which claims
them to be of the same type as the inhabitants
of Asiatic Tartary, and to have emigrated by way of
Kamschatka and Sitka. When we consider the
narrowness of the channel that divides the great
continents of Asia and North America, and that that
channel for about three months in the year is frozen

up, and that the Kamschatkas annually cross it to barter furs, the hypothesis deserves respect. Once across, it follows that as in the course of centuries they multiplied they migrated further into the interior. Other strong evidences of their Asiatic origin are the similarity in language, the resemblance in feature, the same contour of the face, high cheek-bones, sloping forehead, aquiline nose, complexion, and formation of the posterior lobes of the skull, which may safely be taken as proofs of the kinship of Americans with Siberian Mongolians.

The nomadic habits and the untamable spirits which mark the Indians of North America, as well as the wild Mongolian race in Asia, prove that there is not such a radical difference between them. A decade of centuries has not been able to efface the resemblance, and though there are certain peculiarities in the Indian not to be seen in the Mongol, yet these may be attributed to the influences of climate. They have the same indefinite idea of some mysterious being; they regard death with the same stoicism; both believe in an after life; one imagines death but an entrance to Elysium, where they can enjoy bliss unutterable, with beautiful houris; the other believes death but the bridge to the "happy hunting grounds." Women are looked upon almost in the same light. One race regards her as a slave to dally and toy with in the joys of love; the other treats her as a slave, makes her cook his meals, make his bed, manufacture his moccasins, and perform laborious operations. They both possess the same natural dignity in language and bearing. Like the Tartar's, the Indian's language is full of short sentences, but more florid and poetical.

The tribes now scattered over the New World, from the Arctic regions to the Antarctic Sea, have degenerated greatly from what they must have been at a former period. If they were the builders of those ruined temples, the deserted cities, and the huge mounds, which contained mining implements of copper and iron, what astonishing degeneracy! Having no means of intercourse with other nations, we may suppose they gradually relapsed into barbarism—barbarism so profound that it will take a century to wean them back.

In some mounds have been found ten cartloads of stone hammers, copper chisels, copper gads with heads much battered, and copper knives. Charcoal has also been found in many places, and pits have been explored, which had been sunk some fourteen feet, following the course of copper veins. Sunken pits have been discovered extending below the ground in continuous tunnels.

Shafts have been found in the Rocky Mountains which had been sunk to the depth of thirty feet, following the gold lode. In a few of these were found crowbars, and sacks containing unwashed ore, pyrites of iron and gold dust, which assayers asserted were valuable. Majestic temples, standing solitary and alone, in Arizona and Mexico, monuments of national glory ; cities filled with stately mansions, with wide streets totally deserted, imposing edifices of worship which in their ruins appear as if weeping for the departed prestige, and valour of the past. Who has not read and heard of these ?

Who were these people ? What of their names, their religion, their history ? Were they Toltecs, Aztecs, or Chalcoes ? Are they of a different race to the present Indians of the plains ? Did the Aztecs not occupy the country which is now called Arizona, New Mexico, Colorado, and Wyoming ? As they migrated to the southward, might they not have left these cities sleeping in silence, through adverse circumstances of which we have no note ? I am inclined to think that the ancestors of these wild Indians were the devastators of semi-civilised America. But we have not space enough to continue the interesting subject.

Between Julesburg and Junction Cut Off there are two large mounds, which can be distinctly seen for a distance of eighty miles as the traveller passes through the Platte valley. Some people say they are natural. There are several mounds, the exact counterpart of those near Julesburg, scattered over the American continent, containing more or less relics of bygone ages of a people who have silently disappeared from the face of the earth. These memorials are a marvel and a mystery. Whether they are the receptacles of the remains of Indian tribes or landmarks of defunct nations, we must fain wait till some devoted searcher of the future explores them before we can have our doubts resolved.

The Indians have several traditions, many of them calculated to raise a smile, at their very absurdity, all of them highly poetical. Old warriors love to sit on their mats before the door of their lodges, and recount the legends handed down from time immemorial from sire to son, surrounded by wondering children and amateur warriors. Yellow and wrinkled beldames delight in weaving romantic legends of some daring, noble young brave, who died for love of some Indian damsel, supremely beautiful. These fanciful legends are carefully treasured up by the young maidens of the tribe, who in like manner relate them to their children. Their language, songs, and proverbs, like those of the Arabs, are highly poetical, and from this we deduce the fact that poetry and nature are inseparable.

The Sioux nation have a firm belief in a Great Spirit. When there is lightning and thunder the Great Spirit is angry with His red children, and speaks His displeasure in the thunder. The Delawares have also a similar belief in a Spirit, who possesses supernatural powers—one who is able to punish them for their misdeeds. The Dacotahs style their chief deity Oank-tay-hee, but being superstitious they are afraid of calling him by that name, and therefore call him Tako-wak-au, or that which is supernatural. This mighty God manifests himself as a large ox. His eyes are as large as the moon. He can haul in his horns and tail, or he can lengthen them as he pleases. From him proceed invisible influences. In his extremities reside mighty powers. He is said to have created the earth. Assembling in grand conclave all of the aquatic tribes, he ordered them to bring up dirt from beneath the water, and proclaimed death to the disobedient. The beaver and others forfeited their lives ; at last the musk rat went beneath the water, and after a long time appeared at the surface, nearly exhausted, with some dirt. From this the great Oank-tay-hee fashioned the earth into a large circular plain. The earth being finished, he took as a deity one of his own offspring, and after grinding him to powder he scattered the dust upon the earth, which produced many worms ; the worms became full-grown Dacotahs.

All the Indians in the west of whom we have any knowledge believe in one Supreme God, and the immortality of the soul. All good and all power they attribute to Manitou, as they call the Supreme Being. They also believe in many subordinate deities who live in the sun and moon. Supernatural powers are ascribed to serpents, especially rattlesnakes and eels. They pay religious honours to rocks and venerable objects. In their belief brutes have animated souls as well as men. They also believe in the existence of an intelligent evil principle, whose wrath they endeavour to avert by prayer and sacrifice. Their after life they style the " happy hunting grounds," wherein they expect to enjoy with greater pleasure the same delights they experienced in this world. They have some vague idea of a future punishment awaiting transgressors.

Each Indian holds some particular animal in reverence, which he calls his totem, and which he can by no means be induced to kill, or eat when killed, for fear of some terrible misfortune. The Indians believe in sacrifices. To their invisible Manitous they sacrifice tobacco, worn-out clothing, strings of wampum, ears of corn, the skins, and often the whole carcasses of animals. These offerings are seen along difficult or dangerous roads, on rocks, and on the shores of rapids, as so many offerings made to the presiding spirits of the place.

In honour of the sun, and, also, of inferior spirits, they throw into the fire a part of everything they use, as an acknowledgment of the power from which they derived their possessions. To Indian corn they sacrifice bear's flesh ; but to deer and bears they sacrifice corn. When an Indian has dreamed of seeing some superior being demanding a deer or a bear, he goes and searches for the animal, and when found brings it to the altar. The "medicine man" conducts the ceremony. He surrounds it with hot stones, and as the smoke ascends chants the following prayer : "This brave offers unto thee a fine fat deer. Have mercy upon him, and grant good luck unto his family."

Every tribe possesses a medicine bag, to which they attach great importance. This bag is filled with boiled bones, eagle and hawk feathers, sometimes moss and dried herbs. The Indians regard their "medicine men" with superstition and reverence, which the medicine man is not slow to take advantage of. He is the image of the African Obi—a compound of cunning and double-distilled impudence, but not more so than the white medical quacks who advertise their universal pills as infallible specifics for all diseases.

When an Indian is sick the medicine man is in immediate requisition. Clad in fantastical manner, with horns on his head, and a wolf's scalp on his face, he proceeds to exorcise with incantations the sick man, of the animal, insect, or enemy that torments him. He is not always successful in purging the tormented, but if he fails he blames the devil, very much as we do. Still, the Indian doctors have been of great use to the United States pharmacopœia. They have discovered several valuable herbs, for which those suffering from ague and fever should be grateful. Vapour baths they frequently have recourse to for the care of their sick. Catarrhal and rheumatic affections, asthma, coughs, dropsy, diarrhœa, and amenorrhœa, they generally treat with great skill, but venereal diseases they do not seem able to treat with any degree of success.

As the Romans reckoned the days of the months by kalends, nones, and ides, so the Indian counts his days by suns and moons. As the Romans wore the *toga* and the *pallium*—so the Indian wears his flowing robe with a native dignity and simple elegance not to be surpassed by a crowned despot ; and similar to the escutcheons of noble families in France and England are the symbols or tokens of Indian tribes and families represented by a bull, bear, wolf, horse, elk, arrow, or anything that may have captivated their fancy. Every article of dress is ornamented with beads. Their breech-clouts are gradually disappearing before the common-place toggery of the white man, but their barbarous finery and gaudy trappings they still adhere to.

An Indian feast is accompanied by great and imposing ceremonies. While at North Platte a party of us were invited to a feast given by Spotted Tail in honour of Generals Sherman and Harney.

On our arrival, we found the supplies of Indian delicacies commensurate with the quality of the guests. The cooking was simple enough, without salt or condiment. We all squatted ourselves on the ground and the old and young squaws volunteered to serve us on the occasion.

Before proceeding, the great calumet of peace was passed around. Whenever this calumet is brought forth it is a token of great respect. It is adorned with brass tacks, blue and golden feathers, beads of coral, and carved in the most unique manner. After the pipe had been passed around the circle the chief commenced the feast by eating, regardless of his guests.

There were all kinds of wild meat spread out, but the most esteemed of all was dog meat. In huge dishes of wood might be seen a juicy lump of buffalo, a hind quarter of an antelope, meat, venison, wild ducks, geese, and turkeys, surrounded by dishes of wild beans, Indian corn, rice, and some strange herbs which appeared to be very palatable. These various vegetables were boiled separately, with a sprinkling of buffalo fat, giving the whole an exceedingly unctuous appearance.

In the centre of the circle were three dogs, of a dropsical appearance, the hair merely scorched, which had been roasted entire, intestines and all. Over this Indian delicacy was poured the gravy, dog's grease. The dripping had been collected in bone dishes. The dogs appeared plump and young, and all seemed to pay especial attention to the three young pups, which were to them what the *pièce de résistance* is to the civilised whites. For appearance sake we partook of a very small piece ; and, could we but have conquered our prejudices, we might have made a very hearty meal. As it was, we were satisfied. The meat appeared to be of a brownish colour, somewhat resembling porpoise meat. If we might judge by the oily streaks about the capacious mouths of the chiefs, and the pleasure which sparkled in their eyes, we should pronounce dog meat delicious.

After the feast was over there were three canine skeletons left on their respective dishes. Tomahawks answering the purpose of pipes, as well as instruments of bloody deeds, were handed to us ; and as this was an important epoch in Spotted Tail's life, he caused them to be filled with a leaf of native tobacco. Generally the tobacco they use is composed of the dry leaves of the sakakorni plant, or the kinnikinnick, a species of willow bark.

During our stay in camp we saw several strange scenes. Sitting near his lodge was an old Indian, on the wintry side of seventy, decrepit and almost useless. His sole occupation and delight was to relate accounts of conflicts in which he was the hero. The young boys were gathered around him listening eagerly, hanging, as it were, on the words of the ancient warrior. His scars were numerous, and spoke to embryo braves of deeds of daring and renown.

Around another lodge, which seemed to belong to a chief of consequence, were squatted a group of braves, who were stripped to the buff, and whiffing out of their steatite pipes sharp jets of blue smoke, which curled above their heads, while they muttered gutturally their opinions of the whites then and there assembled. To two forked stakes planted in the ground was slung a red cradle containing a copper-coloured papoose, while a female, doubtless related to it, pushed it now and then, droning forth in "accents mild" a song which had for its component parts some "War Eagle's" prowess.

Seated on the ground, not far off, was a squaw most worthily employed in killing vermin that infested the straggling locks of a boy.

On the stillness of the night broke forth the unearthly chantings of an Indian priest engaged in his devotions to some griffin or satyr unknown to modern naturalists. Under a cover of tanned buffalo skins were a bevy of giggling girls employed in discussing our respective merits, and chatting unceasingly, exhibiting rows of teeth that fairly glistened.

Little boys rivalled each other in gymnastic feats, and wrestled Indian-hug fashion ; others largely patronised the game called " Plum Stone." This last game is played in the following manner, as near as we could find out. A lot of plum stones were marked with certain unknown hieroglyphics not unlike Cufic. They placed the stones in a wooden bowl, and after shaking them thoroughly those with certain characters turned up, and the game was won. This seemed to be a very amusing play, if we might judge by the peals of laughter that the winners indulged in. We saw several other things equally strange and novel to us, but as twilight had waned and darkness had come, we rose and bade the hospitable old chief Spotted Tail a good-night, and departed with a higher appreciation of a peaceable Indian than ever we had before.

When a boy has arrived at the age of sixteen he begins to manifest a disposition to become a warrior. This is the darling wish of his breast. He has been incited to it by the words of the war doctor, by the oral records of other heroes, and by the injunctions and hopes of his father. After making known his wish, he commences the fast, which is to test his

powers of endurance, and is the first important cere
mony preparatory to being launched on the warpath,
in the train and company of tried warriors. The
lessons inculcated in his young breast must now bring
fruit worthy of the son of a brave. For three days
he keeps the fast, hidden from human eyes, and constantly engaged in invocations to his deity. On
coming out of his retreat he is saluted by his whole
tribe with the sound of gongs, drums, loud rattles,
and reed flutes.

The chief of the tribe presents him with a bow and
arrow, suitable for a brave. He then is dispatched
on his errand of death—to secure the scalp of an
enemy. On his return with the trophy he is pronounced a brave, and is for ever emancipated from
the submissiveness of boyhood. He is admitted to
the councils of the tribe, and gradually wins his way
by merit to the powers and positions of a chief.

Like all other savages of the Missouri, the Sioux
and Cheyennes occupy themselves in war and hunting, leaving to the women the making of tents and
garments, beside their usual household avocations.

Many of the braves have six or eight wives, one of
whom, however, is usually the favourite ; the others
the husband is willing to barter with the whites, often
for a small compensation. But although thus indifferent to their squaws, infidelity on the part of the
wife is punished severely. The offender's nose is first
cut off, and then she is thrust from her husband's
presence. From the time of her banishment she is a

marked object ; no one will marry her, and she is condemned to eke out a miserable existence by performing the most menial offices in the camp. Often the wife is killed in the first moments of rage, which bursts on the discovery of her faithlessness. In this case no one interferes, and if the husband avenges himself on the paramour by taking away his horse or other valuable property, the offender must quietly submit.

When an Indian wishes a wife he sends a friend to the father to make the bargain. A price is soon fixed upon, and when this is paid the lover takes the damsel to his wigwam, and she becomes his without any ceremony. When the warrior wishes a divorce, he merely sends his wife back to her parents. She takes her property with her, the children remaining behind, and no disputes ever arise in consequence of the repudiation.

The Indians do not bury their dead in the ground if it can be avoided, but sew the body up in a buffalo robe after dressing it in its best clothes, and painting the face red. It is then laid in some retired place, in a ravine or forest, sometimes in the cleft of a rock, and often on a high, steep bank, where it will be safe from wolves. When a warrior dies, however, his favourite horses are killed over his grave. The relations of the deceased cut off their long hair, smear their faces with a whitish clay, and wear their worst clothes, in token of mourning. Sometimes they sever a joint of a finger.

There are ten different dances with the Sioux. These are the mosquito dance, dog dance, the dance of the buffalo with shin bones, the dance of the prairie dog, the dance of those who carry the raven, the soldier's dance, the old bull's dance, the dance of the imprudent, the medicine dance, the scalp or war dance. It would take too large a space to touch upon any of them, and we could have gone further with our subject upon the manners and customs, but the limits of our space will not permit us.

P.S.—

NORTH PLATTE, NEBRASKA, NOV. 25TH, 1867.

FROM Laramie we have come in hot haste here to conclude the last treaty of peace with the Brule and Ogallalla Sioux, and the Northern Cheyennes. The Indians agree to live on their reservations, and cease molesting travellers, emigrants, etc.

The U. S. Government on their part agree to pay each tribe at the rate of $15 per capita annually. One-third every spring and two-thirds every autumn. They also agree to build agencies on the reservations, which are to be located in the neighbourhood of the White Earth or Cheyenne Rivers.

And now comes the natural question : What has the Commission done ?　In answer to which I append the following brief statement of facts, which will show what results have accrued from their work.

By the act of General Pope in establishing the Powder River or Boseman road to Montana, right through the last and only reliable hunting ground of the Sioux, and planting along it Forts Reno, Phil Kearney, and C. F. Smith, without their consent, and in the face of their protests, war had broken out and raged with great fury along the Platte, and along the route of the military road just mentioned. Such was the status of affairs when the Fortieth Congress convened in its second session in July of the current year.

The Congress, acting upon the suggestions of Commissioner Taylor, after an earnest and intensely interesting debate, proceeded to provide for the appointment of a mixed Commission of military officers and civilians supposed to be most familiar with Indian affairs, with instructions to proceed at once to the plains to treat with hostile Indians, if practicable, to examine the sections of the country supposed to be suitable for Indian territories, and to make report to Congress, etc.

When they entered upon their work the war was flagrant, North and South ; the border citizens were flying from their burning homes ; the bloody implements of death were gleaming in hundreds of hostile hands ; the newspapers every day were teeming with accounts of outrages and atrocities perpetrated on the plains. Now, peace reigns all over the plains.

The Commission have met many thousands of Indians in council, and turned their thoughts and

I. U

feelings from war to peace. They quieted and pacified
the bands of Cheyennes, Brules, and Ogallallas, along
the Republican and Platte rivers, at North Platte.
They have made new treaties with the Kiowas,
Comanches, Apaches, and Southern Arapahoes, and
solemnised a treaty of peace and friendship with the
scourge of the plains—the Southern Cheyennes.
They have visited most of the friendly Indians of the
Missouri River, at their reservations, and confirmed
their resolutions to avoid hostility with our people.
They have visited Fort Laramie, and met there many
members of the hostile bands of the North, who agree
to go no more on the war-path. They have met a
large delegation of chiefs of the Mountain Crow
Indians, and sent them home to the borders of
Montana, the fast friends of the white man. It is
true they did not meet Red Cloud, who is the leader
and soul of the war on the Powder River road ; but
they have assurances from him that he will meet the
Commission in a grand peace council at Fort Phil
Kearney when the grass grows in the spring.

The Commission could not reasonably have expected the Northern hostile tribes to come to Fort
Laramie. The lateness of the season, the consequent
shortness of the grass, and the severity of the weather
in that latitude, rendered it a difficult undertaking.
When it is also remembered that to meet the Commission at Laramie, Red Cloud and his bands must
have been compelled to travel in coming and
returning a distance of more than six hundred

miles, just in the season of their preparation of winter supplies of meat by the chase, most readers will agree that a meeting under such circumstances was out of the question.

We will now close our correspondence from the Indian expeditions with a few words which I obtained from General Sherman.

He thinks large expeditions to distant posts will be needless. He intends to build posts all along the road between Denver and Montana. The cavalry under General Custer will continue scouring the belt between the Arkansas and the Platte rivers. By these means he believes that the plains may be safely traversed from East to West, by all who desire to reach the Gold-fields of Colorado and the Pacific.

INDEX.